. Anonymous

Outlines of Sermons on the Old Testament

. Anonymous

Outlines of Sermons on the Old Testament

ISBN/EAN: 9783743333970

Manufactured in Europe, USA, Canada, Australia, Japa

Cover: Foto ©ninafisch / pixelio.de

Manufactured and distributed by brebook publishing software (www.brebook.com)

. Anonymous

Outlines of Sermons on the Old Testament

OUTLINES OF 300 SERMONS.

The Clerical Library.

THIS series of volumes is specially intended for the clergy of all denominations, and is meant to furnish them with stimulus and suggestion in the various departments of their work. The best thoughts of the best religious writers of the day will be furnished in a condensed form, and at a moderate price.

The first volume, in crown 8vo, is now ready, price $1.50, entitled,—

THREE HUNDRED OUTLINES OF SERMONS ON THE NEW TESTAMENT.

AUTHORS OF SERMONS.

WILLIAM ALEXANDER, D.D.,
    Bishop of Derry.
HENRY ALLON, D.D., London.
ALFRED BARRY, D.D.,
    Canon of Westminster.
G. S. BARRETT, B.A., Norwich.
ROBERT BICKERSTETH, D D,
    Bishop of Ripon.
PHILLIPS BROOKS, Boston.
WM. M. TAYLOR, D.D.,
    New York.
JOHN CAIRNS, D.D., Edinburgh.
GORDON CALTHROP, M.A.,
    London.
W. BOYD CARPENTER, M.A.,
    London.
JAMES CAUGHEY, America.
R. W. CHURCH, D.C.L.,
    Dean of St. Paul's.
S. COLEY (The late), Leeds.
E. R. CONDER, M.A., Leeds.
HOWARD CROSBY, D.D.,
    New York.

BISHOP CUMMINS, America.
T. L. CUYLER, D.D., Brooklyn.
R. S. STORRS, D.D., Brooklyn.
C. H. SPURGEON, London.
W. G. T. SHEDD, D.D., New York.
R. W. DALE, D.D., Birmingham.
C. F. DEEMS, D.D., New York.
MARCUS DODS, D.D., Glasgow.
J. T. DURYEA, D.D., Boston.
J. OSWALD DYKES, D.D., London.
JOHN EDMOND, D.D., London.
F. W. FARRAR, D.D.,
    Canon of Westminster.
T. C. FINLAYSON, M.A.,
    Manchester.
DONALD FRASER, D.D., London.
GEORGE GILFILLAN (The late),
    Dundee.
ALBERT GOODRICH, B.A., Glasgow.
E. M. GOULBURN, D.D.,
    Dean of Norwich.
WILLIAM GRAHAM, D.D., London.
JOHN HANNAH, D.D., Brighton.

[*See next page.*]

Sent on receipt of price, charges prepaid.

OUTLINES OF 300 SERMONS.

EDWIN PAXTON HOOD.
THOMAS JONES, Swansea.
BENJAMIN JOWETT, D.D., Oxford.
JOHN KENNEDY, D.D., London.
JOHN KER, D.D., Edinburgh.
G. W. KITCHIN, M.A., Oxford.
W. J. KNOX-LITTLE,
    Canon of Worcester.
HENRY PARRY LIDDON, D.C.L.,
    Canon of St. Paul's.
J. B. LIGHTFOOT, D.D.,
    Bishop of Durham.
ALEXANDER MACAUSLANE, D.D.,
    London.
JAMES MCCOSH, D.D.,
    Princeton, New Jersey.
JAMES A. MACDONALD, D.D.,
    Princeton, New Jersey.
ALEXANDER MACLAREN, D.D.,
    Manchester.
HUGH MACMILLAN, D.D.,
    Greenock.
W. C. MAGEE, D.D.,
    Bishop of Peterborough.
SAMUEL MARTIN (The late),
    Westminster.
WALTER MORRISON, D.D.,
    London.
JOSEPH PARKER, D.D., London.
JOHN PEDDIE, D.D., New York.
JOHN PULSFORD, Edinburgh.

WILLIAM PULSFORD, D.D.,
    Glasgow.
W. MORLEY PUNSHON, D.D. (The late), London.
ROBERT RAINY, D.D., Edinburgh.
ALEXANDER RALEIGH, D.D. (The late), London.
J. C. RYLE, D D.,
    Bishop of Liverpool.
ADOLPH SAPHIR, D.D., London.
R. PAYNE SMITH, D.D.,
    Dean of Canterbury.
WALTER CHALMERS SMITH, D.D.,
    Edinburgh.
W. ROBERTSON SMITH, M.A.,
    Edinburgh.
A. P. STANLEY, D.D., (The late),
    Dean of Westminster.
A. C. TAIT, D.D.,
    Archbishop of Canterbury.
FREDERICK TEMPLE, D.D,
    Bishop of Exeter.
S. A. TIPPLE, London.
C. J. VAUGHAN, D.D.,
    Dean of Llandaff.
JAMES VAUGHAN, M.A., Brighton.
MARVIN R. VINCENT, D.D.,
    New York.
HENRY WACE, M.A., London.
BROOKE FOSS WESTCOTT, D.D.,
    Canon of Peterborough.

NOW READY:

OUTLINES OF SERMONS ON THE OLD TESTAMENT.

IN PRESS:

OUTLINE SERMONS TO CHILDREN, WITH NUMEROUS ANECDOTES.

The series will probably extend to twelve volumes, and the price will be $1.50 each volume, EACH COMPLETE IN ITSELF.

Sent on receipt of price, charges prepaid.

The Clerical Library.

OUTLINES OF SERMONS

ON THE

OLD TESTAMENT.

New York:
A. C. ARMSTRONG AND SON,
714 BROADWAY.
1883.

[*All rights reserved.*]

PREFATORY NOTE.

IN deference to the wishes of many, the outlines in this volume have been made much fuller than those in the previous volume, and they are consequently fewer in number. A large part of the book is here printed for the first time, and the rest is almost exclusively from fugitive sources, very few of the outlines having appeared in book form.

AUTHORS OF SERMONS.

G. S. BARRETT, B.A., Norwich.
E. BICKERSTETH, D.D., Dean of Lichfield.
E. H. BROWNE, D.D., Bishop of Winchester.
J. BALDWIN BROWN, B.A., London.
T. P. BOULTBEE, LL.D., London.
J. P. CHOWN, London.
R. W. CHURCH, D.C.L., Dean of St. Paul's.
E. R. CONDER, D.D., Leeds.
T. L. CUYLER, D.D., Brooklyn.
A. B. DAVIDSON, D.D., Edinburgh.
J. OSWALD DYKES, D.D., London.
E. HERBER EVANS, Carnarvon.
F. W. FARRAR, D.D., Canon of Westminster.
DONALD FRASER, D.D., London.
J. G. GREENHOUGH, B.A., Leicester.
W. F. HOOK, D.D. (The late) Dean of Chichester.
W. BASIL JONES, D.D., Bishop of St. David's.
JOHN KER, D.D., Glasgow.
EDWARD KING, D.D., Canon of Christ Church.
J. B. LIGHTFOOT, D.D., Bishop of Durham.
H. P. LIDDON, D.D., Canon of St. Paul's.
J. A. MACFADYEN, D.D., Manchester.
ALEXANDER MACLAREN, D.D., Manchester.
W. C. MAGEE, D.D., Bishop of Peterborough.
THEODORE MONOD, Paris.
ARTHUR MURSELL, Birmingham.
JOSEPH PARKER, D.D., London.

E. H. Plumptre, D.D., Dean of Wells.
John Pulsford, Edinburgh.
W. Morley Punshon, D.D. (The late), London.
Robert Rainy, D.D., Edinburgh.
Alexander Raleigh, D.D. (The late), London.
C. P. Reichel, D.D., Trim, Ireland.
Charles Stanford, D.D., London.
A. P. Stanley, D.D. (The late) Dean of Westminster.
W. M. Statham, B.A., London.
W. M. Taylor, D.D., New York.
S. A. Tipple, B.A., London.
H. J. Van Dyke, D.D., America.
C. J. Vaughan, D.D., London, Dean of Llandaff.
James Vaughan, B.A., Brighton, Prebendary of Chichester.
M. R. Vincent, D.D., New York.
W. J. Woods, B.A., Manchester.
C. Wadsworth, D.D., America.
G. H. Wilkinson, M.A., London, Canon of Truro.
C. Wordsworth, D.D., Bishop of Lincoln.

OUTLINES ON THE OLD TESTAMENT.

I. The Creation. GEN. i. 1. "*In the beginning God created the heaven and the earth.*"

How familiar to every child are these opening words of the Bible; and yet how pregnant with interest, the interest of instruction, but also with the interest of difficulty to the strongest minds! What is creation in this primary biblical sense of the term? Clearly it is not mere production of any kind. The natural sense of the passage in the translation, as in the original, is that the universe originally owed both its form and substance to the creative fiat of God.

The Christian Bible, like the Christian creed, begins with stating that all that is not God owes its being to the will of God. The Bible solution of the creation is the only one which seriously respects the rights, the existence of a God. Pantheism buries Him in moral filth. The atheistic materialism denies Him outright. The other supposition that the universe and God are both eternal makes two Gods.

The Bible doctrine of creation does not only protect the supremacy, the personality, the sanctity, the reality of God; but it sheds light upon His nature and character.

I. It illustrates the boundless resources of God's self-existent life. He called into being the very material which He subsequently fashioned. He called it into being out of nothing.

II. Observe as an element of creation the gift of life, that gift which is in its essence so entirely beyond our power of analysis.

III. God creates in majestic and perfect freedom. No force was put upon the Creator. He made it; but He might have left it unmade.

No created being could add to the bliss of God, none could lessen it; and yet the Divine love willed to summon a whole creation into being, upon which in its perfectness and beauty and even in its misery and shame that love might lavish its caresses.

Both in creation and in redemption there is a shadow which is a foil to the eternal love. His love burns bright; but it is ever and anon robed in mystery. For the sinner there are gifts superadded to the gifts of creation; the precious blood of redemption washing out all sins even the foulest, the illuminating Spirit, the sacraments of life. Awake! thou that sleepest, and as thou contemplatest that thou existest and must exist for ever, remember that Christ now and in eternity will give thee light if only thou wilt receive it.

H. P. L.

II. The Spirit of God. Gen. i. 2. "*The Spirit of God moved upon the face of the waters.*"

IT was not peculiar to the Hebrews to believe in spiritual existence. All nations of antiquity of whom we have certain knowledge, had words to express the difference between matter and spirit, and all used more or less the same metaphor to convey the thought, namely breath or blowing. What fitter metaphor could men use! The living, willing mind of man they likened to air; his active energy was the breathing out. Air is invisible, but it is not unsubstantial. So we deem of spiritual existences if we believe in them at all. When God created man, He is said to have breathed into his nostrils the breath of life. When man's breath goeth forth, he dies, he gives up the ghost—the breath—and his life principle is gone. With the Hebrews God was believed to be a spirit, a person, a unity. Yet we may observe, what in the light of after revelation is most observable, that whilst the first verse of their most ancient Scriptures teaches that God is personal and one, the second verse pictures to us God sending forth His Spirit to brood over the chaos and breathe into it light, order, and life.

Here we see the shadowing out of a truth which Christians believe but of which the Jews could only catch a glimpse, that God is over us, God is in the midst of us and God is within us.

He who sent forth His Spirit to breathe order into creation, sent forth His Word to dwell amongst those, who in His likeness had yet become likened to the Evil one. The Word wrestled for them with that enemy and breathed forth fresh spiritual life for those who would enlist into His company.

The victory is sure, for inspired by that Divine Spirit we can expel the Evil one and triumph over him.

At present the battle sounds are loud, but though the waters may prevail upon the earth, still the ark floats over them, and the Spirit of God is moving upon the face of the waters.

E. H. B.

III. Light. GEN. i. 3. "*Let there be light.*"

THIS is the very first expression which the Bible contains of the Divine Will. It is, according to the conception of the sacred writer, the first voice which broke the silence of eternity. It is a tribute to the paramount greatness, the inestimable value of light over darkness for all the coming ages of the world then first struggling into existence.

I. This Divine command is the keynote of the whole Bible. False religions say "Let there be darkness!" They have their refuge not in light but in darkness. But true religion has always said, "let there be brightness and warmth and cheerfulness, let there be openness, and knowledge, and enlightment." Doubtless so long as we linger in this "valley of the shadow of death," we must see "as through a glass darkly," but nevertheless the object of Revelation is to diminish the shadow, to illuminate the darkness as far as possible.

II. Christ was the light as well as the life of the world. One main purpose of His work in the midst of men was to make them not children of the mist, but children of the light.

III. The last words of the Book of Revelation agree with the first words of Genesis; describing the perfection of the blessed it says, "And there shall be no night there, and they need no candle, neither light of the sun, for the Lord God giveth them light, and the Lamb is the light thereof."

A. P. S.

IV. The Creation of Man. Gen. i. 27. "*So God created man in His own image, in the image of God created He him.*"

It will probably be found upon examination, that one thread of unbelief runs through every form of modern scepticism. This is either a direct or a virtual denial of God's personality. If there is any one doctrine which is more certainly scriptural than another, it is that of the Divine Personality.

I. "God created man in His own image." It is not that the God whom we worship is like man: but that man is created in the likeness of God. And therefore we do not draw Him down to us; we rather seek to raise ourselves up to Him.

There is between God and man a real resemblance, or rather a real community of nature, which the Bible announces at the very outset.

We may interpret that image of God of which we read in the text, to be that which is distinctive of man in the creation, and that by which he comes nearer to God than any other earthly creature.

Man knows himself; can think, reason, choose, distinguish between good and evil, and love good rather than evil. At this point he touches the nature of God, while he is in these respects more or less sharply divided from the beasts that perish. It is true that even in these things the image of God is partially defaced; but so long as there remains in him any sense of right and wrong, any sting of conscience, his nature has in it something akin to God.

II. The image of God may be defaced in all, but it is wholly destroyed in none. It may be repaired and developed by careful intellectual and moral training; but even this will not suffice for man's perfect state. For there is a "new creation," as there shall be "a new heaven and a new earth;" only the new creation, which shall be consummated in eternity, is begun in time, and "they that are Christ's," have here "put off the old man with his deeds, and have put on the new man, which is renewed in knowledge after the image of Him which created him."

W. B. J.

V. Walking with God. GEN. v. 24. "*Enoch walked with God: and he was not; for God took him.*"

IT is never safe when you are reading the Scriptures to judge from mere appearances, for sometimes in the least likely places you will meet with the most precious passages. What an odour of refreshing from the better land comes wafted to us in the words, "And he was not, for God took him." It blossoms here like a flower growing in the crevice of a venerable tomb, and just when we are becoming saddened with the dull refrain, "and he died," it lifts our thoughts to a life that is beyond life.

Let us study the record, that we may be helped thereby to earnest holiness on earth and happy immortality in heaven. Let us get at a definite idea of all that is implied in walking with God.

It describes a habitual course of conduct, and not a mere isolated act. A walk is something more than a step. It is a way of life, and a constant progress in that way.

We shall find underlying the history which is summed up in these words, three distinguishing characteristics.

I. There is faith.

He that walketh with God must believe that He is. We cannot walk with an abstraction, and so we conclude that Enoch must have had a very real sense of the existence of the unseen God. He was to him as one continually by his side, and that is the explanation of the grandeur of his life.

II. There is fellowship implied in this experience.

The talk is the great feature of the walk. This is a favour you reserve for those you love. And so when it is said of one that he "walks" with God, we conclude that he and God are familiar friends. The fellowship of the believer with his God is a very real thing. There is a consciousness in his soul of God's friendship with him, a sense of God's nearness to him, and an experience of helpfulness from God. "Thou God seest me," is with him as it was with Hagar, an ejaculation of delight and gratitude and not of dread, for he knows that under such supervision no evil can befall him.

III. There is assimilation. We become like those with whom we constantly associate. He that walks with God, shall be at length God-like. In the measure in which he walks with God, he obeys the precept, "Be ye holy; for I am holy."

This God-likeness which is thus associated with walking with God is a progressive thing. The believer grows in holiness through increasing and prolonged fellowship with God.

Thus it is evident that the man who walks with God has a peculiar aim in life, for he seeks something different from that which is merely seen and temporal; that he has a new rule for life, for he endeavours to follow always the law of the Lord; that he has a special model in life, for he desires likeness to God in Christ Jesus; and that he has a strong support through life, for "he endures as seeing Him who is invisible," and the approval of God is more to him than the opinion of his fellow-men.

Where is this walk with God to be maintained?

In the minds of many it is particularly associated with special religious exercises so called—the study of the Scriptures, or the devotions of the closet, or the observance of the ordinances of the sanctuary. But when a man's communion with God is confined to what are called distinctively religious duties, it is not real communion with God even in them.

This walk is a continual thing, and does not, and cannot, cease when the man rises from his knees or closes his Bible.

Neither is this experience an adjunct to a particular occupation.

The notion that it is easier for a minister to walk with God than it is for other men, is only a fragment of that priestcraft which had so long possession of the minds of men.

Lastly, consider the consummation of this experience. "Enoch walked with God: and he was not; for God took him," or as Hebrews expounds the words, "He was translated that he should not see death."

He passed into heaven as the saints who shall be on the earth at the coming of the Lord will do; without undergoing death, and simply by receiving that change which fitted the body of this life for the immortality of the life that is to come.

The true readiness for death is this walking with God, and if we can but have Enoch's character, it makes no difference how or where we are required to die, for however it comes that will be unspeakable gain, as introducing us into the presence of the Lord.

W. M. T.

VI. **Harvest.** GEN. viii. 22. "*While the earth remaineth, seedtime and harvest, and cold and heat, and summer and winter, and day and night shall not cease.*"

THIS was God's first promise to a pardoned and restored world, and if for this reason only, that it recalls this great promise, harvest-time is a most solemn time of the year.

I. The harvest carries us back to the oldest days of the world. It binds us all together—the old world and the new—it makes us feel that after all we live the same life at bottom and depend on the same bounty of God to sustain us.

II. The harvest is a solemn time, since it reminds us of what our earthly life depends upon. In the year is grown the year's food only, and the world each year literally depends for its subsistence on something which is newly given it, and which it cannot provide for itself.

III. It suggests a time of trial and of reckoning. Here, as in other things, our God calls us to be fellow-workers with him. If we have not sown, neither shall we reap. If we have sown bad seed, we shall reap accordingly. When the harvest-time has once come, there is no opportunity for mending or altering

The harvest was often used by Christ as the image and likeness of the judgment of the world. When the reapers are at work in the fields, can you help thinking of those other awful reapers of whom the Lord and His apostles have told us? It seems almost as if the parable of the world's judgment was being acted before our eyes. Now is our sowing time against that great harvest. Sow not the unblessed seed of selfishness and forgetfulness of God's benefits and of a soul dead to the wants and sufferings of others. Sow not the wind of sin and vanity, for they that thus sow shall reap the whirlwind. God who keeps his promise in the seedtime and the harvest, will keep it in yet greater things. He will keep it in things eternal who keeps it so surely in the things of time.

R. W. C.

VII. **Lessons from Lot.** GEN. xiii. 10-12. *"And Lot lifted up his eyes, and beheld all the plain of Jordan, that it was well watered everywhere. Then Lot chose him all the plain of Jordan."*

IT was the will of God concerning Abraham that he should be ultimately isolated from all his kinsmen. Terah died in Haran, before Canaan was reached, and now he separates from his nephew Lot. Up till this time Lot was happy and prosperous, but his troubles begin now.

I. Notice the evils which may follow from one wrong step in life. Under the influence of the love of this world Lot decided his habitation, without taking the interests of his soul and the souls of his household into account. Let us think of Lot every time we have to decide whether we shall go to the right hand or to the left, and let us see to it that no well-watered plains allure us toward Sodom, to our soul's detriment. In every choice we must take the elements of tendency and direction into account. Towards Sodom is ultimately in Sodom.

II. Notice the stealthy insidiousness of sin. There is a wide difference between Abraham's household and Lot's, but that difference was not a thing of sudden growth. We have the key to it in the question addressed by Lot to the angel: Is it not a little one?

III. Notice the necessity of watchfulness against sin throughout one's earthly life. The noon and the afternoon of life are beset with dangers as great as those of its morning, and our only safety lies in constant vigilance.

We cannot say much of Lot's eternal portion. All our hope regarding him is based on Peter's words, when he speaks of him as a "righteous" man. We know that if he did acknowledge his sin and seek God's forgiveness, that blessing would not be withheld.

W. M. T.

VIII. Prevailing Prayer.

GEN. xviii. 32. *"And he said, Oh let not the Lord be angry, and I will speak yet but this once: Peradventure ten shall be found there. And He said, I will not destroy it for ten's sake."*

MOST remarkable and most encouraging is this instance of prevailing prayer. It may well stimulate us to exercise sublimer faith when we behold a mortal thus wrestling with Omnipotence—wrestling with such holy boldness that justice suspends its inflictions and cannot seal the sinners' doom. Pious men, in all ages of the world's history, are the true strength of the nations in which they live! Oftentimes averting calamity, and restoring strength and blessing.

I. Who are pious men? (1) They are pious who avowedly separate themselves from surrounding wickedness. (2) They are pious who cultivate firm attachment to the doctrines of Christian truth. (3) They are pious who cultivate cordial brotherly love. (4) They are pious who endeavour to spread the Gospel and convert the world.

II. The effects which we may expect to ensue from such piety. This is the doctrine of the text, that Sodom would have been spared if the ten righteous men had been there. God preserves nations for the sake of pious men. Pious men will preserve a land's prosperity, and spiritual prosperity will also be secured. There will be the defeat of erroneous opinions, and truth will prevail. The salvation of souls will be secured also. The conversion of a soul is an infinitely greater triumph than the eradication of a false opinion. Convert a man's soul and his opinions will come right by-and-by.

If you are not personally pious, you will be accomplices in drawing down the thunderbolt which will ruin your country. The saint and believer is a patriot as well as a saint. The worldling may sneer and scorn, but we have a noble revenge, for it is pious men that have kept the conflagrating elements away from this long-doomed world up to the present moment of its history. Oh for the increase of these pious men! Be you of the number of this unostentatious but valiant host.

W. M. P.

IX. Blessing through Abraham's Seed. GEN. xxii. 18. *"And in thy seed shall all the nations of the earth be blessed."*

THE history of the whole Church of God in every age lies in the promises made to Abraham. There is not a blessing that any child of God under any subsequent dispensation ever received, which is not the result of the covenant which God made with Abraham. Every Gentile travels to all his mercies through the Jews.

Notice that even Abraham had the purpose of God respecting the Jews unfolded to his mind very gradually. Little by little God gave him revelations, and at last He said: "And in thy seed shall all the nations of the earth be blessed;" adding, "Because thou hast obeyed My voice." From this we gather the general rule—that a course of practical obedience is the nearest road to the understanding of prophecy.

I. How is Abraham's seed in its natural sense the blessing of the whole world?

It was a "blessing" to all our race when God made Abraham's seed the depository of His truth, committing to them His word.

Nobly and faithfully, in every generation, have the Jews done their work for the world in the guardianship of God's ancient word.

It is a blessing, because in God's dealings with Israel we see warnings for our instruction and our peace. Again, it is a blessing because Gentile Christians are indebted to the Jews for whatever spiritual privileges they enjoy. Again, the present state of the Jews should be regarded as the great standing evidence of the truth of revelation.

II. How is Abraham's seed in its spiritual sense the blessing of the world? God had a particular intention when He made the promise to run in the singular, and not in the plural number, and that He said, "Not in thy seeds, as of many, but in thy seed." The Lord Jesus was the "Seed" in which all nations receive blessing. It is an argument of deep consolation to know that the nature of the great Elder Brother places Him in fellowship with our bodily trials—that He is still a man, "Abraham's Seed." Through Christ we become of the seed of Abraham, and there is not a prophecy of love of which I may not say, "It is mine because I am Abraham's seed."

J. V.

X. **In the way.** GEN. xxiv. 27. "*I being in the way, the Lord led me.*"

THIS chapter is full of beautiful things, but the words of the text are its brightest gem. It is only when we are in a certain way that we have a right to expect that God will lead us; and, even in that way, there is only one kind of leading that we are warranted to look for.

I. The Way.

(1) This servant Eliezer was evidently in the way of duty. He had accepted a commission from his master, and thus far he had faithfully followed the instructions he had received. It was not, therefore, until he had done all that he could, that he awaited the guidance of Jehovah. Now in all this there is much to direct us, for the way to get more light is to follow fully that which we already possess. This applies to intellectual doubt, and when we are perplexed as to the truth of great doctrines; it is well to remember that the path to peace lies through the performance of those duties in regard to which we are already certain. Ask, "Is my conduct abreast of my conscience, or am I living below even that standard which I have accepted?" Let a man hold fast by those things which are yet certain to him, and faithfully and earnestly act up to them, for it is by these that God will ultimately lift him out and set his feet upon the rock of faith. The same thing is true in reference to conduct. When in our daily lives we are brought to a stand and see no outlet, then if we are where we are because we have been faithfully doing what we believed to be right, let us stand still and wait, assured that God will open up our way. It makes all the difference in the world as to matters of conduct, whether we are simply seeking our own gain, our own pleasure, our own honour, or whether we are striving to meet the obligation which God has laid upon us.

In the former case we have no right to expect God's guidance; in the latter, we may be sure that it will not be withheld. Cultivate then the habit of walking in the way of duty, and you will find it a way of light. It is when you want an excuse for evading duty that anxiety begins.

(2) This servant was in the way of faith. He had a firm, child-like, and sincere belief in God. God was to him a real personal Being, as interested in the success of his mission as he was, and able to help him in his present emergency.

Now we do not wonder that such an one was guided. We may, perhaps, find the secret of our harassments and daily worries in the fact that to most of us God is little better than a mere abstraction.

Unbelief is at the root of our worry. If we had the same faith as this Oriental servant we should be very seldom in difficulty, and when we were we should be willing to wait peacefully and trustfully for His guidance.

(3) This servant was in the way of prayer. That follows from what has been remarked of his faith, but there is a plain, direct, earnest purpose in his supplication which is most striking. He even specifies the way in which he wishes his prayer to be answered. This man was a child and therefore he spoke as a child and was answered in a style which he could understand. As compared with the weakest Christian, Eliezer was but as a child is to a full-grown man. This request of his was born of trust in God, and not of suspicion of God; and therefore, being a real application to Him, it was answered by Him.

While we may well hesitate to present our petitions in such a form as this, we may be encouraged from the answer which even this prayer received, to go to God in every perplexity.

This servant went to the very root of his anxiety. He did not ask for blessings a long way ahead, but said, "Give me good speed this day," and having unburdened his heart, he waited God's answer. So it should be with us. When a man is in earnest he will take the shortest way of telling his distress.

II. The leading of God, when we are in the way.

This leading is to be looked for by us, in and through God's ordinary providence.

Through natural law and common-place incidents God is leading His people to-day, as really as He led Israel by the pillar of cloud and fire. If you are in the way of duty, of faith, and of prayer, be sure that somehow, through the common incidents of a common day, He will guide your feet into the right path. How near this brings God to us! How sacred, too, in this aspect of them, do the events of our lives become! They are new revelations of God to us, and we too, have, like these old patriarchs, our Hebrons, and Bethels, and Peniels, and Moriahs. Let us go on in this faith, and we shall feel our hearts lightened as we sing, "The steps of a good man are ordered of the Lord."

W. M. T.

XI. Jacob's Dream. GEN. xxviii. 12. *"And he dreamed, and behold a ladder set up on the earth, and the top of it reached to heaven."*

So wonderfully rich is this singular passage that it would be unwise to seek to exhaust it. Let us look at the most luminous points in the narrative and not seek to reach the intermediate parts, which lie deeper and, perhaps, beyond us. The transactions are recorded in the history of a man, of all the patriarchs perhaps most like ourselves.

I. Notice the circumstances in which this part of Jacob's history took place.

It was when he was setting out in life and leaving his home for the first time.

And whatever consoling power this vision and history has, it has it especially to the young on the threshold of life, when they are taking the first step on the dark unknown road of activity, which we call living,—to all such going out into life is this vision sent.

Or when one no longer young is now for the first time taking on him the part he is fitted to play in life, and at last awakening to the duty of doing God's work in the world, this vision comes to such with strong encouragement.

And there are many others of those who have already entered on life, who also are entitled to take encouragement from this vision, not now to begin, but to carry on life. For few there are who on looking back will feel satisfied with the past. And with the memory of former difficulties and falls that is painful, there is a need of encouragement, and this encouragement is to be found in this vision given to the lonely patriarch.

II. Jacob's dream. His dream was not a baseless fabric like our own, but a vision sent him from God. What Jacob saw was not some new thing created to be shown to Jacob, it was something already there which Jacob was enabled to see. He knew it to be a real thing, the only wonder was the opening of his eyes to see it. These things Jacob saw are always to be seen—they are real things if we had but eyes to see them. This ladder always exists, it always binds earth and heaven together. Jehovah is always standing at the head of it. Angels are always crowding up and down upon it, ministering to them who shall be heirs of salvation.

Does not it often seem to us—to us who want the eyes to see what Jacob saw—that there is no communion between earth and heaven—that God is far away—that no cry or influence of ours can ascend, and no help can come down?

Jacob, no very young man at this time, calls such a period the day of his distress. His distress was chiefly made up of the feeling of being alone in the world, and of the feeling that he had now taken himself in charge, and must think and resolve for himself, and fight his own battles henceforth, and meet foes he was little able to cope with.

God meets him with these words of encouragement: "I will keep thee in all places whither thou goest." What strange sights a little faith helps us to see, how it transforms the complexion of the world, how it helps our eyesight to pierce through the veils that are hung across the face of things and see marvellous things beyond!

Till God opens our eyes we see little.

This wanderer thought the wilderness a weary, God-abandoned spot. God opened his eyes, and he found himself lying at the gate of heaven. And we think the earth far from God, and our life lonely and ourselves unheeded, while, if we would but look, heaven is opened, and God standing looking down in unspeakable love upon us.

III. The vision itself. Jacob felt lonely and he felt weak; and when the darkness came down, his heart filled with sensations he had never known before. And God used the thoughts that had been working all day in his mind to attach His revelation to. This is the way in which revelation generally came. It came in such a way that it seemed to grow out of the mind of the prophet who gave it. Like any other weary and troubled man, Jacob dreamed, and his dream was woven out of the materials that had all day long been troubling his spirit.

The vision is described in words that express the simple but extreme wonder of the seer. He dreamed, and *behold* a ladder, and *behold* the angels, and *behold* the Lord. Wonder after wonder unfolds itself. And then a voice comes rolling down the steps: "I am the Lord God of Abraham thy father." As to the ladder's appearance, we need not enquire; the truth taught was the connection of earth and heaven, the nearness of heaven to earth, and the close and rapid intercourse between the two. The Lord was very visible; He was so near that His whisper could be heard down from above, so lowly are the heavens, so closely do all heavenly things brood over and embrace the earth.

All that was revealed to Jacob was that there was a ladder—a way to heaven; at least a way, however steep and narrow. To us it has been shown Who the way is. Christ said to Nathanael, "Hereafter ye shall see heaven open and the angels of God ascending and descending upon the Son of Man. I am the Way: no man cometh unto the Father but by Me." Lying at the foot of this Ladder we have visits of the angels; lifting up our eyes we see the Lord standing looking upon us in love and hear Him speaking to us.

Notice the attitude and words of Jehovah Himself. He is standing, attitude of interest. He is looking down, attitude of sympathy and knowledge, bending over His sleeping child.

But Jehovah's sympathy is not exhausted with silence: He speaks, He introduces Himself to Jacob, and with marvellous humanity. "I am the God of thy father." Jacob was loved for Abraham's sake. This is a great mystery, but God loves us for our father's sake. The children of God's people are from their birth under the peculiar love of God. Jehovah's promise to Jacob is twofold: a promise of salvation, and a promise of guidance in life's journey. Jacob stipulated for bread to eat and raiment to put on, for outward help. But then such was the relation between God and these early simple men, that these outward things were the symbols and assurances of things far deeper.

IV. Jacob's response to God's offers.

Jacob vowed a vow. He responded to this marvellous vision. He made a resolution, a determination. Religion needs this. Particularly in beginning life this is needful. We need to resolve firmly that the Lord shall be our God— not business, not pleasure, not affection—the *Lord*. Jacob also set up a stone. He made the inner resolution, and having taken it, he also set to this strange outward seal of it. And it is well to commit ourselves to a godly life—to let others into the secret of our vow. It is well, too, for others, to set up our outward sign of finding God; to strew the world over with monuments of God's presence and grace.

For there are always men in the world seeking after God, and often wearied and disheartened by the search. How cheering to some such wanderer it would have been to find such a monument as Jacob reared!

The Lord, after years had gone by, and the fervour of Jacob's purpose began to fade, commanded him to return to Bethel, to renew old memories. And at the sight of Bethel he grew young again. The crust, the hardness put upon him by life fell off, and he was softened by these old memories, and he shook off habits that were tightening themselves about him, and became again as of old, resolutely the Lord's. And so let us do! Keep our Bethels in mind—live over again the feelings—it will keep the world from bearing in upon us, and sin from gaining the mastery over us.

A. B. D.

XII. Hindrances to Faith.

GEN. xxviii. 15. "*Behold, I am with thee, and will keep thee in all places whither thou goest, and will bring thee again into this land: for I will not leave thee until I have done that which I have spoken to thee of.*"

A BELIEF in God is more effectual for man's happiness

than all the flowers of Paradise, and we can all help in the maintenance of the belief in God.

All those who are conscious of moral freedom, and all who know themselves to be persons and not things, not mere machines, but men endowed with the awful dower of personality, we would ask to help in this maintenance of belief. What are some of the hindrances and difficulties that you will meet with, if you endeavour by a life of daily duty, to give the evidence of your moral fceedom, and of your separate personality in the midst of the great forces in which you live?

I. The feeling of your own littlenesss. One has said, "Two things fill me with awe; the starry firmament, and the responsibility of man." We so often trifle with our powers of thought, and consider the powers that make up our separate personality so insignificant, that their littleness fills us with awe. But God made us, and He made us for Himself. That feeling of weakness is but a right consciousness of true creaturely dependence. All we have to do is to awaken like Jacob, from a dream, and admit that this world is still the House of God: that the Lord is in this place, though we knew it not.

II. Another hindrance is your sense of sin. The sense of duty, more or less, in all of us, must produce the consciousness of disobedience. God did not refuse to be with Jacob though he had sinned, and His presence preserved him from further sin; his old sin was constantly before him, but it never overcame him. It gave him suffering and trouble, but it did not rob him of God's continuing presence. The fear of the past need not rob you of the hope that you may yet give your life as evidence of the existence of the one true God.

III. Another difficulty is the sense of singleness which arises from personality. No two lives can follow exactly in the same steps. The text offers the consolation of a personal presence, and again the Son of God has promised to be with us always, even to the end of the world.

E. K.

XIII. Jacob at Bethel. GEN. xxviii. 16. "*Surely the Lord is in this place, and I knew it not.*"

THE site of Bethel is described as an unimpressive scene, with nothing whatever to attract the eye or fire the imagination. Yet this was none other than the House of God, this was the gate of heaven. Why should this one spot be chosen to plant the foot of the ladder which connected heaven and earth?

The paradox of Bethel is the paradox of the Gospel—is the paradox of God's spiritual dispensations at all times The Incarnation itself was the supreme manifestation of this paradox. Look at the accompaniments of the Incarnation. Could any environment of circumstances well have been imagined more incongruous, more alien to this unique event in human history! And the same paradox which ruled the foundation of the Church extended also to its building up.

So then in its accompaniments, not less than in its main idea, this incident at Bethel is a type of the Gospel of Christ. This exile prefigures a greater outcast, the whole family of man. This ladder reared up from earth to heaven is the Incarnation of the Eternal Word. To those whose sight is purged by faith, to those who are gifted with the eye of the spirit, the vision of Bethel will be vouchsafed with a far more exceeding glory: "Verily, verily, I say unto you, hereafter ye shall see heaven open and the angels of God ascending and descending upon the Son of Man:" and on thyself too, man, for thou art one with this Son of Man, one with the Father in Him.

If the capacity of vision be absent, then the heavens are riven asunder and the glory streams forth in vain. Only the cold bare stones beneath, only the midnight gloom overhead, these alone are visible otherwise. To realize God's presence, to hear God's voice, let this be the aim and discipline of our lives. So at length we shall pass from Bethel to Peniel, from the palace courts to the presence chamber. We shall see God face to face. The blessing is won at length by that long lonely wrestling under the midnight sky. The fraud, the worldliness, the self-seeking, is thrown off like a slough; all is changed and old things have passed away. J. B. L.

XIV. Mysterious Providences. GEN. xlii. 36. *"All these things are against me."*

JACOB was indeed brought low when he could speak thus; and though we may not vindicate him for murmuring, we understand his state of heart too well to upbraid him for giving way to his grief. But natural as this outgush of feeling was, we cannot but observe that it was essentially atheistic. He makes no mention of God in his exclamation. He had for the time forgotten Bethel's God.

This sentiment was also quite untrue. These things were really working for his good. We all feel that there are times when we are prone to fall into this despair. Let us see what considerations we may draw from the Book or from our experience, wherewith we may fortify ourselves against this temptation.

I. We have the unqualified assurance that God is the Friend of His people, directing and controlling all things for their highest good.

II. We have the evidence of God's love to us, in the death of His Son on our behalf.

III. We have the testimony of many of God's people to the fact that the things in their lots apparently hardest were after all the most blessed to them.

There can be no strength without strain, and the very wrestle of our soul with difficulty, when we wrestle according to the will of God, leaves behind it a residuum of reserve power.

Let God finish His work, and when you too can see the end from the beginning, you will not need that any one should vindicate His ways to you, and you will see that none of these things were against you.

W. M. T.

XV. Stability. GEN. xlix. 4. *" Unstable as water, thou shalt not excel."*

JACOB'S first-born son seems to have been distinguished by levity of spirit, weakness of will, and fickleness of disposition. He was not an out-and-out bad man. He at first meant to do right, but between the purpose and the performance other things intervened, and so he seldom carried out his intention and never attained eminence.

It is remarkable too, that the same characteristic reappears in the Reubenites, who were distinguished for nothing but their poor mediocrity. No men of eminence or influence sprang from that tribe during the long course of Jewish history.

But apart altogether from their reference to one of the tribes of Israel, the words of the text enunciate a general law which holds good in every age of the world and in every department of life. Wherever there is fickleness you may say with infallible certainty to the man who is characterized by it, "Thou shalt not excel."

And if we are flippant, fickle and unsteady, we may never hope to rise to true Christian excellence. If we vibrate between principle and passion, or change from acting now as the sons of God to acting again as the children of the world, we shall never become eminent as Christians, but may, even like Reuben, be deprived of our birthright or, like his descendants settle down on the wrong side of Jordan, and short of the Land of Promise.

I. Foremost among the elements of Christian stability is a perception of the supreme importance of the Christian life. If we once get that firmly rooted in our hearts, then, naturally, we will give ourselves entirely to its attainment. How are we to obtain such a conviction of the pre-eminence of Christian holiness? It is by earnest investigation of the subject itself. Let any man seriously set himself to ponder the statements of the Word of God, and he will be led to see that if there is anything in them at all, everything is in them, and they must be entirely put aside, or everything else must be put aside for them and made subordinate to them.

II. A second element in Christian stability is strength of will to turn aside from all those things which are inconsistent with the attainment of the excellence we seek.

The Christian must resolutely set himself to refuse all enticements to the commission of sin, and endeavour so to keep his worldly business within bounds that attention to it shall not hinder his progress in holiness. This firmness of will is to be acquired by prayerful exertion. We have only to begin to resist and to go on resisting until by the strength of God's Spirit the habit is acquired by us. Mark, it must be prayerful exertion. Prayerful, because it is only in God's strength that we can acquire it ; exertion, because it is only through the forth-putting of our own efforts that God will strengthen us. "Work out your own salvation with fear and trembling, for it is God that worketh in you, to will and to do of His good pleasure." God works in us, but the willing and the doing are our own, and so it is only in the union of prayer and effort that we can obtain strength of will.

III. Another element of Christian steadfastness is concentration of soul.

This may seem identical with what has been specified before, but there is a difference between them.

A man may shut out all external intrusion, while yet he may lose all benefit of this seclusion by allowing his mind to wander in a fantastic day-dream instead of chaining it to some particular topic. He may have a merely negative excellence, and may be remarkable more for the absence of evil than for the presence of positive holiness.

Hence we must not only strive to keep our souls from sin, but also seek to centre them on the attainment of the measure of the stature of the perfect man in Christ Jesus as the great end of our being. Holiness is a character ; it is not doing but being. Religion is a growing in holiness, and is not to be confounded with religious services. You cannot indeed be always engaged in what are commonly called religious exercises ; but a man may be religious—growing in holiness—in his shop, in the market, at his fireside, as well as in the church and at the table of the Lord. There is a holy and an unholy way of doing even the simplest and commonest things, and the man who has the concentration of soul here spoken of, will seek always to take the holy method.

This concentration is to be acquired by prayerful, personal exertion.

Think of Christ in everything, and let everything you do be offered up in loving sacrifice to Him.

If this be not done, the great uniting bond which makes your life a harmonious whole will be broken, recklessness will characterize your career, and when men come to write your history they will do it in the words of the text, " Unstable as water, he did not excel."

W. M. T.

XVI. The Secret of Trust. GEN. l. 20. "*But as for you, ye thought evil against me: but God meant it unto good, to bring to pass, as it is this day, to save much people alive.*"

WE cannot but admire the conduct of Joseph in this remarkable interview. He had learned to look at his whole life in the light of God's Providence, and in his resignation to that he found it easy to forgive his brethren. "Ye thought evil against me: but God meant it unto good."

Here is the "open secret" of that marvellous equanimity which is so characteristic of his demeanour. He traced God's hand in every incident of his history. He accepted the lot which God assigned him, and wherever he was he had the unfaltering conviction that "God meant it unto good." If we had the same trust in the wise and loving arrangements of an all-superintending God, we, too, might continue peaceful amid all the changes and surprises of our unsettled and fleeting lives.

I. The Providence of God preserves and controls all the operations of the physical universe and all the actions of moral agents.

As the shorter catechism has succinctly expressed it, "It is most holy, wise and powerful, preserving and governing all His creatures and all their actions." That there is such a thing is clearly taught in the Word of God, is matter of daily observation, and follows naturally and necessarily from the very fact of creation. That which could be produced alone by the will of the Omnipotent can be maintained and regulated only by the same volition. Hence, unless we are prepared to adopt the ancient doctrine of the eternity of things as they are, we must accept that of the all-sustaining and all-governing Providence. "Of Him, and to Him, and through Him, are all things.' "By Him all things consist."

II. The Providence of God is universal, having respect to every atom of creation and every incident of life.

There are some, however, who conceive it to be derogatory to the greatness of God that he should interest Himself in minute details. There are two obvious answers to this.

(1) There can be no perfection without the arrangement of details.

(2) Small things are often the hinges on which the most momentous matters turn, and it is therefore impossible to overrule the greater without taking cognizance also of the less.

III. This universal Providence is carried on in harmony with those modes of operation which we call natural laws. We shall not here attempt to explain how the Providence of God is so carried on as to be a controlling and governing thing, while yet it does not infringe on the moral freedom of man. That it is so carried on is plainly taught in the Scriptures and confirmed by experience. It is necessary to notice particularly that the actions of men, as well as the operations of natural law, are under the control of God, because it is in reference to the moral sphere of Providence that the faith of most of us is weakest. How often, for example, one is tempted to say, when a fellow-man has deliberately injured him, "If it had been a visitation of God I could have borne it." Now, of course there is an immense difference between what God does directly and what He simply permits others to do, yet the fact that the actions so permitted by Him are wrought into His plan of our lives ought surely to have some importance in our view, and we should seek, like Joseph here, to trace the goodness of His overruling hand and to forgive those who have injured us.

IV. God's Providence is carried on for moral and religious ends. This will be at once allowed so far as the sphere of spiritual things is concerned. But we find that the primal curse was, "Thou shalt surely die," and in that, physical was connected with moral evil. So in God's dealings with Israel we find that physical calamity came as the punishment of their iniquity. God's Providence is conducted now on the same principles as it was then, and we must still expect that moral evil will be attended by physical calamity. Thus in the universe of God the moral and the physical go hand in hand and still the law is vindicated in morals, as in the fields of the agriculturist. "Whatsoever a man soweth, that shall he also reap."

V. The Providence of God contemplates the highest good of those who are on the side of holiness and truth.

"All things work together for good to them that love God"; observe the condition, "to them that love God;" remember that if we would love God, the first indispensable thing is that we accept God's love to us.

W. M. T.

XVII. Training Children.
Exod. ii. 9. "*Take this child away, and nurse it for me, and I will give thee thy wages.*"

God's care over the infant Moses is but an illustration of the Divine watchfulness over all children. Pharaoh's daughter spoke better than she knew when she uttered the words of our text. God spake through her lips.

I. The first qualification for the training of children is the love of children. This means something more and better than the instinctive fondness which men and women, in common with beasts, have for their own offspring. It is a perception of the intrinsic beauty of childhood, a sympathy with its simplicity and freedom from guile, a profound yearning towards its helplessness. They who do not love other people's children, do not love their own in the sense upon which we are insisting. Miriam's heart beat and her cheek glowed with its impulse when she "stood afar off to wit what would be done." She is the type of multitudes of single 'sisters whose unselfish devotion is among the richest treasures of the family and the Church. Pharaoh's daughter was constrained by this love when she had compassion on the weeping child. Jesus Christ exercised it in perfection when He took infants in His arms and blessed them.

II. The second grand essential is to receive children as sacred trusts from God to be nursed for Him. Our success in the prosecution of any work in life must depend upon the motives with which we enter upon it, and the end we propose to obtain by it. When the little one is laid in our bosom and we ask, "What manner of child will this be?" the answer is "Just what you propose to make of it." We should regard a child as a being of unbounded susceptibilities, and destined to eternity, which God has committed to us to train for His glory.

III. A third essential is the requirement of unanswering obedience. This is the first element of all social virtue, and of all religion. This requirement does not involve any harshness in the manner of its enforcement. It is saturated through and through by the love of the children. It is lifted above the impulses of selfish petulance and passion by a sense of the Divine trust given to us.

IV. Parents ought to cultivate and win the absolute confidence and affection of their children. We must not take too much for granted on this subject. If the plastic period of childhood is not improved to sow the seeds of a rational affection and confidence which after years will cultivate and develop, the natural instinct will amount to nothing, even if it does not turn again and rend the bosom that has nursed it. It is not easy to obtain this absolute confidence and affection except so far as love makes easy the self-denials and unselfish devotion which it suggests.

There are cases, indeed, where after long years of self-sacrificing love, a broken-hearted father and mother can only come to Christ saying, "Have mercy upon me, O Lord! my son, or my daughter, is grievously tormented with a devil." For surely there is no worse form of demoniacal possession than the filial ingratitude that tramples on a father's or mother's heart in its way to everlasting orphanage and remorse.

The most important thing connected with home is the atmosphere which pervades it. If it is warm with love, and bright with the recognition of God's presence, then it is indeed a garden of the Lord.

H. J. V. D.

XVIII. God's Revelation to Moses. Exod. iii. 6.

"*I am the God of thy father, the God of Abraham, the God of Isaac, and the God of Jacob. And Moses hid his face; for he was afraid to look upon God.*"

THIS verse has been rendered for ever memorable by the use our Lord made of it, in replying the Sadducees, as the great proof of the Resurrection of the dead drawn from the old Testament Scriptures: "As touching the resurrection of the dead, have ye not read that which was spoken unto you by God, saying, I am the God of Abraham, and the God of Isaac, and the God of Jacob?" (Matt. xxii. 31, 32). It is not strange the multitude were "astonished when they heard this," for the argument is so new and unsuspected, and yet so conclusive, that it still fills us with the same wonder at the depth and originality of Christ's interpretation of these words, and suggests to us what unexplored riches there may lie beneath the most familiar words of Scripture.

The whole chapter in the Book of Exodus, from which this text is taken, is one of the great chapters of the Bible, and like the call of Abraham, or the giving of the law at Sinai, or the establishment of the kingdom in Canaan, forms one of the great critical epochs in the unfolding of the history of the old covenant.

I. First of all it ought to be noticed that the deliverance of Israel from Egypt, and the call of Moses as the deliverer, begin with the personal revelation of God to Moses. It is not without meaning that the history of the Exodus begins with the history of the burning bush. All the servants of God who have been called to any great work by Him, have commenced their work with the vision of God. Abraham, Elijah, Isaiah, Jeremiah, Ezekiel, in the Old Testament, and St. Paul and St. John in the New, are illustrations of this great truth. And in the case of Israel, the revelation of God was specially needed, not merely because there had been none for some hundreds of years, but because the revolt in Egypt was emphatically a religious revolt, and the deliverance from Egypt was emphatically a Divine deliverance. It was a "Redemption," and the supernatural character of the redemption is stamped upon it from the very first.

II. And yet—how significant it is—this revelation of God to Moses comes to him in the midst of his ordinary and daily work. It was as "he kept the flock of Jethro, his father," he suddenly beheld "this great sight" of the bush burning, but unconsumed, and heard the voice of God speaking to him out of the bush. It is a witness to the old but ever new truth, that the highest manifestations of God are not to be seen by those who "seek some great thing," but are to be found in the faithful performance of the "common round, the trivial task;" and that only those who are content thus to be "faithful in a very little," are ever called by God to "rule over ten cities."

III. The successive stages in the revelation itself are equally significant.

(1) It begins, as all revelation of the Infinite to the finite must begin, with a symbol: "The angel of the Lord appeared unto him in a flame of fire out of the midst of a bush; and he looked, and behold, the bush burned with fire, and the bush was not consumed."

(2) But the symbol passes into the higher spiritual truth it was meant to reveal. The fire becomes a voice. "God called unto Moses out of the midst of the bush, and said, Moses, Moses. And he said, Here am I. And He said, Draw not nigh hither; put off thy shoes from off thy feet, for the place whereon thou standest is holy ground." The lawgiver of the Old Covenant is learning its first lesson— the lesson of awe. Revelation begins with reverence.

(3) But not of awe alone. For the next words of God, the words of our text, are a demand for trust, and the demand is founded on the history of the past: "I am the God of thy father"—the personal relation of God to Moses coming first, and the wider relation to the patriarchs now following—"and the God of Abraham, the God of Isaac, and the God of Jacob." But the pledge which the past relation of God to Israel affords of coming deliverance is now to be finally sealed by the Revelation of God, culminating in the communication of that awful and ineffable Name which at once shall declare His eternal unchangeableness as well as His eternal Being; the Name that for all the ages to come was to witness to the most sacred and tender relation of God to His people; the Name which no Jew ever dared to utter with his lips, lest he should be consumed, and which no Jewish scribe ever dared to write, without first lifting his pen from the scroll, and as he dipped it freshly in the ink, devoutly breathed a prayer for mercy—the name of JEHOVAH.

One last and solemn act in this revelation of the name of God has yet to be accomplished. The New Covenant Name must be solemnly affixed to the ancient patriarchal title of God, as the sign to Israel that all that was precious in the dealings of God with their fathers may be looked for in His coming dealings with them. And therefore

Moses is commanded to go forth with this as his first message to his people—at once the pledge of his own commission and of the changeless faithfulness and pity of God—"Jehovah God of your fathers, the God of Abraham, the God of Isaac, and the God of Jacob, hath sent me unto you."

Such, in brief, was the revelation of God to Moses. And it had the moral effects upon him that the vision of God always has on His servants. It makes him just as humble in the presence of God, as it makes him strong in the presence of man. Before God Moses "hides his face" and is "afraid to look upon God," and imploringly deprecates his being entrusted with a mission for which he confesses himself profoundly unworthy. Before Pharaoh he is as "bold as a lion;" he has lost all the former timidity and fear of man which, forty years before, had sent him flying a fugitive from the wrath of the king, into the land of Midian, and with a voice as of thunder, he utters the command to Pharaoh, "Thus saith the Lord God of Israel, Let my people go." The figure of Moses that the genius of Michael Angelo has sculptured, and which in stern and awful grandeur frowns down upon the beholder from the walls of *S. Pietro in Vinculi* in Rome, looking as strong and unyielding as the rock from which it was hewn, is only the image of what "the meekest man above all men that are on the face of the earth," may become under the vision of God. It is the sublimest illustration in the Old Testament of the experience St. Paul has recorded in the New, as the crowning revelation of the Lord Jesus to himself, "He said unto me, My grace is sufficient for thee; for My strength is made perfect in weakness;" and it teaches even the humblest and weakest among us how he may say, "When I am weak, then am I strong."

G. S. B.

XIX. The Golden Calf. Exod. xxxii. 1. "*The people gathered themselves together unto Aaron, and said unto him, Up! make us gods which shall go before us out of the land of Egypt . . . we wot not what is become of him.*"

It is all-important for us to study the manifestations of

God's government and God's relations to man, and man's dealings with God, as we find them unerringly traced for us in the Jewish history. We see there, as it were condensed, intensified and so made sharply and clearly visible, one of those slow processes of Divine government and judgment, which in other nations rolled themselves out through the length of centuries. Let us consider one such feature of the dealings between God and man in history as it is given us in our text.

We find that it is really the history of a most remarkable religious revolution occurring in the nation of the Jews. The essence of the scene lies in this, that you have a nation rejecting God and His law, that you have that nation immediately plunged into the wildest and foulest licentiousness, and then that you have that nation judged and chastened by a sore and bloody judgment.

I. We have here an instance of national corruption and ultimate rejection of the true faith.

From what source did this spring? who were the movers in this great act of national apostasy? There appeared in it the priest and the people. Aaron puts out all his skill at the people's bidding. You have a distinctly marked case of priestcraft in its very surest form. But the people are the inciters of that priestcraft. Here are true history and true philosophy. Never yet in the world's history were the priesthood so separate a caste in the nation, as that they invented their belief, and then imposed it on the nation. It is not so often the priests who deceive the people, as it is the people that will have the priest to deceive them. So, "The prophets prophesy falsely and the priests bear rule by their means, and my people love to have it so, and what will ye do in the end thereof"! It is this imperious multitude, craving for novelty, which imposes upon the priest and the teacher the duty of pleasing them. Do we hear nothing like this from the multitude now? Is it not rung in our ears in all our modern literature? "You priests, what have you to teach us! Give us less of your dogma, and imbibe the spirit of the age; learn of the multitude. Make us gods that shall go before us, for as for this Moses—this Christ—we wot not what is become of them." Woe to us if we listen to any such entreaty. High above the priest and people stands the mount of the law of the Lord. In so far as we bear this law faithfully and honestly in our hands have we the right to teach you.

Priestcraft then springs from the people—this is the first lesson that we learn from this incident.

II. The real cause of this impatience of the people with their old faith.

It was this : " As for this Moses, we wot not what has become of him."

Their teacher had become invisible. They needed something that they could see, and touch, and handle, and these were to be their gods. They could not " endure as seeing the invisible."

This is the temptation of the human heart in all ages. Men's heart craves to see its god ; and the answer to that craving of humanity—God's answer to that—has been the incarnation of Jesus Christ, and to the soul of man that desires to see God there has been revealed " God manifest in the flesh."

But He too has passed away from earth, and He has told us that it is for our good. The reason of this is that we may learn to have faith in the invisible.

And so the nation or the soul that gives itself up to resting only on the visible, believes only in what can be demonstrated, worships, lives, cleaves only to that which is close to it, and it makes itself gods that may go before it. It takes off its ornaments, which the priests took off the Jews.

This nation takes off its ornaments—of its wealth and learning and philosophy and art, of its statesmanship, its literature, its poetry—and it makes for itself new gods, and there comes out ever this calf. There comes out ever some degrading and debasing form of self-worship—the god that the man worships who worships but himself is, after all, but a beast which he worships for a god.

III. The result of this national apostasy, of this worship of the visible.

(1) There immediately follows gross licentiousness. Why is it that a sensuous and low life should follow upon an intellectual error in a man's creed ? Why is it that idolatry, or the worshipping of many gods, is always accompanied in the history of the world with the grossest sensuality ? The reason is clear. Each idol that men worshipped in pagan

days, or that they now worship in heathen nations, is some portion of nature deified—some power in nature—some attribute of man—which the man takes and worships as his god. Now it is the very nature of all such properties or attributes, that they are monstrous and mischievous. For instance, love without purity is appetite; wisdom without truthfulness is cunning; courage without mercy is ferocity; justice without compassion is horrible cruelty.

It is only as men recognise that there is one supreme perfect unseen Being, in whom all these differing fragments as it were, of being and of life, are united and harmonized in their true properties, it is only in that degree that they gain a pure conception and a true ideal of their own life to which they may conform it. And just in the degree in which men lose this idea will they become like unto the things they worship.

The idol, be it what it may that we worship, degrades our souls and makes us base and sensual. Are there no idols of the day that we are in danger of worshipping now? Is there not the idol of public opinion, the voice of the multitude, which they tell us is the voice of God.

Another idol of the day is the temptation to follow party—to make party a god.

Then there is the coarser and lower idolatry of self—mere sensuousness that leads a pleasant luxurious life and forgets the death that comes to all, and seeks to make life a continual feast, with no eye to see the hand that may be writing on the wall "mene, mene, tekel, upharsin," at their feast.

Then there is the intemperance of the people, which so often drowns their souls.

May God deliver us, one and all, teachers and taught, preachers and people, from the idols of the age.

(2) There also follows fratricide.

It is one of the incidents of the story that those who slay are specially commissioned to slay, but it is of the essence of the story that licentious and selfish life is ever, in mankind's history, cleansed with fire and with blood. When religion that men have attempted to banish from them, has no longer its lessons of a Divine fatherhood or of a Divine brotherhood, the hand of every man is against his fellow, and lawless anarchy prevails.

And so ever does the false faith lead to the foul life, and ever is the foul life cleansed by the terrible judgments of God. May God give us grace to shun the sin of idolatry, and so may He preserve us from the suffering of judgment.

W. C. M.

XX. Sojourners with God. Lev. xxv. 23. *"The land shall not be sold for ever: for the land is mine: for ye are strangers and sojourners with me."*

THE singular institution of the Jubilee year had more than one purpose. As a social and economical arrangement, it tended to prevent the extremes of wealth and poverty. As a ceremonial institution, it was the completion of the law of the Sabbath. As the Sabbath in the week, so was the seventh year among the Jews—a time of quiet and rest. It was appointed to enforce and to make the whole fabric of the national wealth consciously rest upon this thought contained in the text. The land was not theirs to sell—they had only a beneficial occupation. While they held it, it was still His, and they were only like a band of wanderers settling for a while, by permission of the Owner, on His estate. Their camp-fires were there to-day, but to-morrow they would be gone. They are "strangers and sojourners." That may be sad, but all the sadness goes when we read on—"With Me." They are God's guests, so though they do not own a foot of soil, they need not fear want.

I. Here is the lesson of God's proprietorship and our Stewardship. "The land is Mine," was of course true in a special sense of the territory which God gave by promise and miracle, which was kept by obedience and lost by rebellion. But it is as really true about our possessions, and that not only because of our transient stay here. Length of time makes no difference in this tenure. Undisturbed possession for ever so long does not constitute ownership here. God is possessor of all, by virtue of His very nature, by His creation and preservation of us and of all things. When we talk of "mine" and "thine" we are only speaking a half truth. There is a great sovereign "His" behind both.

(1) This thought should nurture constant thankfulness. Blessed are they who, by the magic glass of a thankful heart, see all things in God and God in all things. To them life is tenfold brighter, as a light plunged in oxygen flames more intensely than in common air. The darkest night is filled with light, and the loneliest place blazes with angel faces, and the stoniest pillow is soft to him who sees everywhere the ladder that knits earth with heaven, and to whom all his blessings are as the messengers that descend it on errands of mercy, whose long shining series leads up the eye and the heart to the loving God from whom they come.

(2) Here is the ground for constant thankful submission. "The Lord gave, and the Lord hath taken away." We have no right to murmur, however we may regret, if the Landowner takes back a bit of the land which He has let us occupy. He does not take it away for His advantage, or at His own whim, but "for our profit." His only reason for ever disturbing us is that we may be driven to claim a better inheritance in Himself than we can find even in the best of His gifts.

(3) There should be a constant sense of responsibility in the use of all which we have. All is His, and He has given all to us for a purpose. We are but stewards or trustees, and are bound to employ everything according to what, in the exercise of our best judgment, we believe to be the Owner's will.

II. We have the teaching of the transiency of our stay here. "Ye are strangers and sojourners"—pilgrims who make a brief stay in a foreign country.

(1) How vividly this word of the text brings out the contrast between the permanence of the external world and our brief stay in it. In Israel there would be few vineyards or olive-grounds held by the same men at two, and none at three successive Jubilees. The hoary, twisted olives yielded their black berries say to Simeon, the son of Joseph, to-day, as they did fifty years ago to Joseph, the son of Reuben, and as they will do fifty years hence to Judas, the son of Simeon. "One generation cometh and another goeth, but the earth abideth for ever."

(2) The constant change and progression of life are enforced in this metaphor. The old emblem of a journey

suggests how, moment by moment, we hurry on, and how everything is slipping past us, as fields and towns do to a traveller in a train.

A long, patient discipline is needed to keep fresh in our hearts the sense of this transiency. Let us set ourselves consciously to deepen our convictions of it, and amidst all the illusions of these solid-seeming shows of things, keep firm hold of the assurance that they are but fleeting shadows that sweep across the solemn mountain's side, and that only God and the doing of His will lasts. So shall our life pierce down with its seeking roots to the abiding ground of all being, and looking to eternal things we shall be able to make what is but for a moment, contribute to the everlasting ennobling of our character and enrichment of our life yonder.

(3) These words tell of the true home.

Ye are strangers—because your native land is elsewhere. How short this phase of being must look seen from above! If we reach that safe shore, and look back upon the sea that brought us thither, as it stretches to the horizon, miles of billows so terrible once will seem shrunken to a line of white foam. Cherish, then, constant consciousness of that solemn eternity. Use the transient as preparation for the eternal.

III. We have here also the teaching of trust—" With Me." That gives the true notion of our earthly life. We are strangers indeed, passing through a country that is not ours, but whilst we are, we are "sojourners" with the King of the land. Since we are "with Him," we have companionship even when most solitary. Whoever goes, He abides. So will it be while we live, and when we are called to die—well; the King of this land where we are strangers, is the King of the other land beyond the sea, where we are at home. Death the separator shall but invite us to the King whose presence indeed fills this subject-province of His empire with all its good, but who dwells in more resplendent "beauty," and is felt in greater nearness in the other "land that is very far off." Whether here or there, we may have God with us if we will. With Him for our Host and Companion let us peacefully go on our road, while the life of strangers and sojourners shall last. It will bring us to the fatherland, where we shall be at home with the King, and find in Him our "sure dwelling, and quiet resting-place, and peaceful habitation for ever."

A. M.

XXI. The Benediction. NUM. vi. 24–26. *"The Lord bless thee and keep thee: the Lord make His face shine upon thee, and be gracious unto thee: the Lord lift up His countenance upon thee and give thee peace."*

THIS was the form divinely appointed, according to which Aaron and his sons were to pronounce their benediction upon Israel. While humbly receiving the blessing the Israelites must have felt that in the form of it a mystery was involved which they could not comprehend.

I. When they found that the Sacred Name Jehovah was pronounced three times, and each time with a different accent, this feeling of awe was deeply rooted in their hearts. What was a mystery to the Israelites has, through the Gospel, become a revelation to us. It has been clearly revealed to us that in the one Divine nature there are three distinct Persons, the Father, Son, and Holy Ghost. We should not expect on the one hand to find the fact of the Trinity clearly revealed to the Israelites. They were not in a state of sufficient intellectual advancement to receive that fact; but on the other hand, the fact itself having existed from all eternity, we should expect to find intimations of that fact in every part of the Bible, intelligible to us to whom a revelation has been made. So we are not surprised when learned Hebraists inform us that in upwards of two thousand instances "God" is described by a plural substantive, the adjuncts of which are in the singular number.

II. There is a particular reference in our text to the distinct and peculiar blessings conferred by the Godhead on the members of His Church. Each Person in the one Godhead peculiarly undertakes to discharge special blessings.

God the Father gives His love to His children, and causes all things to work for their good. God the Son makes His face shine on them, and is gracious, giving them to see God in Him reconciling the world to Himself. God the Holy Ghost lights up His countenance upon them and gives all the comfort which results from a conscience at peace with God.

W. F. H.

XXII. Our true Leader. NUM. x. 29, 31.
"And Moses said unto Hobab, Leave us not, I pray thee; forasmuch as thou knowest how we are to encamp in the wilderness, and thou mayest be to us instead of eyes."

THE fugitives, whom Moses led, reached Sinai in three months after leaving Egypt. They remained there for at least nine months, and amidst the solitude of these wild rocks they kept the first Passover—the anniversary of their deliverance.

"On the twentieth day of the second month," they began again their march through the grim, unknown desert. One can fancy their fears as they looked forward to the enemies and trials which might be awaiting them. In these circumstances the story comes in most naturally.

Some time before the encampment broke up from Sinai, a relative of Moses by marriage whose precise connection with him need not trouble us now, Hobab by name, had come into the camp on a visit. He was a Midianite by race, and knew every foot of the ground. So Moses prays him to remain with them and give them the benefit of his practical knowledge—"to be to us instead of eyes." It is noteworthy that the narrative does not tell whether the persistent request succeeded or not. We find, indeed, his descendants enrolled in the great Domesday Book of the Conquest as possessing land, and probably incorporated among the Israelites. It may, therefore, be supposed that, either then or afterwards, Hobab forsook his country and his father's house to shelter himself beneath the wings of the God of Jacob.

The silence of the record is significant, especially if taken in connection with the verses immediately following. The historian does not think it worth while to tell whether Moses' attempt to secure the help of sharp Bedouin eyes succeeded or failed, but passes on to describe at once how "the ark of the covenant of the Lord went before them to search out a resting-place for them;" and how "the cloud was upon them when they went out of the camp." He puts the two things side by side, surely expecting that we shall not miss what is so plain. He would teach us that it mattered little whether Israel had Hobab or not, if they had the ark and the cloud. Perhaps he meant us to ask ourselves whether it was not a wavering of faith in Moses, to be so anxious to secure a human guide when he had a Divine leader.

I. There are times and moods in which our forward look brings with it a painful sense of the unknown wilderness before us.

The general complexion of the future may be roughly estimated. We know very early in life, unless we are wonderfully frivolous and credulous, that the thread of our days is a mingled strand, and the prevailing tone a sober, neutral tint. The main characteristics of what we shall meet we know well enough. "That which is to be hath already been." But the particular events are hid, and it is strange and impressive when we come to think how Providence, working with the same uniform materials in all human lives, can yet, like some skilful artist, produce endless novelty and surprises in life. For every one of us, the road is new day by day. "We have not passed this way heretofore," is always true of each day's new tasks and incidents; for even if they be the same as those of a thousand days before, yet we who tread the road are not quite the same, and the bearing of the events on us is somewhat different. The solemn ignorance of the next moment is sometimes stimulating and joyous. To young life it gives zest and buoyancy and secures many a glad surprise. But to all there come times when the blank curtain between us and the next beat of the pendulum is felt to be very near us and very thick, and when the ignorance is saddening, and when the shapes we paint on its folds are gloomy and threatening.

It is a libel on God's goodness to speak of the world as a wilderness. He has not made it so; and if anybody finds that "all is vanity and vexation of spirit," it is his own fault. But still, one aspect of life is truly represented by that figure. There are dangers, and barren places, and a great solitude in spite of love and companionship, and many marchings and lurking foes. Who knows what we shall see when we top the next hill or round the shoulder of the cliff that bars our way? The great crises and trials of our lives mostly come unlooked for. Our Waterloos have a way of crashing into the midst of our feasts, and generally it is when all goes "merry as a marriage bell" that the cannon shot breaks in upon our mirth, which tells that the enemy have crossed the river and the battle is begun.

II. We have here an illustration of the weakness that clings to human guides. For men who have God to guide them, it argues weakness of faith and courage to be much solicitous of any Hobab to show them where to go and where to camp. Of course we are meant to depend on one another. No man can safely isolate himself either intellectually or in practical matters. To live without dependence on human help and guidance, is to be either a savage or an angel. A very large part of God's guidance is ministered to us through men. But we are ever apt to feel that we cannot do without the human leader, and are all apt to pin our faith on some trusted guide, and so put the teacher between ourselves and God.

The highest eulogium that the human teacher can receive is when his scholars say to him, "Now we believe, not because of thy saying, for we have heard Him ourselves."

III. The true Leader of our march. The contrast which is brought into prominence by the juxtaposition of this section and that which follows it makes this thought emphatic. "The Lord went before them by day in a pillar of cloud to lead them the way." If Moses had remembered how their marching and their encampments were fixed, he had not been so anxious to secure Hobab's sharp eyes.

We have the same Divine guidance if we will; in sober reality we have God's presence; and waiting hearts which have ceased from self-will, may receive leading as real as ever the pillar gave to Israel. It is wonderful how much practical wisdom about the smallest perplexities of daily life comes to men who keep both their feet and their wishes still until Providence—or, as the world calls it, "circumstances"—clears a path for them. Be sure of this, that if we are content to see but one step at a time, and take it, we shall find our way made plain.

Do not let your wishes get in advance of the pillar and

the ark, and you will be kept from many a mistake, and led into a region of deep peace. The old injunction is still our duty and our wisdom, " Go after the ark, yet there shall be a space between it and you ; come not near it that ye may know the way ye ought to go." If we impatiently press too close on the heels of our guide, we lose the guidance. There must be a reverent following which allows vindications of the way full time to develop themselves, and does not fling itself into new circumstances on the first blush of apparent duty. " The meek will He guide in judgment, and the meek will He teach His way."

IV. Our craving for a human guide has been lovingly met in the gift of Christ. Hobab's experience was his qualification. We have a Brother who has Himself travelled every foot of the road by which we have to go, and His footsteps have marked out with blood a track for us to follow, and have trodden a footpath through the else pathless waste. He knows "how to encamp in the wilderness" for He Himself tabernacled among us. His life is our pattern. Follow your leader, and plant your feet in his footprints. That is the sum of all ethics and the vademecum for practical life. To Him transfer all those feelings of confidence and affection too often lavished on men. The noblest use for the precious ointment of love, which the poorest of us bears in the alabaster box of the heart, is to break it on His head.

If we only ask him to be with us "instead of eyes," and accept His gentle leading, we shall not walk in darkness, but may plunge into thickest night and the most unknown land, assured that He will "lead us by a right way to the city of habitation."

A. M.

XXIII. Two Prayers. NUM. x. 35, 36. "*And it came to pass, when the ark set forward, that Moses said, Rise up, Lord, and let thine enemies be scattered;* . . . *and when it rested, he said, Return, O Lord, unto the many thousands of Israel.*"

HERE we have two prayers—one for the hours of warfare and journeying, another for the hours of repose and recreation. Both turn to the one thing, the symbolic presence of

God in that ark of the Covenant; and we can picture to ourselves the glad confidence with which the leader of the hosts set forth on the morning march, and the quiet security with which the tents of Israel couched themselves like sleeping figures round the vast Tabernacle as the night fell, and went quietly to rest with an unslumbering eye upon the many thousands of Israel. We may very fairly take these two prayers as representing for us the temper in which we ought to set ourselves to the various works of life, and the temper in which we ought to give ourselves to the restful hours of quiet and repose which come in every life however stormy or turbulent.

I. Look first at the prayer which pertains to the warfare and journeying. "Rise up, Lord;" that is all he asks; simply that He will arise; and then the petition rises into prophecy, "and thine enemies shall be scattered, and them that hate Thee flee before Thee." Look at the magnificent confidence—simply calling upon God. And then, to take the figure of the text, he represents to himself, as it were in a moment, all the antagonism and opposition disappearing.

(1) But how have we a right to identify our poor struggles and conflicts, with Him and with His cause, when we say at the beginning of our various work and warfare, "Rise up, Lord, and let Thine enemies be scattered?" These people had a good reason for it, for they were entitled to believe that all their enemies were God's. There is a very plain answer to this question.

Many a man has fiercely and fanatically identified his wishes and designs with the Divine purpose, and the hindrances and oppositions he has met with he has identified with the enemies of God. But we have no right to do so unless we are quite sure that we are upon God's side. If we are quite sure that we are fighting not for our own will but for His, then we may be quite sure that all which hinders His will is His enemy as well as ours. Knowing the defects of our own hearts, and trying all we can to fulfil His wishes instead of our own, we may venture then to take this prayer for ours, and identify our cause with His, and to appeal to Him to guard us from the foes that oppose us, because they are His foes as well as ours.

(2) Here we get the true attitude in which we ought to

set ourselves to the effort, and do the work of daily life. The confidence that God is with us gives rise to the prayer that He will be with us. Remember the remarkable language of the text—"It came to pass, when the ark set forward, that Moses said, Rise up, Lord." It was done. It was done before he asked it; he asked it before it was done. Here is confidence and faith which comprehends and believes a thing as a fact already before we cry, and makes it a perpetual fact because we cry. Or to put it in other words to Christian men and women, if you want God with you in your labour, if you want to secure Him at all times, to make His presence perpetual, to have Him by you in the hurly-burly of life,—pray! He has arisen for your help, but if you want that He shall stand by your side ready to help you,—pray.

Unless we found our confidence upon past experience of His mercies and upon present faith, they are not prayers like this of my text. The prayer of the Christian should be the prayer that comprehends the fact of God's loving presence and help, and makes that fact perennial, and tries, as it were, to verify it continually in the circle of our experience, as in that wonderful story when the two disciples were walking, and by the way their heart burned within them. When the Unknown came by them, and the evening was falling, and they were near the little house where they were to tarry for the night, the stranger made as though he would have gone further on the straight road, when they came, perhaps, to the little bye-path which led to the house. But they said, "Tarry with us, for it is toward evening, and the day is far spent." And so He went in with them. If they had not asked Him, He would not have abode with them—He would not have continued with them except for their cry.

So He who has risen to help you, and who stands ready to help you at the beginning of all tasks, needs as it were to be bound to us by the prayer of our faith, lest in the thickest of the fight we shall lift up our eyes, and lo! He is not there, and we are exposed, undefended and unaccompanied, to the assaults of the enemy.

II. We have also a prayer for the hour of rest, "And when it rested." When the tabernacle was pitched and the curtain was spread about it, when the stars were coming out by ones and twos about the desert sky, and when the smoke of the simple evening meal was perhaps rising, and the night was slowly drawing on, he said, "Return, O Lord, unto the many thousands of Israel." They laid themselves down to sleep, and as the darkness deepened, the fiery cloudy pillar glowed across the sands, and they were safe beneath the guardianship of the Almighty. The lesson is, that we want God's felt presence quite as much in our times of rest as in our times of work. Plenty of people believe that they want Him in the morning's fight who do not think they need Him nearly so much in the evening's repose. Many realize the fact that when the great difficulties and trials come upon us we need His help. But a great many do not realize the fact that for the quiet moments, when no sinew needs to be braced for effort and no heart needs to be nerved and steeled to courage and endurance we need Him even more; but it is true. The hour of rest has its own temptations—times of self-complacency, times of undue depression. When the wearied body and the jaded mind are fit for very little, then, as perhaps at no other time, do certain forms of evil visit us; and just as when the vitality is low and depressed, a man will catch any kind of fever that is going, so when we are wearied out with work and have come to rest, we are exposed to the assaults of all insidious temptations. I believe that for every Christian man or woman that lose the purity, tenderness, and the simplicity of their Christian character in the midst of work, there is a dozen that lose it amidst the luxury and ease of rest. It is the way in which you spend your evenings and your leisure that will determine whether your Christianity will be vigorous. It is of no use going out in the morning to the struggle of daily life with the prayer, "Rise up, Lord," unless when you come home to rest yourself at night, you say, "Return, O Lord."

Is it not beautiful to think that the one Presence takes any shape that a man wants? When he needs it to be a spear and a shield, it is a spear and a shield for him; when he needs it to be a pillow on which to rest his head, it is a pillow on which he reposes.

May we return to the better rest, where the fight is done and the ark of the Lord shall be no more remembered nor brought to mind, for all the holy Jerusalem shall be called the throne of the Lord ; and there shall we beat our swords into ploughshares, and our spears into pruning hooks, and the nations shall study war no more.

A. M.

XXIV. Even from Thence. DEUT. iv. 29. *" But if from thence thou shalt seek the Lord thy God, thou shalt find Him, if thou seekest Him with all thy heart and with all thy soul."*

THE Book of Deuteronomy was designed not purely for for those to whom it was first addressed by Moses, but for all the Jews of all after times. In the subsequent history of the Jewish nation, this promise was not unfrequently the only light that shone upon them in the cheerless night of their calamity, and guided by it they returned to the God of their fathers and obtained deliverance. Particularly was this the case in the time of their captivity in Babylon.

But this book was not written for Jews alone, and the promise before us is not to be restricted to the seed of Abraham according to the flesh. It contains within it the principles of God's merciful procedure with men yet, and assures them that they shall find God if they seek Him with all their hearts.

I. Look at the case specified. It is not that of the sinner who is hearing of God and of His mercy for the first time.

The first reference of this promise is to the Jews, who had been brought up in the knowledge of the oracles of God, but who, in spite of manifold privileges, had become idolaters. Now where shall we find the parallels of these sinners under the New Testament dispensation?

Not in the heathen abroad, not in the heathen at home; but this promise speaks to those whose guilt is of deeper dye than theirs, because they have been favoured with far higher privileges and have disregarded them. It appeals to those who have been taught to pray beside a parent's knee, who have been members of the Church, but who have lapsed into one or other of the many forms of idolatry that have been set up in the land—as the worship of mammon of fame, of power, of self, of pleasure,—yet even to them this promise comes, the assurance that if they return God will pardon.

II. The blessing promised " Thou shalt find Him."

To many this promise would read very like a threatening, inasmuch as they know that they have sinned against God, and their guilty consciences associate Him with vengeance. But when it is said that the contrite souls shall find God, the meaning is not that He will reveal Himself to them in their punishment, but rather that He will make Himself known to them as He would have done if they had never wandered away from Him. They shall find the God whom they had lost, and they shall find Him toward them precisely as He was before they lost Him. Nor is this all: the contrite sinner shall find God restoring to him the title to the heavenly inheritance which he had forfeited.

III. The qualification annexed to the promise. " If thou seek Him with all thy heart and with all thy soul."

Now what is it to seek God! It cannot be a mere outward search. We need not look for Him in outward forms or ceremonies of worship, we need not seek Him in fasting, or in prayer, or in almsgiving. We need not seek Him in mere external reformation of conduct. The search we make must be spiritual. Now God has told us that He is to be found in Jesus Christ, when we come to Jesus in simple confiding faith. Christ is the meeting place of the sinner and his God. Jehovah has come in Christ seeking to reconcile us to Himself, and if we wish that reconciliation we must go for it to God in Christ. There must be no half heartedness in the search, no mental reservations; nothing but our unqualified submission of the soul to be saved on God's terms, and in God's way. This is seeking God with all the heart and soul.

IV. The grounds warranted that the promise is to be believed. " Whereby shall I know that I shall inherit it?"

Remember that this is God's promise. But we have something more than the word of God to rest on here, for He has made this promise over sacrifice. Go to Calvary and behold the confirmation given there to this precious promise.

Then God has performed this promise in numberless instances. Manasseh, the penitent thief, Saul of Tarsus, the Philippian jailer, all found God by seeking Him with all their heart.

God is faithful who hath promised, and His word is as stable as His throne.

W. M. T.

XXV. The Sabbath. DEUT. v. 12. "*Keep the Sabbath day to sanctify it, as the Lord thy God hath commanded thee.*"

LET us enquire—first, on what ground and on what authority is one day in seven set apart from all other days and dedicated to Almighty God? secondly, on what ground and by what authority is the first day of the week to be set apart and hallowed with special reverence by itself? and, thirdly, in what manner ought that reverence to be paid?

I. First, then, on what ground is one day in seven to be set apart as holy? In replying to this question, we may observe that it is a natural law of universal application, that Almighty God is to be worshipped; and since man is created in order to exist in society here and for eternity, therefore the worship of God ought to be social. But the social worship of God cannot be maintained until stated times be appointed for that purpose. It is clear, then, even from natural reason, that some stated portion of time ought to be set apart for God's service, but it does not appear from reason alone what that precise portion ought to be. But here Divine revelation comes to our aid—holy Scripture informs us that God finished the work of creation in six days, and that on the seventh day God ended His work which He had made, and God blessed the seventh day and sanctified it. That is, He set it apart from all other days, because that in it He had rested from all His works which God created and made. Thus the setting apart of one day in seven days from the creation, not from the giving of the Law on Mount Sinai to the Israelites. The manna was given from heaven before the Law from Mount Sinai; and when the manna was given the seventh day was holy. Thus Almighty God brought the sanctity of the Sabbath from the very clouds of heaven from which the manna came. Besides, in the Decalogue the obligation of hallowing one day in seven is grounded on the creation itself. Again, the promulgation of the Decalogue was not the enactment of a new code, but it was a declaration of original law—a republication of the Divine edicts given to man at the beginning. And if the other commandments of the Decalogue have a moral meaning and universal application, as undoubtedly they have, can we imagine that the fourth commandment, which was placed among them by the hand of Almighty God, and which prescribes the sanctification of one day in seven, has no such moral significance, and that virtually and in substance it has no such perpetual application? Can we suppose that a code graven with the finger of God was so incoherently framed? No. Almighty God Himself declares the indissolubility and unity of the code. He calls it in Holy Scripture, not the nine commandments, but the ten commandments. And our Lord says, "If thou wilt enter into life, keep the commandments"; and St. James teaches, that if a man break one commandment he is guilty of all.

Further, it is indeed true that we do not see the moral fitness of setting apart the seventh portion of time for sacred uses; but it does not therefore follow that there is not some moral fitness in so doing. On the contrary, it is probable that there is such a fitness even in the very constitution of things. Almighty God does everything in number and in weight. We do not as yet understand all the sacred harmonies of the Divine arithmetic. They may be fully revealed to us hereafter, when we listen to the music of heaven. Perhaps also the fourth commandment may be better adapted than any to be the instrument in our moral probation, and to try and test our faith and obedience to Almighty God, which are the very essence of our moral being. In doing things of which we ourselves see the reason, we may be obeying ourselves, and not be obeying God; and therefore Almighty God often tests our faith and obedience by things of which we do not see the reason.

II. Let us now pass on to consider upon what ground is the first day of the week to be hallowed by us. According to the argument just now used, ought we not, it may be asked, observe the seventh day of the week and not the first day? Ought we not to keep Saturday only and not

Sunday? To this we may reply, we should be obliged to do so if we had only one Testament. But we have the Gospel as well as the Law, and Christ who preached the Gospel came to explain and to fulfil the Law. He showed by His mighty works that He is equal to and one with the Almighty Being who delivered the Law upon Mount Sinai. He proved Himself to be what He came to be—the Lord of the Sabbath. But He came to infuse into it a new life, to breathe into it a new spirit, and to invest it with fresh dignity. He came to separate what was merely ceremonial and temporary in the fourth commandment from what is moral and perpetual. He came to confirm the separation of one day to God, and to change the position of the day dedicated to God. He came to teach us that we still owe the seventh part of our time to God, and that this debt is to be paid, not at the end of every week, but at the beginning of it. And so the first fruits of every week of our lives are to be consecrated to Almighty God. There is something significant in the fact, that Jesus Christ having rested the seventh day in the grave, raised Himself from the tomb very early in the morning on the first day of the week, and vouchsafed His presence to His assembled apostles on that day, and said: "Peace be unto you." There was something significant in the fact that He did not present Himself again to His assembled apostles till the first day of the week had again come round. Thus we may say that the seventh-day Sabbath died and was buried with Christ, and that it rose with Him from the tomb, and emerged with fresh beauty on the first day of the week, and received a new name, and was baptised into Christ, and became the Lord's Day.

Further, when Christ ascended into heaven He did not forget the first day of the week, His own day. He imparted another privilege to it. On the first day of the week He gave His best gift to the Church; on that day He sent the Holy Ghost from heaven. Thus, then, we see the ever blessed Trinity united together in consecrating the first day of the week. The first day is holy to God the Father, who began to create the world on this day; it is holy to God the Son, who rose from the dead on this day; and it is holy to God the Holy Ghost, the Comforter, that came down from heaven on this day. Thus for more than eighteen centuries this day has been singing a weekly hallelujah to the ever blessed Trinity.

Further, the practice of the apostles proclaims the sanctity of one day in seven, and declares the sacredness of the first day of the week, and Jesus Christ Himself, sitting in His royal majesty in heaven, poured down a blessing upon that day, by revealing Himself three times in glory to the beloved apostle and evangelist St. John in the Isle of Patmos, and the Holy Spirit has shed His holy unction on this day by putting into St. John's mouth the words at the beginning of the Book of Revelation : "I was in the spirit on the Lord's Day."

III. It now remains to answer in what manner the Lord's Day is to be observed by us.

(1) It is the day of rest. It is a great mistake which some commit in imagining that by treating the Sabbath as a day of rest from worldly pleasure we imitate the Jews. Let any one examine the writings of the ancient Christian fathers, and he will find that they often censure the Jews because they would not work on the Sabbath, yet they did not scruple to spend it in worldly pleasure. The fact is, that those persons are the real Judaisers who observe the Sabbath by worldly amusement. The Christian Sunday is a day of rest for this lower world. Here is not our rest. Here we have no continuing city, but we seek one to come, where the Christian Sunday is a day of rest from this world's cares and toil, and it is a day of rest to God.

(2) But the Christian Sunday is more than a day of rest, it is the Lord's Day—not our day, not man's day, not the Tempter's day, but the Lord's Day—and profaned whenever it is spent in secular business or worldly pleasure.

(3) Again, it is the day of resurrection. It is the day of Christ's resurrection, and the day of the spiritual resurrection of every true member of Christ. Every successive Sabbath ought to find us more disengaged from earth and nearer to heaven.

(4) It is also a day of light. On it the light of Christ sprang forth, the Light of the world rose from the grave, the light of the Holy Ghost came down from heaven. Let us, therefore, cast off the works of darkness, and put on the armour of light. Our Sundays are the days on which we open our hearts to the melodies of the blessed. Thus we

may become more fit for heaven. Thus, though in our earthly course we have lain among the pots in the brick kilns of Egypt, yet we may plume our feathers and gird them for the heavenly flight, and our souls may have the wings of a dove, whose wings are as silver and her feathers as gold.

C. W.

XXVI. The Finality of the Ten Commandments. DEUT. v. 22. "*And He added no more.*"

THESE words may be very sad or they may be very joyous. We cannot tell what they are merely from reading them—it is needful to go a little into the circumstances in order that we may catch their precise significance. Moses has first copied down the commandments as they were given to him by the Lord, and having gone through the whole Ten Words, as these commandments were anciently called, he says: "He," that is "God," "added no more." He did not give eleven commandments; He gave ten. Man must stop where God stops as he must begin where God began. The words would be sad if the Lord had turned away in anger, saying, "I will not speak again unto you"; but they may be very joyous, yea, musical after a heavenly sort, when God has said just enough to meet the necessity and the weakness of man, and when He forbears to add one word that would overtax his strength and throw his dying hope into melancholy and despair.

I. You have something like completeness of law in these ten commandments—a completeness adapted to the time in which they were delivered. God Himself puts the full stop to the legal literature which He has written on the two tables of stone. His delight is, as little as may be needful for proper discipline, and to secure loyal, loving and sufficient obedience. Has He written all the universe over with commandments? He has written the universe over with promises and blessings, and here and there His commanding word is written—for too many benedictions and promises, untempered by these severer words, might lead us into presumption, and might end in making us molluscous instead of strong and grand. This is a kind of

E

authority which begets love and thankfulness. God never shows me His power merely for the sake of inspiring me with awe. When I see the universe I see the suppression of His almightiness, not its extent, not its abundance. God has given me a memory short and shadowed. He could have turned it into a daily plague by the multitude of His commandments and requirements; He gives me ten, it is enough, by and by He will shorten them into one. Here is the authority of gentleness, authority limited to my condition, stooping to my capacity.

II. What marvellous commandments these are when looked at in their simplicity. They are ten speeches to little children. These are not commandments for the manhood of the world, but for its child-age. "He added no more." It was beautiful in its tenderness, it was divine in its pathos. The commandments are not abolished, they are fulfilled, glorified, carried up to their highest interpretation and most beneficent meanings. Jesus Christ said, "Think not that I am come to destroy, I am not come to destroy the law, but to fulfil it," to carry it on to its higher meanings. Now how does He deliver the ten commandments? "Thou shalt not steal," becomes "If you would like to steal, you have stolen." He digs down the outer wall and searches into the chambers of imagery, and there, on the walls around, are seen symbols and images and faces and pantomimes of evil that the heart does and that the life would like to do. So we who are in Christ are not under the law, and yet we are under the law as Israel never was. Jesus Christ has given one commandment—will it be easier to keep one than ten? "A new commandment I give unto you, that ye love one another," and we all must confess "I count not myself to have attained, but press towards the mark."

III. How easy for Christ to lay down the law. No, He did not lay it down; He did it. He became obedient unto death, even the Cross-death, that He might redeem us. "By this shall all men know that ye are My disciples,"—not if you utter the same theological Shibboleth, but by this "if ye have love one to another." Love is the highest exposition, love is the profoundest criticism, of Christianity. Love repeats the cross and sets the crown above its bleeding head.

J. P.

XXVII. The Feast of Tabernacles. DEUT. xvi. 13–17.

"*Thou shalt observe the feast of tabernacles seven days, after that thou hast gathered in thy corn and thy wine: every man shall give as he is able, according to the blessing of the Lord thy God which He hath given thee.*"

THE three great feasts of Israel—the Passover, the Feast of Weeks or Pentecost, and the Feast of Tabernacles—were not only commemorative of national blessings or prophetic of yet greater spiritual blessings to be bestowed, but they were conspicuously connected with the three great seasons of the tillage of Palestine—the barley and the wheat harvests and the vintage. This Feast of Tabernacles was the most joyous of them all. Above and beyond all other marks of joy and utterances of thanksgiving, the law laid stress on the thankofferings of love. Men were not to appear before the Lord empty. The law, "Freely ye have received, freely give," applies to the natural as well as to the spiritual life, and there can be no true fulfilment in the latter if it is neglected in the former. Harvest festivals are valuable in this age.

I. They tell us of the truth which we are constantly tempted to forget—that the God of grace is also the God of nature; that the Son of God is also the Divine Word, the Eternal Wisdom, by whom all laws of nature are ordained; that the Holy Ghost is also the Lord and Giver of life, and that not only are all holy thoughts and desires His gifts, but that even the skill of the artist and the builder speak of a wisdom for all manner of workmanship which is His gift. Harvest thanksgivings help us to look out on the world of nature and of men with more large-hearted sympathies.

II. They bear their witness that we believe that the laws of nature are the expression of an Almighty Father's will, and that we accept its workings, not with simple submission, but with thankfulness and trust.

III. They bring us into fellowship with the old religious life of Israel. It adds to the interest with which we think of this feast, to remember that one large and important part of our Lord's teaching was connected with it. The history of one Feast of Tabernacles occupies four chapters of St. John's Gospel. Its ritual was present to the eyes of men, and to His own thoughts, when He stood and cried, "I am the Light of the world. If any man thirst, let him come unto Me and drink."

E. H. P.

XXVIII. The Dwelling-Place of the Soul. DEUT. xxxiii. 27. *"The eternal God is thy refuge, and underneath are the everlasting arms: and He shall thrust out the enemy from before thee; and shall say, Destroy them."*

IT is not a little significant that the last words of Moses, the lawgiver of the old covenant, should have been words of blessing (ver. 1). The man whom we associate with the tremendous judgment that fell on Egypt, and with the awful majesty of Sinai, and whose very name has become almost synonymous with the terrors of the law, here closes his life by blessing Israel. Moses' first public act was slaying the Egyptian; his last, as he stood on the borders of the eternal world, and when, if ever, the true meaning and end of all God's dealings with Israel would be most clear to him, was the pronouncing a solemn and formal blessing on the people he had loved and served so well—a blessing that, at the end of such a life as his, came like the benediction after prayer. It is only one out of many proofs of which the Old Testament is full, that just as we have a law in the Gospel, so to the ancient people of God there was a Gospel in the law. The lawgiver dies with words of mercy on his lips.

And how infinitely precious would such a promise as that contained in our text, and which is the sum of all the blessings that had gone before, be to Israel at this time. They had been wandering, homeless and houseless, in the desert for forty long years; now they hear the "Eternal God" is to be "their dwelling place." They had often been tempted to doubt whether God was really with them or not, and to give way to doubts and fears: now they are assured that though God is in heaven, He is also with them on earth, and stoops to lay "underneath them the everlasting arms," bearing them and their cares too. They were looking forward to the promised land, but its possession was to be gained only after a terrible conflict with, and overthrow of, their enemies, and now they are taught this same God shall fight their battles for them: "He shall thrust out the enemy from before thee, and shall say, Destroy them." And so Israel found every blessing it most needed contained in this single promise: an abiding and unchanging dwelling-place where "no evil" could ever "befall" them; an "everlasting arm" to sustain and support them, strong enough to bear every burden and every care; and a Divine Presence pledged to go before them, whom no foe could affright, but who would beat down all their enemies beneath their feet.

Read in this way, the words of our text are as full of meaning and comfort for us as they were for the Jews, and we may try and learn some of the lessons they ought to teach us.

The key to the whole promise is in the opening words, "The eternal God is thy dwelling-place." Let us endeavour to understand what this means.

I. There is a sense, it hardly need be said, in which God is the "dwelling-place" of every human soul. "In Him, says St. Paul, and he is speaking of mankind generally, "we live and move and have our being." To use a very imperfect illustration, but the only one that gives even a feeble conception of the truth, just as the atmospheric air encompasses the earth, the breath of all life, within us quite as much as without us, itself unseen though everywhere making its presence felt, so the "Eternal God" is Himself the One Infinite and Invisible Life in which "all things subsist." The creature lives only as it lives in God.

II. But, in a far higher sense than this, the people of God "dwell" in Him. They are not only sustained, in common with all living things, by His life, but they actually and consciously share it; through their union with the Lord Jesus Christ they have "become partakers of a Divine nature," and their life, to use St. Paul's words, "is hid with Christ in God."

III. Now, if this be true, some very grave consequences follow. Many Christians are accustomed to go to God as their strength in times of weakness, or to flee to Him as a "very present help in trouble;" but they forget that God has just as much to do with their life when they are strong and glad, as He has when they are troubled and heavy-laden. When the clouds gather, and the sunshine of life is darkened, and the storm breaks upon them, they turn to Him to protect them; but when the storm has passed by, and all is bright and fair again, they leave Him, as if now they could walk alone. They make God their "refuge;" they forget He is "their dwelling-place." They are thankful for Him as a "hiding-place" for a little while; they do not remember He is more than this, He is their *home*. But if they were continually mindful of this fact, how completely it would alter their lives! To think there is not one thing in my daily life that I have to do alone, not one trouble that comes to me that I have to bear alone, not one joy I have to share alone, not one purpose I may make alone, not one sin I am to fight alone; to know that the least event in my history, quite as much as the greatest, does not happen to me alone, but that God shares my life with me, and that at every moment I am dwelling in Him; to realize this would be almost a revolution, although a most blessed one, in many lives. How many things would be left undone that are now done, how many troubles that crush us now would seem easy to be borne; what a new sanctity and sweetness would fill our joys; what deeper responsibility would invest all our plans and purposes for the future; what victories we should gain over sin where hitherto there have been only defeats; what greatness and sacredness of meaning would attach itself to the common things of our daily life, if once we felt the truth of these words, "The Eternal God is thy dwelling-place."

Of course everything else that Moses declared was contained in this blessed fact we should find true. We should never be crushed with the care or the burdens of life. How could we, when we were not bearing them by ourselves, but "underneath were the everlasting arms"? We should never be afraid of meeting any foe, and never despair of victory in the most desperate fight. How could we when we knew that "greater was He that was with us than all they that were against us," and were trusting in Him to "thrust out the enemy from before us, and to say, Destroy them"? Very few of us can tell what our lives might become if once we realized all the meaning of the words,

"Whosoever shall confess that Jesus is the Son of God, God dwelleth in him and he in God."

G. S. B.

XXIX. **Courage.** Josh. i. 5, 6. *"I will not fail thee, nor forsake thee. Be strong and of a good courage."*

THE leading trait in the character of Joshua as given to us in Holy Scripture is courage. There are indeed other points of character well worthy of consideration and imitation, as the Christian might well expect. The character of Joshua, unlike that of many of God's servants, stands before us without reproach. In his famous address we see the habitual humility of his character, in ascribing all the past successes of his life to God—"for the Lord your God is He that hath fought for you." God gives him, in the words of our text, the assurance of His support and presence.

I. The real lesson of Joshua's character is not merely the example of a soldier's courage, but of intrepidity built on faith. Loss of hope, despondency, and then indifference, are distinct forms of temptations to young Christians in the present day. Too many who should be the natural leaders of the young to fresh victories, and a securer peace, bring back, as it were, an evil report of the land, and discourage the people. Either they say the land is altogether unknowable, a land of mist and cloud, or they speak of Christianity as powerless to win the land that may be yet before the people. The cross is too old a weapon; we must look for something new. This is all an untrue report. Christianity has plenty of untrodden ground before her; it is not all mist and doubt around us; we can see already many points where new victories may be won. In the region of the intellect there is uncultivated ground, and not less so is there in that of morals.

II. Another lesson may be gathered from the life of Joshua, namely, that before the battle of his life began, before he became the leader of his brethren, he was with Moses in the Mount. This is a true preparation for a brave life, a youth spent in communion with God. To be a leader implies standing out alone, and for solitude there is but one remedy, the remedy of our Divine Master: "And yet I am not alone, because the Father is with me." If you would be free of all fear, begin early to fear God. A youth spent with God will make you independent of the terrors of the world. Then, when difficulties arise, Joshua's God will make Himself known, assuring you of His loving presence: "I will be with thee, I will not fail thee nor forsake thee."

E. K.

XXX. The Untrodden Path. Josh. iii. 4. "*Ye have not passed this way heretofore.*"

THE tribes of Israel had come to the brink of Jordan when Joshua spoke the words of our text. The crossing of the river was the only difficulty lying between them and Canaan. Joshua had issued minute directions to the host as to the order and manner of crossing, and as if to ensure careful attention to his instructions, he adds, "Ye have not passed this way heretofore."

I. The crossing of the Jordan may stand to us for any new experience of peculiar uncertainty through which we are called to pass; the ark of the covenant may be taken for God's presence with His people, and the direction to keep it in view as being the true safeguard of the Christian, letting nothing come between him and the perception of the truth that God in Christ is reconciling the world to Himself, and guiding His people to safety and blessedness. Put the ark of God in the river before you and keep it in view, then, though it be overflowing all its banks, you shall go over dry shod.

II. This principle is appropriate to those who are face to face with a difficult duty which is new to them.

III. This principle applies to those who are called upon to bear some heavy trial for the first time. Sorrow in some form must come upon us in the world. But the commonness does not make it one whit less bitter. No matter what else we look to, we shall still find ourselves in the swelling of the river; but the moment we see Jesus our feet stand on dry ground.

IV. This principle applies to our own death. Nothing

can acquaint us with this path but the treading of it for ourselves. But Jesus by His own death and resurrection has put the ark before us, and looking at that we shall find the river dry.

W. M. T.

XXXI. Success in God's Work. JOSH. iii. 5. "*And Joshua said unto the people, Sanctify yourselves, for to-morrow the Lord will do wonders among you.*"

A FRESHNESS and purity as of morning dew, a glory as of sunlight, seems to gather round those words, spoken in the morning of a nation's youth. As they were spoken there lies behind the speaker and the hearers a past altogether unique, and there lies before them a certain future, certain because assured by Divine promise of it. God's purpose was ripe, and the hour of conquest was on the stroke; all that remained for them to do was to prepare themselves for its fulfilment. "Sanctify yourselves."

Let us look at these words as transparent with the light of an inner meaning, a wider and more glorious hope. They set before us the cause and the condition of the Church's success, the cause being Divine power, and the condition personal consecration.

I. The condition of success in the work of God to which the Church is called, is holiness, or personal consecration. Three ideas naturally occur to our minds as included in this word "holiness" as used in the Bible—purity, consecration, and obedience.

(1) Spiritual purity means power, and it means beauty. It has a passive side set forth in many parts of Scripture. "Then will I sprinkle water upon them, and you shall flee from all your iniquity, and from all your transgression will I cleanse you." But it has just as truly an active side. "Cleanse your hands, ye sinners, and purify your hearts ye double-minded."

(2) Consecration is a giving to the Lord. That person, possession, thing, or whatever it may be, is consecrated which is given to God according to His will and pleasure. The greatest type of consecration in Scripture is that of the priest.

(3) The idea of obedience. How is any real practical idea of holiness possible without obedience? For what is sin but disobedience? But these three—purity, consecration, and obedience—do not set before us anything like a complete idea of what the Bible means by holiness. It must have an inner life of which these are but the outer manifestations. The very heart of it is the indwelling presence of God's Holy Spirit. "If any man has not the Spirit of Christ, he is none of His." Is not this the highest testimony to the glory and greatness of our nature, that nothing else can be salvation but the indwelling of God's Spirit, making our very bodies temples of the Holy Ghost? Therefore, this inner life of holiness must needs include a spiritual renewing—a heavenward, Godward direction of the affections.

There can be no greater mistake than to confound feeling with affection, except the still more fatal mistake of confounding feeling with faith. There may be a great show of feeling in a very shallow soul; and there may be deep roots, both of faith and feeling, where the upper surface of the soul is all charred over with the fires of trial, all frosty with sorrow or trodden down under unsympathising feet. There may be a deep and faithful love in the very heart that is perhaps chiding itself and wearying itself with bitter self-rebuke, because its love to God is so cold. There is something deeper still. These affections may have a rooted holiness, as the Bible signifies—a loving hold upon a loving Saviour.

One thing seems to follow very plainly, that holiness is an intensely practical thing, a principle of Christian activity. There can be no holiness without effort, without work. If God works in us, He works in us "both to will and to do."

II. The cause of the Church's success is the Divine power. Christ has not said "Follow Me" to any one to whom He has not also said, "My grace is sufficient for thee, My strength is made perfect in thy weakness." When God says "Sanctify yourselves," it is the height of presumption and unbelief for us to sit down and say we cannot do it. Is it true that the light is waiting for the lightbearers; that the power to be put forth is waiting for the condition on which it has pleased God to suspend it? Yes, the power is there. We dare not doubt that the Lord is able to do wonders. "Awake, awake, O arm of the Lord. Put on thy strength as in the ancient days." Hark! what is the answer? "Awake, awake, O Jerusalem! put on thy beautiful garments. Arise, and shake thyself from the dust, O captive daughter of Zion."

"Sanctify yourselves," and doubt not that the Lord will, yea, to-morrow, do wondrous things.

E. C.

XXXII. The Covenant of Joshua. JOSH. xxiv. 25.

"So Joshua made a covenant with the people that day, and set them a statute and an ordinance in Shechem."

"THAT day" was a very notable day in the annals of Israel; its transactions might well be recorded in the volume of the book and engraven on the monumental stone. All the favours which God had promised to their fathers while yet in Egyptian bondage had now been fulfilled, and the promised land was theirs. In the meantime their captain, Joshua, waxed helpless and old! he felt that there gathered around him the mists and shadows of the coming change. He summoned the tribes, therefore, to Shechem, where he gave them his parting charge. He made a covenant with them and stamped it with a sacramental and with an authoritative value, and set it up for a statute and for an ordinance in Shechem.

We must see in the narrative some suggestions of searching application to ourselves.

The nature of the covenant. The burden of the summons which Joshua made was that they should serve the Lord. Joshua could not have served the Lord if he had neglected the Divinely appointed institution of sacrifice. Although the Mosaic and the Christian economy differ in many things, they are alike in this, that the foundation of each of them is a recognition of sin. They are both dispensations for the recovery of the tainted, not for the preservation of the pure. They both of them recognise an alienated treasure, and furnish provision for its recovery to the Divine favour.

Whenever the Israelite was urged to serve the Lord, he would at once understand that, as the earliest condition of his service, the daily offering, and all the sacrifices of the day of atonement, must be reverently maintained. We must recognise the atonement also, and rely upon it alone as the condition of service. God will have no service from us which is based on false pretences or on fictitious character.

Joshua could not have served the Lord, nor could any Israelite in the camp, if he had not obeyed the Ten Commandments of the law. This would be admitted as an indispensable element of Divine service.

The great principles of morality are the same in every age, and these precepts of the former time, with a new spirit put into them by the exposition of Jesus on the Mount, are binding on our conscience to-day.

In entire union with Christ, power to obey may be obtained. Let us make a covenant with God. Come to Christ and keep His law, and you will be fit for earth and fit for heaven.

W. M. P.

XXXIII. The Benedictions of Life. Ruth i. 8.

"The Lord deal kindly with you, as ye have dealt with the dead, and me."

We are to consider Naomi's sweet benediction. The Hebrews were fond of benedictions—" The Lord bless thee and keep thee," " The angel which redeemed me from all evil, bless the lads," " The Lord bless thee out of Zion." The keynote of the text is in that word " kindly." The argument is this. We can understand kindness in the sphere of the human, and rise from that to a prayer for the Divine kindness.

I. The Lord knows best what kindness is. Has He been kind? At times we should have been tempted to answer, No! The vine is blighted, the fig-tree withered. Kindly? Yes, we shall answer, one time, when we stand in our lot at the end of days. For kindness is not indulgence, and God's kindness to us may take forms which surprise us. At the heart of His surest judgments there is mercy; in the bitter spring, there is healing water.

II. The Lord knows best what others have been to us.

Naomi says with a voice that trembles with remembrances of the old days, "As you have dealt kindly with the dead and me." What a blessing so to live, so to fill our places as sons and daughters, so to sanctify life, that others may make our conduct a plea, and say, "The Lord deal kindly with you, as ye have dealt with the dead and me."

III. The Lord alone will be with us all through our future pilgrimage.

IV. The Lord looks for our love to Him in our love to each other. If we love Him we shall feed His lambs, forgive our enemies, and fulfil the whole law of love.

W. M. S.

XXXIV. God's still Voices. 1 SAM. iii. 10. "*Then Samuel answered, Speak, for Thy servant heareth.*"

THE subject is God's voices; how they may be heard, and when expected.

The world is full of God's voices, but they are not heard, or rather, God is always waiting to speak, but His voice is kept back, and there is no utterance because men's minds are not in the posture really to listen. God will not speak to minds that are not set to the note to which His voice is pitched.

Four times the Lord called Samuel before He spoke to Him. He waited till there was that frame of mind which the text conveys: "Speak, for Thy servant heareth." Little Samuel had been working all day for God. When lying down for rest, God gave him a wonderful communion with Himself. When we are very quiet, after we have been very busy for God, is the occasion above all others for God's still voices.

What is that state of mind which is a pre-requisite for being individually spoken to by God?

I. A mind disengaged. The door is open, the conscience is free, and the heart bids welcome.

II. Another necessary feature is a mind unbiassed. There was a simple desire to hear only the truth. Let God speak what He will.

III. Evident expectation. God has something definite to say, and the heart longed to hear it. The ear was bent to listen. The message from God was an advent, and there was a "now" in it—an importunity of strong, earnest desire.

IV. There must be a sense of personality. Observe: "Speak, Lord, for Thy servant heareth." How close the speaker and the hearer come together! The heart is a little sanctuary for God, and a whisper comes into the ear, and it is assuring and endearing. If you do not expect it personally, it will be no voice at all.

V. There is humility. "Thy servant." And when the servant hears he hears to serve. With such a state of heart God's voices will come soon, they will come satisfyingly, and you will walk about hearing voices.

J. V.

XXXV. Playing the Man. 2 SAM. x. 12. *"Be of good courage, and let us play the men for our people and for the cities of our God: and the Lord do that which seemeth Him good."*

THESE grand words are, even more remarkable if we take notice of the lips from which they came. The speaker is one of the least attractive and least devout of all the Old Testament characters. That fearless, domineering, rough soldier, Joab, who all his life long was a thorn in David's side, and whose death appeared to the dying king the means which afforded even a chance of peace for his successor. And yet this man, rough, harsh, with not a touch of religion in him, so far as we see in all the story of his life hitherto, when he is brought into a great peril is stirred into an utterance which discloses the grandest courage and the profoundest sense of godly philosophy. And as he looks at the handful of men by his side arrayed against the greater number of men opposed to him over there, he says, "Be of good courage: let us play the men." He then falls back upon that which is the only strength of man, "The Lord do that which seemeth Him good," but at the same time no mere fatalism, no Mahommedan resignation, "but be of good courage, and let us play the men," etc; and then, when we have done that, "the Lord do that which seemeth Him good." That is all the more striking and beautiful from the lips out of which it comes, the fountain playing sweet waters and bitter.

I. The first point I mention in connection with these words is that we may take them as the religion of an irreligious man in times of danger, when the pain and the stress come. There are so many of us who—some of us for mere momentary emotion, some of us as a mere piece of hypocrisy, and some of us, too, I do believe, because the pain and the stress get down to the true man—are in the habit of starting up into something greater and nobler and devouter than in the ordinary character of our lives. I do not say that is good—it is bad ; but, on the other hand, some man who has all his life forgotten God, when his favourite child has been smitten down, when his world of business comes crashing about his ears, he then falls back upon the truths which in bright and prosperous times he held very lightly. Don't let us say that is all bad. God sometimes thrusts His sharp spear through the skin of sensuality and selfishness into the quick of the man. Then comes to life what has been lying more than half dead within him, and Joab is found, when the enemy is yonder, when there seems to be no help in the world else, he too is found facing God.

I don't say that that is desirable ; but there are such instances, and let us be thankful if even in such equivocal way a soul finds its true peace, and a life's energy is dedicated to its Saviour.

Suppose in all these people round about him, David had been asked : "Do you think there is any religion in Joab ?" and the answer should have been, "Certainly not," and yet here is a bit of language rooted from the heart. Let us leave that ticklish question of determining what lies below the surface of other people ; let us lay it to ourselves, that our religion be not a cloak we put on, an umbrella that we lift as long as it is raining, and put down when the sun shineth,—a companion for the night and not for the day. Let us see to it that our religion runs through all the circumstances of our lives, and influences and colours and gilds everything that we do ; and then when the strain and the stress comes, it will be all the more likely to be an all-sufficient strength for us if we have been accustomed to deal with it and to handle it in the quiet of other times. I am afraid that it is not only people whom we call "the world" that are apt to fall back upon religion as a thing for stormy times, but it is deep within us all. And you professing Christians and Church members have the same dangers to guard against. Let us take the lesson. Don't let us treat Jesus Christ as men do the doctor, who, when they are ill, would do anything to see him crossing the threshold, and when the bill comes in grumble and call it a high and unreasonable one ; and don't let us be put in a tight place before we learn to say, "The Lord do that which seemeth Him good." Then there is this reason why one would thankfully admit that here we get an illustration of the way in which sometimes unexpected devoutness bubbles up in unanticipated places. Don't let us forget that here is an illustration of how little worth, after all, a religion of that sort is. This man, however earnest, sincere, in his falling back upon the soldier's faith that God would help them that struck with their own strong arms, his religion did very little for him the rest of his life. It did not refine him ; it did not make him patient, gentle, merciful, or anything which it should have made him. This is the sole instance ; and, depend upon it, unless our religion is the underlying power that moulds our whole character, it will never cover our heads in the day of battle.

II. Well, then, turning away altogether from such a way of looking at the lips that spake these words, let us get a lesson out of the words themselves. They illustrate for us also what I may call the plain practical common sense which cuts all the difficult things about man's part and God's.

Joab had no doubt whatever that his first business was to dispose of his troops wisely in front there,—that the next business was that they should, with all the pith in their right arms, and with bold hearts, strike ; and just as little doubt, when all that was done, "the Lord would do that which seemeth Him good." And one set of men would have said : "Ah ! Providence is always on the side of the strongest battalions ; the strongest arms and the sharpest swords will win the battle anyhow." Others would have said : "Ah ! if you believe in this Divine protection, and that sort of thing, what is the use of throwing the dice at all ? They are cogged. The one thing will be done just the same."

Joab—who had not learned much philosophy in David's camp—just by dint of plain, practical common sense—there was no time to talk about casuistry,—hit the right nail on the head. He knew the two things, and we know no more ; and all the cobwebs of the schools have not got a bit further, and they never will get further ; and so the two great telling facts stand—" Let us play the men," and " the Lord do that which seemeth Him good." If you want it in a more evangelical form : " Work out your own salvation with fear and trembling, for it is God that worketh in you to will and to do His good pleasure."

I have no time to spend in analysing this kind of things, as they are *cobwebby* after all. Let us be quite sure of this, that the one thing that we need to know is — do thy part ; and the one thing to trust is—God doeth all. There is the plain common sense of the whole thing, and sufficient quite for all the daily life, wrapped up in these rough words.

III. And so the last thing about this utterance is, that we may take it as illustrating for us also the noble courage that comes out of absolute resignation. Some men need to have the hope of success before them before they can fight for their own or for a public cause with anything like earnestness and vigour. And so there is the courage that is born of the assurance of victory. When William Carey launched the missionary enterprise in which the two notes were—" Expect great things from God," and " do great things for God ; " these were excellent. But don't you think it would have been grander—" Let us play the men for the good cities of our God," and let consequences alone ? You cannot see into that cloud and mist ; and if we could, there is no ray of duty to be got out of that. The only thing we have got to see is, that it is for the cities of our God that we are fighting ; and then, come weal, come woe, success or failure, leave it alone, and say, " the Lord do that which seemeth Him good."

Ah ! dear brethren, when we have thus brought these rebellious wills of ours into harmony with His will, then we have touched the centre, and have got the seed-root of success, and of something better than success—of peace in our hearts, of resignation—by which I mean the active harmony of my will with God's will. That is the secret of all courage ; that is the secret of all peace. Why, if you have been reading about these Afghan wars lately, you know that every now and then there starts out from the other side there some man who is designated by some term which expresses that he is resolved to fling his life away in—as he thinks—the service of the prophet and of God. And these men, just because their whole nature has been absorbed into the one thought of submission of will to Allah and Allah's prophet, these men come storming through all difficulties, lives in their hands; they do not care whether they live or die, and so nothing can stop them from doing what they want to do. And you and I may come to the very same elevation and grand independence of consequences in our hearts and lives if we only will take it on the lines which this text touches: "The Lord do that which seemeth Him good." Ah! the highest example of courage and of playing the men for the city of God is in Him that prepared Himself for His conflict by this—"Father, not My will, but Thine be done." And if we have the mind that was in Christ, we too shall be brave with more than human courage,—be submissive with childlike obedience. "The Lord do that which seemeth Him good" is the key to all peace, to all courage, and to all happiness.

A. M.

XXXVI. Our Weakness our Strength. 1 KINGS iii. 7. *"I am but a little child: I know not how to go out or come in."*

THESE were the words of a very wise and great man, when he was just succeeding to his high dignities and was on the eve of one of the greatest works which was ever given to a man to do. It is the Moseses, the Solomons, the Jeremiahs, who always feel their nothingness. The higher you ascend in the true scale of manhood, the more unaffected and entire is the acknowledgment "I am but a little child." One only who ever lived and achieved the greatnesses of life never used those words, but even He went as near to it as the omnipotence of the immeasurable Spirit which dwelt in Him would allow, when He said, "I can of mine own self do nothing." The way to "go out" and to "come in" well, is to have always in the mind the sense of utter incompetence.

What is it to be "a little child"?

I. You must every day be born again, that so you may have the freshness of a constant regeneration.

II. Simplicity is closely connected with the freshness. The child is ruled by his heart. He loves more than he knows. Take simple thoughts of everything. What is beyond you, leave it. A mystery is the simplest of all simple things so long as you are content to leave it a mystery. This is what the child does.

III. A third characteristic of childhood is purity. It is a beatitude upon childhood: "Blessed are the pure in heart for they shall see God." And therefore a little child sees more of God than a man does, because of this purity of heart.

IV. Consent in all things to be undertaken for, as the little child does. Go leaningly, trustingly and lovingly. "Go in this thy might," your weakness your strength. The ivy that twines round the rock is surer than the cedar which stands alone upon the mountain. At every door, confess to helplessness and through many doors you will go in and out quite safely.

J. V.

XXXVII. True Aims and False Aims. 1 KINGS iii. 9.
"*Give therefore Thy servant an understanding heart to judge Thy people, that I may discern between good and bad: for who is able to judge this Thy so great a people.*"

THE men whose names the world will not willingly let die are those who find in other's good their chiefest, greatest joy. The names of self-gratifiers, self-seekers die out. Selfishness never has imbibed life from the principle of immortality. The men who come up to the height of a great choice, "Give me these that I may judge Thy people, that I may civilise and educate and evangelise, that I may bless my generation," their names become the echo, ever sounding throughout the ages, of the sacrifice they once chose to make for others.

The two great teachers from amongst the kings of Israel learned in suffering what they taught in song, proverb and parable. The text gives you young Solomon ascending to Gibeon and sacrificing at once a thousand burnt offerings. Solomon found out that very night that these offerings were not wasted. God appeared to him and asked him, What shall I give thee? Solomon came up to the height of a great choice, and the choice pleased the Lord.

I. God comes to every one of us, saying, "Choose what I shall give thee"! We must choose; refusal to choose is itself a choice, and it is this liberty to choose one's aim in life and one's destiny at last that makes life so serious. We must choose between religion and irreligion; one of them must be right, and if we choose aright it is well for us.

"Give me therefore an understanding heart." It must begin with the heart. "The pure in heart alone can see God," and if a man cannot see God in the world, he cannot see anything else in its true proportions. God wishes to have the heart to whisper to and to guide. Choose between good and bad in your companions, your books, your pleasure and habits. You are in a world of temptation, and the great thing is not to play a retreat.

II. The right aim in life chosen. It pleased the Lord that Solomon had asked wisdom and rejected the false. It pleased God that he did not ask for long life. Then is that a wrong desire? Well, it is a nobler thing to act well your part than to be constantly wishing for long life. Life is not measured by length of days. "We live in acts not years." Methuselah lived for 900 years and never said a word worth putting down in the Bible. Jesus Christ was only here for three years of public life, and His name has gone through the earth, filled heaven with its praise, and His deeds shall be spoken of throughout the eternal ages. Life is yours to fill it as Christ filled it with noble deeds of help to others.

It pleased the Lord that he did not ask for riches. Then is it not wrong for us to desire riches? As the great absorbing passion in life it is wrong. Jesus did not teach that riches was the root of all evils, but "the love of riches" was. The evil was here before the riches. There was not a penny in the world when the first sin was committed. But if Mammon be your great aim in life you will be the worse for every coin you gather.

It pleased the Lord that he did not ask the life of his enemies. They say that it is the sweetest thing in life to have revenge upon an enemy. Another has said, "Revenge is mine saith the Lord." Christianity is the only religion that teaches all men to give over their vengeance to the Lord.

III. The reason why it pleased the Lord. That Solomon rejected the false and chose the true aim in life.

(1) Because he chose what enabled him to be serviceable to others. "That I may judge the people."

(2) Because he chose to walk in the statutes of a good father. It is the greatest joy of a good father to have a good son.

(3) Because he chose God Himself as his portion rather than all His gifts. "And Solomon loved the Lord." But God gives more than you ask, abundantly more, His gifts never bring leanness to the soul; but they bring a feast of joy, until the Christian is ready to cry "All these and Christ too!"

H. E.

XXXVIII. The Glory of the Lord. 1 KINGS viii. 11.

"For the glory of the Lord had filled the house of the Lord."

THE "house" of the text is the Temple at Jerusalem just completed, and at this point being dedicated with prayer and praise to the God of Israel. The "glory" that filled it was apparent to the eye in the appearance of smoke.

I. The glory of the Lord. What is it? The cloud was not God, but the sign and evidence that He was there. It showed that God was present for a purpose, for good and merciful ends which the word accompanying the revelation disclosed. The miracle vouched for the word, and identified the speaker. It is not so now. It is not needed now that Christ has been here, filling the world with evidences of His presence and power in a Christian Sabbath, Church, and civilization. Jesus has ascended. The fire comes down; fire and no cloud, light and "no darkness at all." But it is "tongue of fire." Henceforth faith is to come emphatically by hearing, and hearing by the word of God.

II. How can a house be filled with God's glory? We assume the Christian temple to be occupied by human beings sufficiently intelligent regarding the Lord to desire instruction and the knowledge of Him. In the measure in which the worshippers acquire and grow in that knowledge, in that degree will the house be filled with His glory. Not in its walls, however majestic; nor its adornments, however costly; nor in its tempests of sweet sounds, is the temple filled with glory; but when the knowledge of God in Christ is being given out and received, then the house is filled with His glory.

III. What is the advantage of beholding the glory of the Lord? "We all with open face beholding as in a glass the glory of the Lord, are changed into the same image from glory to glory." We unfold the glory of the Lord that men may see it, and come to Him and live. This educates the heart and shapes the life. This joins the life that now is and that which is to come.

J. H.

XXXIX. The Fall of Solomon. 1 Kings xi. 11.

"Wherefore the Lord said unto Solomon, Forasmuch as this is done of thee, and thou hast not kept My covenant and My statutes which I have commanded thee, I will surely rend the kingdom from thee and will give it to thy servant."

SOLOMON'S great sin was the encouragement and the establishment of idolatry in and about Jerusalem. The great providential purpose of Israel was the maintenance of faith in, and worship of, one true God. It was to this inheritance of faith and duty, consecrated by the struggles of so many generations, that Solomon had succeeded. The building of the temple was the great work of his life, and it is this fall which throws his latter apostasy into such painful relief. What was it that could have tempted Solomon to practise and support idolatry?

I. The temptation came to him chiefly through his affections. Solomon's wives could do what probably no one man in his empire could possibly have done: they perverted the heart of the wisest of men.

II. Solomon was the victim of a sort of false cosmopolitanism. His wide range of interests, his immense wealth, his contact with men of all creeds and no creeds, brought to him a temptation which often comes to those who, from the nature of their duties, see many sides of human life. In such cases the difficulty is to be fair, just, generous to the convictions of others, without compromising what we ourselves know to be true. Solomon, within the walls of his palace, breathed at last a purely heathen atmosphere, and it did its work upon him. Carelessness became indifference, indifference under pressure soon became apostasy.

III. There was some subtle, unconquered evil in Solomon's nature which led him to sympathize with the wrong thus recommended to him from without. No outward influence can really overmaster the rectitude of a regenerate will. If outward terrors or attractions prevail, it is because of some rottenness within. Solomon's fall was not prevented by his old age, nor by his knowledge, nor by previous sincerity. We have no means of solving the question of Solomon's final salvation; but this is certain, that his sin brought its penalty in this world: "I will surely rend the kingdom from him."

IV. The practical lesson of such a fall as Solomon's is, that perseverance in God's service is not a matter of course with any one of us, but that it is a distinct gift or grace of God, to be secured by watchfulness and prayer. We who are neither kings nor sages, may well take warning by this history of the wisest of kings. Let us watch the issues, we can never fully explore the depths, of these hearts of ours. Let us grasp the hands that were pierced in mercy for us on the cross. Let us look constantly, humbly, to God, as the source of our strength.

H. P. L.

XL. The Call of Elisha. 1 KINGS xix. 19. "*So he departed thence and found Elisha, the son of Shaphat, who was plowing with twelve yoke of oxen before him, and he with the twelfth: and Elijah passed by him, and cast his mantle upon him.*"

THE prophetical ministry was not a matter of hereditary descent like the Jewish priesthood. Each prophet was the subject of a special predestination to his work, and each was called to his work by some especial token or influence.

Elijah does not seem to have spoken to Elisha; but to cast the mantle on another, was to call him to share the labour, the glory, the responsibility, the dangers of the prophetic office. Elisha perfectly understood the symbolical action and obeyed its purpose. The call of Elisha has its place not merely in the history of his order or of his country, but in the history of humanity, and as such it is an instance of the power of religious influence. The silent prophet passes, he drops his mantle, and the life of another man is agitated to its centre. What must have been some of the motives which led Elisha to obey?

I. Elijah would have represented a great cause and a great truth. Truths are sometimes impersonated in single men. Elisha bent before the truth of which his master was himself the servant. The first condition of a deep religious influence is a clear, positive creed. Elijah was powerful because men knew that he had no doubt about his creed.

II Elijah had personal qualities in harmony with the requirements of the cause he represented, and Elisha would feel attracted by these qualities.

III. Elijah had the influence which belongs to a soul often in communion with God. This is an atmosphere which hovers around the life which we are conscious of breathing when we approach it. It is something beyond character—it is tone. It is beyond goodness—it is holiness. Elisha may well have felt this attraction. This history has two lessons; one for those who exert religious influence, the other for those who yield to it.

Every man is assuredly the apostle of something—of evil if not of good. This responsibility cannot be avoided. Let our lives be decided, consistent, unworldly, as was Elijah's, then our influence will be as sure as his. To listen for the footsteps of the Divine Redeemer, passing by us in the ordinary providences of life, is a most important part of the probation of every man. Let us follow Him.

H. P. L.

XLI. Elijah's Farewell to Elisha. 2 Kings ii. 9.

"And Elijah said unto Elisha, Ask what I shall do for thee, before I be taken away from thee."

THE assumption of Elijah the prophet into heaven is one of those incidents in the Bible history which takes possession of the imagination in the earliest years of childhood, while it also suggests problems of the highest interest as long as we can read our Bibles. This event brings before us the departure of a great servant of God from the world of sense. Let us try to understand the solemnity which is inseparable from such an event.

I. We see the parting of friends. The last command of the prophet, addressed to his follower, was the language of tender and devoted friendship. "Ask what I shall do for thee, before I be taken away from thee." To stand by the death-bed of a friend is one of the most solemn experiences of the human soul on earth. If, before he is taken from us, a dying friend can teach us the responsibilities as well as the privileges of friendship, he will have done us a service of the very highest kind.

II. We see the last act of a great life. We might have expected from Elijah a last denunciation of the house of Ahab, or a word of warning to rouse Israel; but no, he is thinking, just like any humble peasant, of what he can best do for his undistinguished follower. It was an act of pure unselfishness, of simple thought for the needs of another. A death-bed does two things. It puts the finishing stroke on life, and it yields a revelation of character. As a rule, dying men act and speak in accordance with the strongest and deepest motives that have governed them through life, or that govern them at the moment.

III. The solemnity of the scene consists in this, that Elijah is visibly about to take his departure for another world. "Before I be taken away from thee." Elijah was, indeed, taken in body as well as in spirit. His translation reminds us that death is not only the conclusion of one stage of being, it is the door through which we enter upon another; and the light which already streams through the openings, illumines the present scene with a strange interest and awe. Christianity has greatly enhanced the significance of death. Elisha, devoted as he already was, was another man after witnessing the translation of Elijah. And there are scenes in every life which ought to send us back to work and to duty with a deeper sense of the meaning and responsibilities of life and of the world which is to come.

H. P. L.

XLII. Naaman. 2 KINGS v. 1. "*Now Naaman, captain of the host of the king of Syria, was a great man with his master, and honourable, because by him the Lord had given deliverance unto Syria: he was also a mighty man in valour; but he was a leper.*"

THROUGHOUT the Scriptures leprosy is treated as a parallel of sin. The stroke, as men so naturally called it, did for the body precisely what sin does for the indwelling spirit: lurking secretly in the system till its hold was well established; breaking out in spots that met and spread till the whole body became hideous and the man became such an object that the meanest slave in Syria would not change places with him; eating like a cancer into the flesh, pursuing its pitiless course until the limbs rotted and fell away and the body became as a living corpse; a disease so foul and so subtle that medical science for many centuries, without thinking of healing, did not attempt to relieve its pain. Leprosy presented to the eye a ghastly picture in the body of the havoc sin works upon the soul. There is no reason to suppose that leprosy is contagious. Naaman, for example, could scarcely have held his position as a personal attendant to the king, and have been in constant intercourse with persons whose lives were held as the most precious in the kingdom, if it were not well known that there was no risk of contagion in his leprosy. Hence the regulations of Moses with regard to the treatment of leprosy may be regarded as having a religious rather than a sanitary purpose; intended to emphasize the fact of leprosy being a picture of sin. Conversely; it is the healing of leprosy as a parallel to the healing of sin. Every cure of leprosy is, in the Scriptures, attributed to the direct interposition of God, just as the mercy of Heaven is acknowledged in healing the sinner. This brings us to our treatment of the text. That which we note in Heaven's mercy to Naaman is quite consistent with the treatment of sinners like ourselves. Now, look in this sorrow of Naaman how the mercy of Heaven humbles the pride of man, ignores the prejudices of man, and declines the co-operation of man.

I. How the mercy of Heaven humbles the pride of man. Sitting in his chariot, which has many a time borne him to fields of trial, accompanied by many servants in rich attire, followed by horses and camels laden with ingots of gold, talents of silver, and rich garments made in the silk looms of Damascus,—as captain of the host of the king of Syria, a great man and honourable, he travelled in all the magnificence of an Oriental grandee. He was a great man, but he was a leper. When he arrived at the gate of Elisha he took it for granted that it would be flung open and that the prophet would himself rush out, and fall on his knees before him, and pay his obeisance, and call upon God to make haste to heal so great a man. But, on the contrary, the door was shut, and the house is still as if it were the house of the dead, till the great man leaves his chariot. Never before had he been doomed to stand at the gate, and this in the presence of his servants. His language is significant of his disgust: "Behold, I thought he will surely come out to me, and call on the name of the Lord his God, and strike his hand over the place." Presently there comes out, not the prophet, but a message. And such a message; not giving him some great and important thing to do, but such as might have been sent to any beggar in the land—" Go and wash in Jordan seven times." If this treatment of Naaman had arisen from a spirit of ecclesiastical arrogance on the part of Elisha, like that of Pope Hildebrand, who commanded the Emperor of Germany to stand barefoot for three days in front of his palace in the January snow, we could neither sympathize with it nor endeavour to extenuate it. But all that Elisha did was in direct obedience to the commands of Him who resisteth the proud and giveth grace to the lowly. Pride was the sin by which Paradise was lost, and the first step towards regaining Paradise is the subjugation of pride. Naaman himself began by learning that God is no respecter of persons. The ministers of our Churches may make distinctions between the sinner with a ring on his finger and the sinner with rags on his back, but it is not so with God.

Is the difference so great between the greatest monarch who rules on the earth and his meanest subject that the sun should shine warmer or the wind blow softer for one than the other, and must God stoop to note these distinctions and differences. A man may be just as vain of his moral virtues as even Naaman of his gold, silver, and raiment, but let any one who imagines that God may make a difference between him and the vilest reprobate on earth meditate on the infinite disparity which exists between his poor, soiled, broken virtues and the infinite holiness of God. We must come before God stripped of all self-sufficiency and on a level with the most guilty.

II. Mark again how the mercy of Heaven ignores the prejudices of man. It has been remarked, Naaman's "I thought" is the germ of all modern Rationalism. Men set up their thoughts as to the manner in which Heaven's mercy should be dispensed, instead of accepting the teachings of God and His prophets and apostles. Are not the rivers rising from their pure springs, running down the hillside, and imparting their sweetness to the gardens of Damascus, clearer and more crystal than the turbid waters of Jordan? But when man seeks mercy from Heaven it is not for him to dictate the terms on which that mercy may be given. Because the terms prescribed were different from those he had thought, and more simple than he expected, Naaman turned and went away in a rage. Many in our time treat the Gospel of the Lord Jesus Christ with contempt, because it is different to what they thought. And are we not told by Paul that in his time the Gospel of Christ was foolishness to those who could not understand that life should proceed from death, or glory from the cross; and to-day there are vain men who in their self-sufficiency say "the Gospel may be good enough for beggars and common people, but it is not good enough for me." But though I may be simple and you learned, though you may be great and I small, you, like me, must take Heaven's mercy on Heaven's own terms. It may not be as you thought, but you must not dictate to Heaven.

III. Notice finally how the mercy of Heaven declines the co-operation of man. "My father"—and happy in his servants was Naaman. Most servants can see faults in their master, but they are not so quick to point them out with humility and kindness to their master first of all. "My, father, if the prophet had bid thee do some great thing wouldest thou not have done it?" Undoubtedly he would. What sank his pride was that to obtain this mercy it was ordained that he, a great man and honourable, was only to do something which any beggar in the land of Israel might have done. He would have been content to do some great thing, but his pride refused to do a little thing. But Heaven says, "My mercy is a free gift; it is not for me to offer or for me to take any price for it." Yet to-day thousands of men stand outside the pale of Christianity for this very reason, that they want to buy the mercy of Heaven. If the service of the Pope bid a man walk on hard peas from Rome to Edinburgh he will do it, or a Hindoo at the command of his priest will hang himself to an oak tree and remain suspended till he dies. No fast is too long, no penance too severe, no price too great with which to buy eternal salvation. But why should men spend their strength for that which is not bread, or labour for that which satisfieth not? They would die freely and gladly, but they turn away with scorn when the message is of a free salvation—to buy without money and without price. Yet these are the terms on which the mercy of Heaven is offered to you and to me. If you will put aside all thought of purchasing forgiveness, if you will put aside all self-reliance, if you will receive it as a free gift, then in His great name, and as His ambassador, on the authority of His book, I pledge you, on the faith of God and the honour of His Son—I pledge you the faith of God, as I must live or die for my trust, and I do so to every one—"Believe on the Lord Jesus Christ, and thou shalt be saved."

W. J. W.

XLIII. The Reality of the Invisible. 2 KINGS vi. 17. "*And Elisha prayed, and said, Lord, I pray Thee, open his eyes, that he may see. And the Lord opened the eyes of the young man; and he saw: and, behold, the mountain was full of horses and chariots of fire round about Elisha.*"

GREAT outbursts of the miraculous, attesting God's energetic presence at particular times in particular places, appear to recur in the sacred history in cycles, when truth has to be announced or to be saved from extinction. Each period has its characteristic miracles. On the other hand, there is a likeness between them, arising from having more or less of a common purpose or object in view. This miracle of Elisha is peculiarly evangelical. It anticipates such miracles of our Lord as that by which He healed the blind man, in which at the same time He gave the gift of natural sight and the higher gift of spiritual light. Let us recall the circumstances under which this miracle was worked.

The Syrian king, resolved to capture Elisha, surrounded by night the small town of Dothan where the prophet was living. The servant returns with the news in the morning, and the statement of his master that "they that are with us are more than they that are with them," must have seemed at first absurd to him. But Elisha prayed the Lord to open the servant's eyes that he might see that world which is above, around, beyond the world of sense. God gave him a new power of spiritual vision, and he saw and was assured of God's sure protection through the agencies of those ministers of His who do His pleasure. This is a picture of the act of faith in the human soul.

I. Faith is not an act of the natural imagination. Faith deals with facts and realities.

II. Faith is not the final act of a process of natural reasoning. The understanding cannot compel faith. Faith is an act of the whole inward nature. What is it which makes the desire of the heart and the evidence of the understanding result in the perfect act of faith? "The Lord opened the eyes." It is a gift from God which nature cannot rival or anticipate.

III. The lessons to be derived from this history.

(1) We have a remedy against despondency.

(2) We see our true patent of nobility. With eyes open upon the great realities we remember our destiny.

(3) We have the secret of real effective prayer. Prayer is cold and heartless because the danger is not realized, and because men see nothing of Him to whom prayer is addressed. "Lord open mine eyes that I may see."

H. P. L.

XLIV. The Power of the Past. 2 Kings. xiii. 20, 21. *"And Elisha died, and they buried him. . . . When the man was let down, and touched the bones of Elisha, he revived, and stood up on his feet."*

There is no other miracle in Holy Scripture which is exactly like this; and it certainly is much more striking than any of the miracles which were performed by Elisha in his lifetime. It produced a great effect upon the Jews, and they held this miracle to be Elisha's chief title to distinction among the prophets. It is no reason against the truth of a miracle that we men are unable to discover any adequate reason for its having been worked. This difficulty will not weigh with any humble and reverent Christian who does not already consider himself to be a sort of private secretary to the Master of the Universe. And yet we may trace a particular motive for this miracle. Elisha's voice was silenced, and it assured the people that his words were still living; it convinced them that his warnings, promises and encouragements, had not died away with his dying breath.

Every tomb does not contain the bones of an Elisha, but there is that in the past which has power to quicken the present. It may be out of sight, but it only waits the time when the languid wills, the cold hearts, the dying convictions of the present shall touch it, and by it be reinvigorated with life.

I. To a nation the past is a power. It is so powerful and precious an element of its life, that wise patriots and rulers do all they can to preserve it. A degenerate posterity asks itself why, with the same blood in its veins, it should be incapable of the virtues of those who have gone before it?

II. To a Church the past is a power. The sacred Scriptures are largely a record of the past. The great saints and heroes of the Church have lived in the past. In practice and in truth the Church must strive to stand on the old paths.

III. Every Christian soul has its past, its sacred memories, known only to itself and to God. Souls have their periods of depression and decline. There is no such thing as indefectible grace. A deadness may have come upon the soul, and eternal realities may have been displaced in its affections by things of time. Then the memory of the days of old may result in a true spiritual rising from the dead. Do not let us forget the past. It has a great place in God's teaching of His Church, and in His guidance of the soul.

H. P. L.

XLV. Rab-shakeh's Question to Hezekiah.

2 KINGS xviii. 19. *"And Rab-shakeh said unto them, Speak ye now to Hezekiah, Thus saith the great king, the king of Assyria, What confidence is this wherein thou trustest?"*

IT is difficult to say at first what is the motive of a question like this. It may be conscious strength forcing a virtually conquered foe to bite the dust; it may be common sense pleading with the false pride of a weak antagonist against the prolongation of a hopeless struggle.

The Assyrian generals had arrived at Jerusalem, and they asked for an interview with the king to demand surrender. Hezekiah sent three of his trusted officers to parley with them, and the burden of Rab-shakeh's address is the hopelessness of their resistance. "What confidence is this wherein thou trustest?"

But Hezekiah had an answer to give which, as the event proved, was sufficient. He trusted in the Lord Jehovah. Rab-shakeh's question still lives. It is asked year after year, century after century, of societies of men, and of individual men. When it is asked of nations the answer is very various, but there is only one real ground of confidence —a public conscience in a country which can trust God, because it acknowledges and fears God.

The soul of man needs something to rest on. It, too, must have a confidence wherein to trust. Life has its turning points when, at the summons of some Rab-shakeh, the soul is forced to look its real source of confidence in the face. Especially is this the case as death approaches. Then "What confidence?"

I. In some cases it is confidence in self.

II. Not seldom do men trust in Egypt, in something that is external to themselves, the strength or weakness of which they never examine, but which satisfies the need of trust in something. There is confidence in reputation, or in wealth, or in friends. But the true confidence of the soul is the perfect, well-founded trust in the Being who made it. Confidence in God and distrust of self is the secret strength of the soul. To those who know this, the sure ground of confidence, death, like Rab-shakeh, may present his summons, but he finds them prepared. With St. Paul, they exclaim, "I know whom I have believed, and am persuaded that He is able to keep that which I have committed to Him against that day."

H. P. L.

XLVI. The Spread Letter. 2 KINGS xix. 14. *"And Hezekiah received the letter of the hand of the messengers, and read it. And Hezekiah went up into the house of the Lord, and spread it before the Lord."*

THE letter was an insolent cartel of defiance, which the Assyrian king, Sennacherib, sent full of as much blasphemous defiance against God as of insolence to God's servant. And in the true homœtheistic point of view, this same letter represents a conflict between Assyria and Judah as being a duel and struggle between the gods of one nation and the God of the other. And the point of it all is: don't let the god in whom thou trustest deceive thee, saying, Jerusalem shall not be delivered into the hands of Assyria. Thou hast seen what Assyria has done to all lands, and is thy God any better than theirs? And so the king of Judah, very simple and child-like, picks up the piece of blasphemy and goes up to the temple and spreads it all before God. With a very *naïve* piece of unconscious symbolism he takes the letter and spreads it out before God, and the meaning of that follows in the prayer, "Lord, open thou mine eyes," etc. It is for Thee to act!

And so that, as I take it, is the essential meaning of the thing.

I. First of all then, about what I call the meaning of this spreading before the Lord of something which influences and agitates us. It is the appeal to God's knowledge, and in your case and mine it takes this shape and form, and it needs the truth to make it very plain and clear to ourselves, that when some great anxiety strikes its talons deep into our hearts, the Eyes up yonder see all about it. A plain old piece of commonplace, but oh! there is a fountain of deep, unutterable consolation when a man realizes this. And that, as I take it, is what our Lord reiterates over and over again; the Father which is in *secret*, which *seeth* in secret.

> "Think not thou canst sigh,
> And thy Father is not nigh;
> Think not thou canst weep a tear,
> And thy Father is not near."

He spread it before the Lord and said to Him: "Thine eyes behold, and yet I bring it to Thee and ask what Thou wouldest."

II. And besides, that double attitude must characterise all our communion with Him. "Thou knowest it all, and yet hast Thou not said, Come, tell it to me." And there is nothing so very wonderful in that, if the Father's name covers in the Divine heart anything like the paternal tenderness upon earth. Pour out your hearts before Him all ye people! Ye do not tell Him anything He does not know full well before ye begin, but it is something to get the voice of our own hearts, and to get a firmer grip of faith while we are talking to Him. And so he spread the letter before the Lord: "Open Thine eyes, and see; bow down Thine ear, and hear." It is an appeal to God—pardon the apparent irreverence—to look after His own business! He spread the letter before the Lord and said, "Hear the words of Sennacherib which he hath sent to reproach the Living God." I say nothing about myself, but it is Thine honour which is threatened. If this insolent braggart does the thing which he threatens, then I throw the consequences upon Thyself, and if I go down, then it will be said, Forasmuch as this Jehovah was not able to save His people, therefore He has let them perish, and the uncouth gods with the barbarous names and those who worship them, will say, Jehovah is a name without meaning, *Thy* name which is above every name! So, see thou to it. With all humility, yet with all self-confidence, if a man has not got something like that in his prayers, they are poor prayers after all! Ask Him not so much to deliver you, as to be true to His character and true to His promises, to be self-consistent with all that He has been, and feel, as we have a right to feel, that if any human soul, that ever in the faintest, poorest, humblest manner, put out a trembling hand of confidence towards His great hand to grasp it, was suffered to go down and to perish, there is a blight and a blot on the fair fame of God before the whole creation, which nothing can obliterate. But it cannot be but the feeblest cry shall be answered, and the faintest faith rewarded, else shame would cover the Name that is above every name. "Not for your sakes, be it known unto you ye House of Israel, but for," etc. Let us take the string of thought, that not only for our own poor selves—though, blessed be God, He does take our happiness as a worthy object—but because His honour and fair fame are so inextricably wound with our well-being that He must answer the cries of His people.

III. Let us take out of this story, not only what we ought *to do* when we come to Him in prayer, but look at the kind of things which we ought *to take* to God. Nothing that dulls me, nothing that makes a danger, or a difficulty, or a trial, or a temptation, or a blasphemy with which His name is polluted, but should be at once spread out before the Lord.

But most of all, to be a lesson which seems to me to be most precious, the common things of everyday life; if there is a strange piece of furniture to be added to the sacred vessels of the temple, a scrawled letter of a heathen king,—but perhaps there was nothing in the House of God that day that was half so precious as that bit of parchment. And so do you learn this lesson: do not be afraid of asking God about trifles, about common everyday things. The small boy that one of our modern writers tells us of, that used to pray to have strength given him that he might learn his Latin declension, had a better knowledge of prayer than men of the world can understand.

IV. And take the other lesson: If you have not been in the habit of going to the House of God at other times, it will be a hard job to find your way there when your eyes are blinded with tears, and your hearts heavy with anxiety. You will find that this man Hezekiah had cultivated a habit of trusting God and referring everything to him, so he went straight into the Temple as by instinct, where he could have known his way in the dark,—and spread this letter before the Lord, as a matter of course.

It is a poor thing when a man's religion is like a waterproof coat, that is only good to wear when it rains, and has to be taken off when the weather improves a little! If you want to get a blessedness of fellowship with God and help from Him in the dark days, learn the road to the Temple in sunshine and gladness, and do not wait for the bellow of the pitiless storm, and darkness upon the path, before you go to the Temple of God.

V. And then, what do we get by this habit of spreading out everything before God? Well, we get valuable counsel. I do not know anything that has such a power of clearing a man's way, scattering mists, removing misconceptions, letting us see the true nature of some dazzling specious temptations, as the habit of turning to prayer.

The thing that perplexes us is, in ninety-nine cases out of a hundred, that the steadiness of the hand that holds the microscope is affected by the beating of the heart, and the passionate desires and wishes, and so there is nothing defined and clear; it is all a haze. It must be held fast and firm, the light within us. Brother, clearness of vision, sound, worldly, practical common sense—and there is nothing better except God's grace, which does manifest itself in sound, practical, worldly common sense—is most certainly of God, when we keep our hearts in equilibrium.

> Of ourselves we nothing can;
> Full soon were we downridden,
> But for us fights a proper man
> Whom God Himself hath bidden."

So sang good old Martin Luther long ago, and so may we say. God's help is given to the man that takes the letter and spreads it before the Lord. Do you remember that magnificent burst, one of the grandest sonnets of Hebrew poetry, in which this dim prayer of Hezekiah was answered? "Thus saith the Lord of all Israel, this is the word which the Lord hath spoken concerning him. The Virgin of the House of Israel hath heard him," etc., etc., and you and I shall get like answers.

VI. And the last thing I shall notice which we get by this habit of spreading things before the Lord is,—a very accurate and very easily applied test. I do not wonder that so many of us do not like to pray about our plans and about our anxieties; it is either because the plans have got no God in them, and the anxieties have got no faith. And you may depend upon it that anything that we cannot pray about we had better not touch. Any anxiety that is not substantial enough to bear lifting and laying down before God, ought never to trouble us.

. Test your lives, your thoughts, your affairs, your purposes by this,—Will they stand carriage to the Temple?—if not, the sooner you get rid of them the better. And then, "Be careful for nought, but in everything, by prayer and supplication and thanksgiving make your requests known unto God," and, in spite of all the Sennacheribs who have poured out their blatant blasphemies—"the peace of God, which passeth all understanding, shall keep you,"—with a better buckler and shield,—"shall keep your hearts and minds in Christ Jesus our Lord."

A. M.

XLVII. Times and Men. 1 CHRON. xii. 32. "*Men that had understanding of the times, to know what Israel ought to do.*"

IT was a dark hour when Saul and all the strength and pride of the elect nation lay dead on the mountains of Gilboa, and David uttered, as he alone could utter, the wail of the national heart. It was like the funeral dirge of the nation, and it would have been so had there not been men there "that had understanding of the times to know what Israel ought to do." God be thanked that at the worst crisis, men of Divine discernment rarely fail to appear, men who have an eye on the motion of the great Leader's hand, and who, led by Him, save the State.

These words reveal to us very clearly what Churches, saints, and ministers are meant for. They are the world's beacon lights, the pungent salt of its life.

I. The times which these men understood.

Men were then watching and waiting for their king.

They were times in which passionate self-will had brought a nation to ruin, and in which a king who could rule after God's own counsel was needed to save the State.

The demoralisation during Saul's reign was fearfully rapid. As it approached its close we see king and people, God-forsaken, crying out to Satan for help and guidance. The king, in the anguish of his despair, calls up the dead to counsel him; hears, or thinks he hears, from those awful lips the sentence of doom on his house and on his people; rushes desperate to battle, and expiates his reckless misrule by a suicide's death. This is all profoundly symbolic, symbolic of a darker, deeper ruin, from which it needed a stronger than David to save.

God has written in this Israel's history His statute and ordinance of national, domestic and personal life. Its significance waxes rather than wanes through the ages; the last age will read more fondly, more reverently the tale of the infancy and childhood of the world.

When the wreck of their worldly hope was utter, a divinely-commissioned man appeared. David did not dare to touch the sceptre till the Unseen Ruler placed it in his hand. His profoundest conviction, a conviction which never failed him through life, was that the Word of the Lord was the only ruler of men. That man swiftly retrieved the ruin of the nation, and after a prosperous reign left the most splendid monarchy to his son.

The understanding of those times was simply having an eye, not for David, but for David's godly submission to the heavenly King.

II. The men who had understanding of the times.

These were just the foremost men in Israel, the men of whose discernment of God's anointed saved the State. They came by troops to crown him. Their action laid the basis of the broad empire which David and Solomon ruled. Who are our foremost men? The men having an understanding of these times, and God's appointed captains and leaders by whom, as by Gideon's three hundred, He is saving the nation. There are those whom God sets first, with higher advantages, privileges, endowments, than their fellows. God's elect, elect for duty. Children of the election be first in service and make your calling and election sure.

The world cannot prosper under its self-elected king. "We have no king but Cæsar!" cried God's people once, and Cæsar harried them and crushed them to death. Full of misery, the world turns its pleading eye heavenwards. Its woe is always a mute cry in the ear of one as merciful as God. It has a right to ask of those who profess to be His friends and fellow-workers, if they can teach and help it. Show us what Christ can do for a soul, for a home, for a community, that we may know whether God has in very deed visited His world. Think on this, holy brethren, partakers of the heavenly calling, and consider what manner of men ye ought to be in all holy conversation and godliness.

III. Their work as the great pattern of Divine work—work for man, work for God, while time endures.

The work of these men, making David king, is the model, under Jewish forms, of the work to which we have to gird ourselves if we are to be teachers and guides of men. "Ye are my witnesses" is God's word to each Christian. The men who have an understanding of the times, and who know what Israel ought to do, are the men who are spending their whole thought and strength in this work, the enthronement of the Lord Jesus in human hearts. It is the essential patriotism. They made David king, and society arose as from death on the instant. It was the Lord's kingdom which David restored. Men live under the Lord's sceptre, they only exist under Satan's. The life flushes up again from the depths when the sunlight of the Lord's smile beams on it. There is joy and gladness in bounding hearts when the Lord sends His times of revival on the world. It is God's great work in all ages, bringing in His King to sorrowful, sin-stricken human hearts. He who is winning one act of homage for God's truth, or quickening one pulse responsive to His love in one human soul, is accomplishing a work for man for God which defies the strength of the mightiest armies and puts the wisdom of the wisest Parliament to shame. And how is this work to be done, how is the witness to be borne?

(1) Walk by faith. "Nevertheless," said the sad Saviour, "when the Son of man cometh shall He find faith on the earth." Was He looking on our days, our faithless days, we are tempted to ask? Here, at least, among Christ's disciples, Christ's preachers, let men see that there are

those who believe in resurrection, in the far-off interest of tears, the fruit of godly travail and patient pain. Let us try to live a life which simply cannot explain itself except by taking into account eternity and heaven.

(2) Abide in love. The Church is a home where love and peace should reign. There is nothing so saddening as to see the Church a world in miniature, with the same unruly tempers, the same selfish passions, the same class antipathies and isolations, a world all over, of the earth earthy, save that it calls itself the kingdom of heaven.

(3) Abound in noble, constant, self-denying work. Justify your pre-eminent privilege by your ministry to mankind. God looks to the Church to justify His ways to men. Fear no burdens. Let your work reward you. Consider Him and endure. "Cast thy bread upon the waters, thou shalt find it after many days."

J. B. B.

XLVIII. The Transitoriness of Life. 1 Chron. xxix. 15. "*For we are strangers before Thee, and sojourners, as were all our fathers: our days on the earth are as a shadow, and there is none abiding.*"

THE occasion on which these words were uttered was one of the most memorable in the history of Israel. David was approaching the end of his earthly career, and in transferring the crown to Solomon, he was anxious to secure that the cherished purpose of his heart in reference to the building of the Temple should be fully carried out. He asked the people to follow his example by consecrating themselves and their substance to the Lord, and the result was such an overflow of liberality as gladdened David's heart, and he poured forth his thanksgiving in a strain of devotion, which for grandeur, humility and pathos is well nigh unrivalled in the Bible.

I. Notice the fleeting character of our earthly life as suggested by those words.

II. The believer's support under the experience of the transitoriness of the present life. When David says here there is none abiding, he is speaking only of men, for all through this exquisite expression of devotional fervour we feel the pulsations of his faith in the eternity of God. Men come and go, but God abideth, and in His continuous care we have the richest consolation, alike when we see those taken from us whom we loved, and when we ourselves are about to depart.

III. The believer's home after this life is passed. The sojourner is seeking a fatherland. We are going home, and death is but the unrobing vestibule of our Father's House.

W. M. T.

XLIX. Esther's Prayer. Esther vii. 3. "*If I have found favour in thy sight, O king and if it please the king, let my life be given me at my petition, and my people at my request.*"

ESTHER'S appeal to king Ahasuerus is the crisis and turning point of a history well known to all of us. Haman had conceived a bitter hatred against the Jews and resolved to be their destruction. Having well considered how he was to go about it, he approached the king with a representation to the effect that there was in his provinces "a certain people," whose laws were different from the king's laws, and therefore it was not for the king's profit that they should be suffered, and proposed that they should be destroyed.

We are disposed to ask how any man in his senses could agree to so unwise a proposal as this; but we must take into account the peculiar temper in which the king was indulging at this time. He had withdrawn himself from all contact with his subjects and even with his court. It was in fact the assumption on his part of a kind of divinity,—the state of the gods, who dwell in peace and quietness and refuse to be troubled by the touch of mortal anxieties or sorrows. He was in this state of mind when the proposal was skilfully made to him by one who knew his business well. It was put to him on the ground of State policy. This Jewish people would not subject themselves to the king's laws. Haman got the king to commit himself by the publication of the edict, before any time for reflection was allowed him.

It is a very good specimen of temptation, and many temptations to which human beings are yielding every day have their striking analogies to this specimen.

King Ahasuerus had a tempter who precisely gauged the condition of his mind, and knew exactly how to deal with it. What do you suppose was in the mind of the king when this proposal was made to him, about "this certain people"? Was it the thought that they were men like himself, with the anxieties, the susceptibilities, the capacities of joy and sorrow, of which he had had experience — men knit together in those relations of life that gladden it and which enhance its possibility for sorrow. Men capable of experiencing the huge pangs that should be connected with such a massacre as was destined to take place? Nothing of the kind was in his thoughts. They were so many human items in a tax-gatherer's roll, so many of the swarming myriads that floated vaguely before his mind's eye, and they were to disappear.

The tempter winds up the proposal with a subtle and ingenious stroke of policy. Surely it was an ingenious way to hinder the king's thinking of these people as taxpayers, by offering him a compensation for the loss their removal would occasion. Haman said he had felt the difficulty. An economical adviser of a king ought not summarily to dismiss a multitude of taxpayers from the roll, and yet he suggests that it will not do for a king of one hundred and twenty-seven provinces to stand too much upon so many taxpayers, more or less. This was intended to pique the king's pride, and it had the desired effect. Haman was to keep the money and dispose of the people as it seemed to the best.

This view which we have been taking explains the suddenness and the strength of the revulsion which the king experienced when Esther, in an agony of intense supplication, told him her request. His horror is expressed in these words: "Who is he, and where is he that durst presume in his heart to do so?" That decree had been about some shadows of distant men and women, that were to pass out of existence. With Esther in the foreground, there stood behind, rising to view more dimly, yet perceptively, all the spectres that would have a right to haunt him if that decree were put into execution. The whole thing came suddenly before him as something horrible.

This is the case set before us here; and now as to lessons we have to draw from it.

I. This Scripture suggests this lesson,—that sin, contemplated at one time with so little sense of its enormity, that it can be very calmly looked at and done in an easy sort of way, may come afterwards to be the cause of those agonizing feelings. The conviction that gives the measure of what the sin is at the first stage is not inside the man. It is standing outside; it is heard, but not clearly heard. A man can shut the door and bar the windows, and make the fire burn bright, and persuade himself that there is not a great deal to listen to. It is not in, but the man knows it is there claiming a right to be in, and to make itself heard. By-and-bye, when the sin is accomplished, a day comes when conviction is found to have got in and it speaks: "You knew that I was claiming a hearing, you would not hear me then, but you shall hear me now." Yes, there are those who do hear it for evermore.

II. If there are any of us to whom an admonition like this should apply, the case of such will be worse than the case of Ahasuerus.

His crime was not accomplished. God's providence stepped in to prevent the consummation. But what shall be said of the case of him who, awakened to that frightful sense of evil and dismay, shall have to feel that all this tumult and dismay can do just nothing at all to undo the sin—his own sin—which he has made and committed, and which he can never undo or unmake.

III. A man may be his own Haman. It is not a light matter to be shut up within a man's own bosom, directing at oneself the Eye that Ahasuerus directed against Haman.

IV. There is only one remedy for such a case as this. The sacrifice, the propitiation of the Lord Jesus, received by faith, is able to put to silence all these charges.

V. May we not say that one form of evil among Christians in all our Churches is one very much like that which we have been denouncing in this ancient Eastern king—a want of loving sympathy for those benighted people who do not know the Lord. For after all who are these "certain people"? great swarming myriads of dusky people far away, masses of them which the mind wearily recognises and dismisses again. And yet take each man and woman of them one by one, and how differently we look on the case. Let us seek to be redeemed from all such miserable carelessness about our lost brethren, from all such miserable self-indulgence and indolence of spirit.

R. R.

L. The Insinuation of Satan. JOB ii. 4. *"And Satan answered and said, Skin for skin, yea, all that a man hath will he give for his life."*

THE Book of Job is a historical poem, and is one of the most ancient compositions of its kind now known to be in existence. The text is composed of the words of the great adversary, and we shall see their real falsehood, despite the air of plausibility which is thrown around them. It is unnecessary to enter upon the numerous explanations of the proverb, "skin for skin," which have been suggested by modern commentators. In effect they all amount to this, that a man will give up everything to save his life; and the insinuation of Satan is, that Job served God from merely selfish considerations, so that if the alternative should be presented, that he must either give up God or give up his life, he would hold to his life. Now in this Satan was only measuring Job by his own bushel.

Of course, there is a degree of truth in the assertion. A lie, pure, simple, unadulterated, does little harm in the world. To make it in the highest degree injurious there must be some truth mixed up in it. The worst liars are those whose blade is false but whose handle is true. Now the handle in which the blade of this lie is "hafted" is the fact that there is an instinctive love of life in every human being. No one loves death for its own sake. It is our duty to use all proper means for the prolongation of our lives.

But still, in spite of the appearance of truth in it, the affirmation as it stands is false. It is not true to the history of unregenerate men; far less is it true to that of those who have been born again.

I. It is not true to the history even of unregenerate human nature.

The passions of hatred and revenge have stirred men up to deeds which even at the moment of their commission they knew would forfeit their lives; and yet they have deliberately braved the law's penalty. The love of adventure has led many to risk their lives in its gratification. At the foundation of that cruel code in which duelling held place there lay this principle, that truth and integrity and purity of character ought to be dearer to a man than his life. There are some illustrations of the fact that even among unconverted men life is not always deemed the chief consideration.

II. If this be true even of unregenerate men, how much more is it of the renewed heart? That which is the ruling passion in a man rules over the love of life as well as other things in him.

Now in the truly godly one the ruling passion is love to God, and love to his neighbour for God's sake; and that dominates over all things else.

In proof of this, consider this history of the patriarch of Uz. With great cunning Satan enlisted the patriarch's wife and his three friends on his side, and many aggravating things which they said fell like hailstones on the heart of Job; but they did not shake his trust in God. Still through all his trouble he grasped the hand of the Almighty, and, amid the accusations heaped on him, he said, "I know that my Redeemer liveth; and though after my skin worms destroy this body, yet in my flesh shall I see God." And so Satan was disappointed and discomfited,

Think again of those three Hebrew youths in the fiery furnace, of Daniel in the den of lions, of the jubilant shout of praise raised by the noble army of martyrs, and have you not conclusive proof that Satan spoke lies when he said concerning the people of God, "Skin for skin, yea, all that a man hath will he give for his life!"

III. There are two practical inferences to be made from the foregoing remarks.

(1) One of the greatest dangers which beset the soul lies here. Through that self-love to which Satan here alludes, many of his most insidious temptations come to us. He has kept continually appealing to man's love of life, and in many cases he has at least partially succeeded.

He tried it with Abraham, and so made him lie unto the king of Egypt.

He tried it with Isaac, and caused him to lie to Abimelech.

He tried it with Elijah, and he fled from before the face of Jezebel. He tried it with Peter, and the man of rock quailed for the moment before the maid-servant and denied his Lord. He tried it with Demas, and in the hour of Paul's extremity he forsook his friend, "having loved this present world." And he still pursues the same method, and will make similar approaches to us. Wherever we turn, some appeal to our selfishness is made; but wherever it confronts us, let us spurn it from us with disdain, saying: "All these things we count but loss for the excellency of the knowledge of Christ Jesus our Lord."

(2) The truest greatness of humanity lies in falsifying this assertion of the devil. Since we call ourselves by the name of Christ, let us be distinguished by His unselfishness. How our littlenesses and meannesses are rebuked by the story of Christ's life and death! In the presence of that infinite sacrifice how poor and paltry does our selfishness appear! We need to have our entire selves hallowed by a lofty consecration; and when they who bear the Master's name shall be distinguished by the Master's likeness, even Satan himself will be compelled to own his error, and to say: "Skin for skin, yea, all that the Christian hath will he give for his Lord."

W. M. T.

LI. Broken Purposes. Job xvii. 11. "*My purposes are broken off.*"

WHAT those purposes were we cannot tell; but how great and dearly cherished we can readily imagine. Job had been possessed of great wealth, and a thousand purposes had been formed for the enjoyment of it. He had many friends, and a thousand purposes had gathered round their attachments. He had a family of sons and daughters, and he had built a thousand palaces of fancy about their future paths. His sky had been bright and clear, but in one moment the heaven became overspread, and the hurricane carried off at one fell swoop all that he had treasured. "My purposes are broken off."

How many there are who will hear in these words only the echo of their own heart's cry. When one looks back on life, and puts the result and actual attainments alongside the aims and hopes with which he started out, he cannot but be struck with the contrast. We are not, any of us, what we meant to be. God has led us by a way that we knew not of. It is not often that all life's hopes are disappointed, and all its attachments riven by one sudden blow. God is more merciful to our weakness than that. Still, we can all use the words of our text, "My purposes are broken off." Let us consider why our purposes are broken off."

I. Some purposes are broken off because they would work evil for us.

II. Some of our purposes are broken off because they would work evil for others. The purposes which we form for our children are not always the best and the wisest for them, and God, who sees farther than we, takes care that these purposes shall be broken off.

III. Our purposes are broken off, partly for own sakes, partly for the sake of others. They are broken off that others may have the privilege of carrying them out. These broken purposes, which are entirely good, are the hardest to understand of all. A Christian labourer is sometimes called to leave a harvest field, and lie aside useless, with his life's strength ebbing away and his life's purposes disappointed. But God does not leave us altogether without answer. He has hinted at a higher service for which He wants these faithful ones.

IV. They are broken off because God has other and higher purposes for us. God disappoints us that He may more blessedly fulfil. It is well they should be, that so our lives may be fashioned according to a higher purpose, purpose which is never broken.

J. G. G.

LII. Prophecy of Christ. JOB xix. 25, 26. "*I know that my Redeemer liveth, and that He shall stand at the latter day upon the earth: and though after my skin, worms destroy this body, yet in my flesh shall I see God.*"

IN these remarkable words the patriarch Job is speaking of the Resurrection. Although we are unable to assign to with historical certainty the precise period at which Job lived, there is strong reason for concluding that he was contemporary with Moses. He was not a Hebrew, but a Gentile. He was "a perfect and an upright man," and one that "feared God and eschewed evil." He was thus like Melchisedec, a representative of the pure religion of the primitive ages of the world.

The patriarch is here comforting himself with the hope of the Resurrection and of the life of the world to come. In an earlier part of this Book he seems anxiously to inquire into the possibility of a man's living again. "If a man die shall he live again?" But here, in this passage, all doubt vanishes. After a severe struggle of anguish and agony, he arose from his deep dejection, and poured forth these magnificent words, words of which he may not himself have then seen all the significance and force. Far across the space of fifteen centuries this prophecy reaches to our Lord's empty tomb, and onwards to the resurrection of all men at the last great day. Translators have had many difficulties to contend with in giving the full meaning of this passage. But translate it as you will, no antiquity about this or that phrase can obliterate from it the doctrine of the Resurrection and that doctrine as connected with Christ Jesus.

I. "I know that my Redeemer liveth." That is, I Job, who am thus grievously afflicted, I am fully persuaded that my Redeemer is living. The Lord Jesus is a living Person, the same yesterday, to-day, and for ever. The word Goel here translated Redeemer, means one next of kin. And so Christ is our true Goel, having made Himself next of kin to us all by taking our nature upon Him, and has redeemed us from the captivity of sin and Satan.

II. The body is to return to its dust. None, not even the saints of God, are exempt from this universal sentence of dissolution. Every living thing that now moves on the face of the earth will disappear from it. This scene of life and thought and intelligence will be changed into the dark and dismal forms of corruption, and others will occupy our places. And is this, then, the end of all things? "Yet in my flesh shall I see God."

III. The Resurrection of the flesh. Beyond question it is a great demand upon our faith to believe that the body, which has been resolved into its elementary particles, can again be compounded into bone and sinew and flesh.

But even reason may help us to accept this truth, and so become, as it were, a handmaid to faith. Does not Nature continually preach to us of the Resurrection? What are the alternations of day and night but images of the Resurrection? And does not the succession of the seasons tell of the same thing?

But since the faculty of reason is apt to grow dull within us, therefore has Christ given us the example of a Resurrection to raise our drooping faith, and to proclaim to us, as we stand wondering at the empty sepulchre, that as He rose from the dead, so has His resurrection a commanding power to raise us from the dead, and that we in our flesh shall see God.

Now if this be indeed true, that we shall appear, in these very bodies, before the Judgment throne, how careful ought we to be lest we dishonour our bodies by making them the instruments of sin. Let us respect our bodies as the temples in which the Holy Spirit vouchsafes to dwell. The body which has had its part to fulfil on earth has no less than the soul its position to fill throughout eternity. Let us strive in the power of the risen Lord to live the resurrection life.

"I know that my Redeemer liveth." Oh, precious promise, imperishable assurance! The sinner's hope, the believer's strength, our guide in life, our confidence in death! Are we in heaviness through the remembrance of past sin, or the power of present temptations? I know that my Redeemer, my God, my Kinsman liveth.

Are friends taken from us by death? These are amongst the first words with which our Church cheers us when we come to consign them to the dust. And when our last hour comes may we, one and all, be able to claim this promise, and die with the humble hope of its fulfilment to ourselves.

E. B.

LIII. Acquaintance with God. Job xxii. 21. "*Acquaint now thyself with Him, and be at peace.*"

THERE are three steps of knowledge; first, the knowledge of things outside of us; second, the knowledge of what is inside us, the knowledge of our own hearts; and third, the knowledge of God. There is only one knowledge which ever gives or can give true happiness. Some, knowing themselves, are seeking happiness altogether independent of God, and they would escape from themselves every day into excitement. Some are seeking true peace, but they look for the evidences of that peace in something which they are and not what God is. Some seek their evidences in God, but not in the God of revelation—in a God of their own fancy, a God they mistake and misrepresent. To all of them the one remedy lies in the command, "Acquaint now thyself with Him, and be at peace." Fulfil this condition and the result is sure. The great question now comes, Who can acquaint himself with God? How can a man know God? It can only be a distant approximation after all, for no man knows God as He is in Himself. But standing in the hollow of the rock we may try to catch the glimpses of His passing. We put aside the teachings of nature. No man can "acquaint himself with God" in that book.

(1) He who has the Holy Ghost knows God. Only God's mind can know God. The Holy Ghost is the mind of God; therefore, if we have the Holy Ghost we have the mind of God, and so can know Him. The Holy Ghost is a promised gift, and whoever truly asks for it shall have it.

(2) The Spirit's book must be read. If you would know God you must study Him in the Bible, in the person, and the character and life and work of His Son.

(3) The Son represents and declares the invisible Father. "No man knoweth the Father but the Son, and he to whom the Son shall reveal Him."

The Son will lead you along to this great end in His own school of discipline and love. He will afflict you, He will strip you, He will make you feel poor and solitary, He will take you into a wilderness, and there in your sense of nothingness He will betroth you to Himself, and "thou shalt know the Lord."

And great peace follows. When "your righteousness is as the waves of the sea," well then "may your peace flow like a river."

J. V.

LIV. The Light in the Clouds. JOB xxxvii. 21.

"*And now men see not the bright light which is in the clouds: but the wind passeth, and cleanseth them.*"

"MEN see not the bright light which is in the clouds." The light is there but not always visible, and we know of the actual existence of the light which the cloud only partially conceals from us. And from time to time, God in His infinite providence and love, sends the wind and sweeps away the clouds, and brings gladness and brightness to our vision. This Word is an inexhaustible jewel-bed, and one of the gems of purest ray is this text, which will show a light to many a one in the dark hours of bereavement and affliction.

I. We live on the unilluminated side of the cloud. Only needful rays shine through, and yet the rays are quite sufficient for our guidance. We cannot understand the fulness of God's being, nor how three persons can exist in one Godhead; it is quite enough that it is the fact. We cannot understand many of the mysteries connected with the Divine plan of redemption, but that matters little, as long as we know that God so loved us that He sent His only Son to die for us. We have sufficient truth shining through the cloud for us to walk in the paths of obedience, waiting for the time when we shall get above the cloud and behind the cloud into the overwhelming glory there.

II. The Infinite light behind the cloud is Infinite love. That cloud is love, for God means every adversity for our good, and every trial to work out "an exceeding and eternal weight of glory." Perhaps thine eye has been blind to the beauty of Jesus, and thine ear has been deaf to the voice of His love. God may touch thee on the tenderest spot, that thou mayest be brought with the touch that brings tears and blood, to that very Saviour whom thou wouldst not see or hear in all the time gone by. His word is full of illustrations of this.

Suffering has many compensations; not only in its influence upon the sufferer in humbling him, bringing him into a sense of dependence, inspiring in him a spirit of prayer, quickening his faith and working out the principles of righteousness, but it has its happy influence upon others.

III. The future will clear up all mysteries. We often

grow so inquisitive to know what the reasons of dark things and trials are. By-and-by shall come the last great day of revelation, and all clouds shall be cleared away. Let us note some lessons:

(1) Remember that God is often inscrutable, never wrong.

(2) On this side of the cloud we have nothing to do but to receive the truth that comes through, and walk by it.

(3) Never get frightened at God's clouds.

(4) Clouds of trial often rain down truth, as the dark clouds in the heavens rain down showers on the thirsty field. The Gospel comes to each of us, and offers to us Christ and with Him light for every dark hour, strength for every trial, pardon for every sin, guidance for every footstep. He alone can illuminate the darkness of the soul, and alone turn even clouds of trial into harbingers of everlasting blessing and glory.

T. L. C.

LV. Christian Development. Ps. i. 3. *"And he shall be like a tree planted by the rivers of water, that bringeth forth his fruit in his season."*

THIS reference to the tree as the image of a good man's life, this garden which is thus summoned up before our minds, harmonizes with almost all the early, and certainly with the closing, scenes in our Bibles. Adam's unfallen life was passed in a garden watered by four rivers; and the kingdom of the blessed in the Apocalypse is represented as watered by the pure river of the water of life.

It is significant that the image which is chosen is not a tree of the forest, untended by man, but that it is a tree specifically planted by the waterside. This is to be noted because this image of the tree of nature has been freely used by a school of thinkers as against any doctrine of human education whatever. "Man is a tree. Let him throw out his branches freely." But man is not a tree, and is only like a tree in some respects which were in the psalmist's mind when he used the image. Man has intelligence which requires to be developed. He has moral freedom which requires to be developed. Once more, he is a depraved being, and if left to himself, he will only grow in depravity. Man educated is a greater, nobler being than savage man. When Christianity is the educator, the difference is vital. It is the difference between light and darkness, between life and death. The first point of similarity between spiritual and vegetable life is that each is gradual; and secondly, that each is mysterious. So we may say that as a tree requires soil, sunlight, and moisture for its proper growth, so the human soul requires certain conditions, without which growth and development are impossible. These conditions are :—

(1) The life of the soul must be based upon principles. They are the very soil of the soul. They are the basis of truth on which the understanding must lean.

(2) Christianity must expand. As it is based upon principles, so must it expand by love. Beauty attracts love, and God has provided for this side of human education. He has revealed Himself in His blessed Son, whom the prophets saluted before his Incarnation as fairer than the children of men. A personal love of the Lord Jesus is the central element of Christian character.

(3) The will must be disciplined. The will is the summit of the character, just as the heart is at its centre, as the understanding is at its base. Undoubtedly it is the Christian who can say, not in his own strength, but by the grace of God, "I will." The will is strengthened by obedience. God in His mercy does not leave the formation of the will to us. He takes us in His own hand, He disciplines us; He gives us trials. But the time comes at last when we have mastered that hardest lesson of the human heart, when we can say with truth, "Not my will, but Thine be done."

H. P. L.

LVI. What is Man. Ps. viii. 4. *"What is man, that Thou art mindful of him, and the son of man that Thou visitest him?"*

IN this psalm David gives expression to that sense of awe and wonder which is due to the beauty and the mystery of the natural world. For David, nature is not a half personified deity, still less a wall of adamant which marks the boundary of human knowledge and human hopes. For David, nature is first the handiwork, and then the robe of

God. The Epistle to the Hebrews shows that there is a great deal more in this psalm than lies on the surface. What David says here of the race, applies to the one worthy representative of the race, Jesus Christ; and thus the psalm forms a hymn of Christian praise addressed to the glorified Redeemer. We may dwell with advantage upon the original sense of the psalm as referring to the race, and ask, "What is man, that Thou art mindful of him?"

I. He is an animal. He is, in the complexity of his nature, a complete recapitulation of all the lower forms of animal existence.

II. He is a spirit. Not merely a life principle, which sustains and invigorates the bodily frame. Every animal is or has such a spirit as that. When man dies his spirit does not fade away into non-existence. It returns to the God who gave it. This belief has been described as a conceit on the part of man. Is it a vain assumption? There are many replies to the question, but one will suffice here. A mere animal has no idea of progress—of improvement. There is no evidence of any effort on the part of any race of animals to raise itself; whereas man, even when least successful, is never wholly without the aspiration towards better things. Man's spirit is the secret of man's royalty in nature. Man is king of the creatures, because in his inmost seat of life he is distinct from them.

III. He is a fallen being. Experience may teach any man that in his darkened understanding, in his weakened will, in the tyranny of sense over thought, of the body over the soul, he finds traces of the fall. And yet "Thou art mindful of him." God's care for man follows the order of man's being and needs. And therefore we bless Him "for our creation, preservation, and all the blessings of this life, but above all for His inestimable love in the redemption of the world through our Lord Jesus."

H. P. L.

LVII. Help from the Sanctuary. Ps. xx. 2. *"The Lord hear thee in the day of trouble: send thee help from the sanctuary, and strengthen thee out of Zion."*

WE all need help. The burden of life presses heavily upon

us, and we feel in our inmost souls that we are insufficient for these things. We know that our help must ultimately come from God. The unstudied exclamation, "God help me," is often wrung from lips that would scoff at formal prayer.

The Christian delights to acknowledge and feel God to be helper at all times. God sends us help through His words, through His providence, and especially through our fellow-creatures.

The text does not ignore, but embraces these channels of Divine help in a larger generalization when it says, "The Lord send thee help from the sanctuary."

I. God sends help from the sanctuary through the influence of the Church and its ordinances upon all our domestic relations.

How bright is the family life which is pervaded from centre to circumference by the influence of God's house and its holy ordinances! What can bind the hearts of husband and wife, parent and child, brother and sister, together in bonds so tender and yet so strong as the bonds of the sanctuary? How could we bear our household griefs but for the help God sends us from the sanctuary?

II. God sends us help from the sanctuary through the power of the ordinances upon our own religious life. It is chiefly through the public means of grace that men are converted to God, and helped forward in their Christian course. It pleased God by the foolishness of preaching to save them that believe. The happiest and the strongest Christians, and they whose life is most helpful in comforting others, are they whose character from youth to old age is moulded by the hearing of the Gospel, and fitted for heaven by familiarity with God's sanctuary on earth.

III. God sends help through the communion of saints, of which the sanctuary and its ordinances are the visible symbols.

A particular Church of Christ is a body of believers, with their children, covenanted together for the worship of God, for communion in the body and blood of Christ, and for mutual helpfulness in the Christian life. Membership in such an association involves many and solemn obligations. The communion of saints is more and better than "the fellowship of kindred minds." It is an actual participation in Christ and the benefits of His redemption, and in those personal possessions which Christian love for Christ's sake "parts to all as every man has need."

To communicate is to commune, and to do good is to communicate. The apostles use the same word to describe our participation in the Lord's Supper and the sharing of our worldly goods with the brethren of Christ. They are both a communion. The communion of saints is a blessed reality, even though we are not embraced in its helping arms. The sap of the vine does not penetrate the dead branches. There is a divine life in the body of Christ which pervades all its true members.

We must give as well as receive, and count it "more blessed to give than to receive." It is by that which every joint supplieth the whole body maketh increase, to the edifying of itself in love. They who complain most of the coldness of the Church generally contribute least to make it warm; and they who grudge the cost of the spikenard, have little enjoyment of it when the house is filled with the odour of the ointment. They who strive most to be helpful to others will receive most help themselves. Some there are who know this by a blessed experience. They find comfort for their own souls by comforting others. To them God's house is indeed a sanctuary—a refuge—a source of strength to do and to suffer the Divine will. The sanctuary is to them the type and the foretaste of heaven. "They shall dwell in the house of the Lord for ever."

W. M. T.

LVIII. The Solitude of Christ in Redemption.

Ps. xxii. 11. "*Be not far from me, for trouble is near, for there is none to help.*"

THIS is one of the cries of the ideal or superhuman sufferer, of whose agonies, both of mind and body, we have so complete a picture in this psalm. The words were David's, but the thoughts, hopes, fears, anguish and exultation were of another and a higher than David. In this psalm there is one feature of our Lord's sufferings upon which special stress is laid, namely, His desolation or solitude. It is the keynote of the psalm, and nowhere finds more pathetic expression than in the words of our text.

In His sufferings Jesus was alone—alone in spirit though encompassed by a multitude. In His passion Jesus experienced a threefold solitude.

I. The solitude of greatness. The loneliness of the great is one of the ironies of human life. They are lonely because they are great; because, had they peers and companions they would cease to be what they are, at least in relation to those around them. The solitude of the throne is proverbial. Again, genius is by its instinct solitary. The mountain peaks, which are the crowning beauty of a vast and fertile plain, purchase their prerogative elevation at a great cost. They are cold, bleak, inaccessible. Again, true greatness of character is in the main solitary. The unswerving adherence to truth, the resolute sacrifice of immediate advantage to the claims of principle are not popular qualities. Our Lord in His passion was great in these various ways. He felt the isolation of royalty. He lived in a sphere of thought which was impossible for those around, and He was sinless.

II. The solitude of sorrow. Though sorrow is universal, no two human beings suffer exactly alike; each sufferer, whether of bodily or of mental pain, pursues a separate path, encounters peculiar difficulties, shares a common burden, but is alone in his sorrow. Especially was Jesus solitary in His awful sorrow. His bodily sufferings were less terrible than the sufferings of His mind. "He bore our sins in His own body on the tree." But the touch of this burden, which to us is so familiar, was agony to Him. It drew from Him the bloody sweat of Gethsemane.

III. The solitude of death. Death strips from a man all that connects him with that which is without him. Jesus willed to share the misery of the souls who cry in their last moments, "My God, why hast Thou forsaken me?"

H. P. L.

LIX. Seeking the Face of God. Ps. xxvii. 8, 9.

"*When Thou saidst, Seek ye My face; my heart said unto Thee, Thy face, Lord will I seek. Hide not Thy face from me.*"

THERE appears to be a good deal of autobiography in this

psalm. The writer, whom we take to be David, travels back in thought to the past of his life, and his backward glance fixes on two distinct objects. At one time he thinks of the past as God's past, all illumined by the radiance of His favour, and helped by the might of His imparted strength ; at another he thinks of it as his own past, wherein he strove to love and serve his Keeper, God ; and from both these aspects of the days that are gone he draws encouragement to hope that God will be the same, and resolves that he will continue the habit of trust and obedience. Here, in the words of the text, these two ways of looking at the past are woven into one strong cord, that the psalmist may hang his confidence and his prayers thereon.

I. There is here God's voice to the heart. We have here, as it were, summed up in a kind of dialogue of two phrases, the whole speech of God to us men, and the inmost meaning of all that devout souls say to God. "Seek ye My face." Such is the essential meaning of all God's words and works. "Thy face, Lord, will I seek." Such is the essential meaning of all prayer, worship and obedience.

What is the significance of that expression, "the face of God?" It is one of those strong Scripture phrases which escape any danger of misconstruction by the very boldness of their corporeal metaphors. The God whom men need and can know and love, the God who is a Spirit, comes near to us in descriptions cast in the mould of humanity, and loses none of His purely spiritual essence, nor any of His infinitude, because we have learned to speak of the eye and arm and the hand and the heart and the face of the Lord. The eye of the Lord is His all-seeing knowledge ; the arm and the hand of the Lord are substantially the same, and may be said to express the active energy of the Divine nature. The face of the Lord is that aspect or side of the Divine nature which is turned to man, and is perceptible by him. It is almost equivalent to "the name of the Lord," which means the manifested character of God, the net result of all His self-revelation by word and work. Another idea is usually connected with the expression— that of light. "Lift Thou up the light of Thy countenance upon us." The two ideas of the sun rising on an else dark world, and the rising of the Divine countenance on else dark and wintry hearts, are here paralleled. To seek God's face is no long, dubious search, nor is He hard to be found. We have only to desire to possess, and to act in harmony with the desire, and we shall walk all the day in the light of His countenance.

Endeavour to keep vivid the consciousness of that Face as looking always in on you, like the solemn frescoes of the Christ which Angelico painted on the walls of his convent cells, that each poor brother might feel his Master ever with him. Scrupulously avoid whatever might dim the vision of His face.

If this be the meaning of seeking God's face, then note that this invitation is God's merciful voice to us. By the very make of our spirits, which bear on them alike in their weakness and their strength the sign that they are His, and can only be at rest in Him, He says, "Seek ye My face."

By all His providences of joy or sorrow, and the alternations which "toss us to His breast," He says, "Seek ye My face."

And most of all in Jesus, the true "angel of His face," in whom all the lustre of His radiance is gathered, does He beckon us to Himself.

II. We have here the heart's echo to the voice of God. Swift and immediate, as the thunder to the lightning, the answer follows the invitation. If the resolve to seek God's face be not made by us at the very moment when we become aware of His loving call, it is very unlikely to be made at all. The first notes of that low voice fall on the ear with more persuasive power than they retain after it has become familiar with them, even as the first-heard song of the thrush in spring-time that breaks the long wintry silence has a sweetness all its own. It is always dangerous to delay for one moment the uprising of the heart in any resolution which we know to be right.

There is also brought out here the complete correspondence between the Divine command and the devout man's resolve. Word for word the invitation is repeated in the answer. This man's obedience is no partial obedience. "Seek, and ye shall find," is ever true, thank God; but it must be a whole-hearted seeking, and not the feeble, flickering desire and the listless action which mark so many of us.

Note, too, the firm and decisive resolution shining through the brevity of the words. If we are quite resolved that our life's business is to be seeking God's face, we shall, for the most part, say little about it.

Further, we have in this heart's echo to the voice of God the conversion of a general invitation into a personal resolution. The call is " Seek ye ; " the answer is " I will seek." That is what we have all to do with God's words. He sows His invitations broadcast ; we have to make them our own. He sends out His mercy for a world ; we have to claim each our portion. Nothing in all the world is so blessed as to hear that wonderful beseeching call sounding in every providence, travelling to us from every corner of the universe, speaking to us in the light of setting suns and in the hush of midnight skies, sounding in the bound of waves on the beach and in the rustle of leaves in the forest depths, whispering to us in the depths of our own hearts and wooing us by all things to our rest. That is heaven on earth, nobleness, peace and power, to stand as at the point of some great ellipse to which converge from all sides the music of God's manifold invitations, and listening to them, to say, I hear, and I obey. Thou dost call, and I answer, Lo! here am I.

III. There is here the heart's cry to God founded on both the Divine voice and the human echo. " Hide not Thy face from me " is clearly a prayer built upon both these elements in the past. God's invitation and my acceptance of it both give me the right to pray thus, and are pledges of the answer.

As to the former, "Thou saidst, Seek ye my face." "Hide not Thy face from me" is but the vivid way of putting the thought that God cannot contradict Himself.

As to the second ground of this prayer, it rests on my part as well as on God's. It is the confidence that because we seek we shall find. He fills the vessels we bring, be they large or small. My feeblest desire brings answers correspondent to its strength and purity.

Seek His face evermore, and your life will be bright because you will walk in the light of His countenance always. That face will brighten the darkness of death ; and when you reach the land beyond you, you will enter it with the wonderful hope on your lips, "As for me, I shall behold

Thy face in righteousness," and heaven's heaven will be that "His servants serve Him, and see His face."

A. M.

LX. The Fountain of Life. Ps. xxxvi. 9. *"For with Thee is the fountain of life."*

THIS is a grand thought—"fountain of life." If life has a "fountain," surely we should stop and drink at it.

I. Let us ask first, What is life?

(1) Life is a garden, and wants its refreshings. Many feel the burden of life's monotony. What we all want is freshness. Who has not felt the tendency of the highest duties to pass into mere forms? How few of us do not find our prayers stiffen into a mere mechanism? And what we need is a re-kindling of the original motive—a new affection to make an old thing new. Now to meet all such feelings there stands a fountain, not a well, always running, always sparkling. "The fountain of life." A real act of communion with God will do more than anything else to make us live again. Our battles, duties, crosses, prayers, feelings, work, and soul must touch Christ; they must take more of Christ into them; they must lie under the droppings; they must bathe themselves in Christ.

(2) Life is a soiled thing, and wants cleansings. There is the defilement of accumulating sin. It is a solemn thing to think of, that to count years is to catalogue transgressions. Throw all these sins into this fountain, and daily come with each day's sins to wash and be clean.

II. What is the "fountain of life?" God put all life into His Son, and that life which is in Christ is the real spring and essence of all that constitutes true human life. The life that is treasured up in Jesus is a very fountain, and it flows freely. If you are not drinking in life, it is not because that fountain is sealed to you, but because your heart is sealed to it.

J. V.

LXI. Unfailing Hope. Ps. xlii. 11. *"Why art thou cast down, O my soul? and why art thou disquieted within me? Hope thou in God: for I shall yet praise Him, who is the health of my countenance, and my God."*

In every sense the Christian life is a conflict, and our enemies are mostly to be found within our own souls. The psalmist had experience of this, and here we have him remonstrating with himself.

I. The state of mind in which the psalmist was,—the soul cast down and disquieted within him.

This is a state in which many Christians are at varied periods in their earthly experience. Some of them very much more than others. These trials spring from manifold sources; sometimes from the Christian himself, sometimes from those dear to him, sometimes from his mental exercise of trial, when he is ready to say, "Thy waves and Thy billows are gone over me."

II. The desirableness of the investigation the psalmist instituted when he said, "Why art thou cast down?"

It is very often for want of asking this question that Christians continue in the state of despondency. There are many imaginary trials allowed to creep into the soul, which once looked at in the face, in the light of the glory that beams from another world, would vanish in a moment —like mists before the rising sun. This enquiry should be made, because generally it would be found that in the Divine dealings there was no cause whatever for the soul to be cast down. There is not a moment of all this experience of trial but shall minister to the need that has been seen in the soul's condition. The answer to this enquiry will very frequently be found in the soul itself. Prayer may have been neglected, or the sanctuary forsaken, or the Bible may remain unread.

III. The counsel addressed to the psalmist, "Hope thou in God." There is the remedy, the cure for the soul. There is the sunlight for its darkness.

And then after this sunlight has streamed into the darkened spirit, there comes the song of praise. "I shall yet praise Him, who is the health of my countenance, and my God." The Christian life ought to be a life of praise. Praise ought to grow stronger and richer every mile you pass over in the way to the New Jerusalem, for you have so much the more mercy in the past to inspire it.

J. P. C.

LXII. Hope in God. Ps. xliii. 5. *"Why art thou cast down, O my soul? and why art thou disquieted within me? hope in God: for I shall yet praise Him, who is the health of my countenance, and my God."*

THIS verse forms the thrice-repeated chorus of a psalm which some consider finer than any other in the psalter in respect of imagery and structure. The forty-second and forty-third Psalms originally formed a single poem, consisting of three strophes, each of which closes with the slightly varied lines of the text.

The writer of the psalm, whether King, or more probably Levite, is in exile. He is dwelling in the Hermons, a mountain ridge to the east of Jordan, and among men of fierce habits and alien faith. That which is passing within his soul seems to be reflected on the natural scenes around him. He marks the gazelle, as it climbs panting up the rocky bed of some ravine in search of water, and he is at once reminded of his own unappeased longing for that Being who alone can quench the thirst of man's soul. He is overtaken by a violent storm, and the thunder and rain only remind him of that storm of secret sorrow which is beating on his soul, and as thought turns back to bygone years, he remembers how at the three great festivals thousands of pilgrims would gather at the sacred city; and how he himself went out with the multitude in solemn procession, and brought them into the House of God with the voice of praise and thanksgiving. How can he but pray that the light and truth of God may be sent forth to lead him home, that he may spend his remaining years in thankful praise.

The psalmist is in colloquy with himself; he is at once the adviser and the advised. He observes, he cross-questions, he rebukes, he counsels his own soul.

We see here how Holy Scripture addresses itself to the darker moods of the human soul, that it may help us to master them, or to turn them into good account. There are modern poets who throw themselves into the gloomy thoughts of men, only to give them more exquisite and luxurious expression, or even to prolong by refining without consecrating them. Not so the Bible. If it turns the eye upon the sadness and disquiet of the soul it is to bid it hope in God, and so rise into joy and peace. Melancholy is not, even from a purely natural point of view, strictly in order. There is something in this which proclaims it to be an intruder, and which prompts us to challenge it, and to bid it give an account of itself.

I. The psalmist's question is always a very practical one for a large number of human beings: "Why art thou cast down?" One answer to this question would be sought in physical temperament. We may have a constitutional tendency to depression, but we can give way to it until it sways irresistibly, or we can check and altogether overcome it by cultivating an opposite habit of mind. He who made us does not ask at our hands that which He Himself has made it impossible that we could give Him. We have only to hope in Him to keep His way. He will promote us that we may possess the land of joy, whatever may be our physical temperament at the outset of our journey.

II. The second answer to this question is furnished by the despairing philosophy of life. "How," it has been said, "can men think at all and not take a gloomy view of human existence?" It is the thought of God, and all that that thought implies, which makes life tolerable. To live beneath the smile of the Heavenly Father is indeed to understand the worth of life, and the worth of those theories which disparage it.

III. There are other answers to the psalmist's question. There is temporal misfortune. The troubles of life do weigh the soul down. The rule is that trouble does crush men unless men can lay strong hold on One who transcends human life and its vicissitudes.

IV. More depressing still is spiritual trouble, when God's face is hidden from the soul. The temptations of such a time are obvious. Many a man will say to himself that his religion, after all, was but a passing phase of feeling. And yet this is but to mistake an act of Divine discipline for the collapse of truth. Oh, put thy trust in God, cling to His hand, though He lead thee through the darkness.

V. Again, there is the sense of unforgiven sin. Much more reasonably may this depress us, for sin is the true, the deepest secret of the gloom of the soul. If sin were compatible in man with lasting joy and peace, the Maker of the world would not be the perfect moral Being that He is If He is a judge, He is also a physician, and so the truest counsel and the truest wisdom is still to "hope in the Lord."

There are many secrets that are worth knowing, but none surely can better deserve our attention than the secret of peace and joy of the soul. "If we say we have no sin, we deceive ourselves and the truth is not in us; but if we confess our sins, He is faithful and just to forgive us our sins, "for the blood of Jesus Christ His Son cleanseth us from all sin."

H. P. L.

LXIII. God's Doings in the Time of Old. Ps. xliv. 1. "*We have heard with our ears, O God, our fathers have told us, what Thou hast done in their time of old.*"

THIS verse is an act of acknowledgment and praise. The psalm probably was written in those dark times which preceded the final catastrophe of the Babylonish captivity. There was failure abroad and misery at home. At such a time the hearts of religious men turned back upon the past—upon all God had done for Israel then. Was He not the same God? Would He be inconsistent with Himself? Surely it was enough to remind Him of His mercies in the past, and then to be certain that the future would be provided for. The Bible is largely made up of human histories, and in God's conduct and control of man, He reveals Himself. History has thus a distinctly religious use, as showing how God works and what He is.

I. Looking to the records of the past, we are taken out of the present, that is to say, we are taken out of ourselves. History throws us back into the past, and we see how similar difficulties were encountered and overcome.

II. History places us face to face with the infinite and eternal God. "I am Jehovah: I change not." In His dealings with men no less than in His own essence He is the same. And what God has been to men we know from history. We know then from history what He will be to us.

III. There are three departments of human life in which this recurrence to the past is of great religious value.

(1) There is the family. Every family has its traditions of the past—has its encouragements and warnings, its splendid memories of devotion and virtue, and too often its skeletons in the cupboards. All this is part of the providential teaching intended for each member of the family.

(2) There is our country. It should be part of every man's religious education to learn to scan the annals of his country, till he can with fervour and sincerity exclaim with the psalmist, "O God, we have heard with our ears and our fathers have told us, what Thou hast done in their time of old."

(3) There is the Church of Jesus. Her annals are a mighty revelation of the faithfulness and presence of God.

H. P. L.

LXIV. Calling upon God in Trouble. Ps. l. 15.

"Call upon Me in the day of trouble: I will deliver thee, and thou shalt glorify Me."

LOVE that needs to be entreated is not perfect love. So, at least, we judge of all the highest forms of human love. What father, for example, requires his child to come to him and beg him for what the child needs before he will consent to bestow it? We feel that for a father to treat his child thus, would at once show that the father's own heart was wrong and cold. The spontaneity of the gifts of love, the delight it has in anticipating the wants of others rather than in waiting to be asked, are of the very essence of love. If these are absent then we say love is absent. And this is especially true when the object of our love is in distress or trouble, and is thrown helpless and dependent upon us. A mother does not need the cry of her sick child to unseal the deep fountains of a mother's love, and to cause them to flow out in all their tender ministries towards it. The little face, pale and worn with disease, is its own best appeal to the mother's heart; and you would pierce that heart with an unutterable pain if you thought it would give no relief to the child unless it first pleaded for pity.

I. But what is it our text tells us? That He who is the Eternal and Infinite Lord, the "Everlasting Father," the greatness and wonder of whose love to His children makes even the deepest of human love seem poor and cold, that He waits for the cry of His troubled child, ere He will bless; and makes the call for His deliverance the condition of its bestowal? Even so. This is the mystery of prayer; a mystery far profounder than the tangled questions about prayer with which we vex and perplex our hearts, such as how can it be answered in a universe ruled by law, or how can it be reconciled with the unchangeableness of God, and the rest. Why should God impose this restraint on His compassion? Why should He, who holds all blessings in His hand, and who has all love in His heart, refuse to bless His people unless "He be inquired of by the house of Israel to do it for them"? If we can answer this question, we have solved the final mystery of prayer.

And yet those who know the value of prayer, and

"What a change one short hour spent in God's presence
Will prevail to make,"

will be the first to thank God even for the mystery of prayer. Whether there be other and still higher reasons for the necessity of prayer—reasons which lie deep in the nature of God as well as in the nature of man—they may not know; but this they do know, *that prayer justifies itself*, and the very condition, that seemed like a limitation of the love of God, becomes one of its richest gifts to the heart.

And this is one of the reasons which go very far to explain sorrow. It leads men to pray. When all things are bright and prosperous without, and we live in unbroken happiness, with sunlight everywhere around us, we are in danger of forgetting God by forgetting our need of prayer. It is not "Jeshurun" alone who, when he "waxed fat," "forsook God who made him, and lightly esteemed the Rock of his salvation," for we have all fallen into the same sin again and again. Just as the too great brightness of the sun causes the distant mountains to fade away, wrapped in a haze of light, so in our summer day of gladness things unseen and eternal are hidden from us, and this present and passing world absorbs and occupies all our thoughts.

Then God sends us trouble. The clouds gather; the sun is hidden; the storm falls upon us, and we walk in darkness and in fear; and then for the first time, it may be for years, we begin to pray. The voice that through long years of uninterrupted peace and prosperity never blessed God for His mercy, now "in the day of trouble" is heard calling upon Him for deliverance. This is not, it is true, the highest form of prayer; it is better to pray from fear than not to pray at all. The burden of a great sorrow has brought us to our knees at last. So trouble, like prayer, begins to explain itself. We make a sudden discovery of ourselves, of our coldness and worldliness and unbelief, and a thousand promises of God that the glare of day had hidden, begin to shine upon us as the stars do when the night is come. And slowly our prayer itself changes. We begin to be more concerned to be delivered from the trouble we have found in our own evil hearts and in our own evil wills, than from the sorrow that has shown us all this unsuspected and terrible sin in ourselves, until at length the prayer, which began with a passionate cry for deliverance for the trouble, ends in a far holier desire, "Thy will be done."

And when that will is done in us, trouble has done its blessed work. God hears our prayer, and the same hand of love that laid the weary burden on us now removes it, and the thick clouds pass away and the sunshine returns, and we walk singing along the way. But it is a "new song" we are singing now. Before our trouble came, our song was of happiness in ourselves; now it is of happiness in our God. We "glorify Him," and that not only for our deliverance from the burden of sorrow, but for what He is in Himself to us; for the new life we have found in Him, and for the new peace that the surrender of our will to His has brought to us; and, burdened with a new sense of God's goodness, we now can say—

> "Amid my list of blessings infinite
> Stands this the foremost—that my heart has bled."

II. Two other thoughts are suggested by the text. Only a personal God and Father meets man's needs when he is in any deep sorrow or trouble. The pseudo-scientific thought of the present day that robs man of his faith in a living and personal God not only does violence to all the noblest intuitions of his reason, but robs his heart of the solitary refuge to which a human heart can flee in time of trouble. Who can call on a law or a force or on a vast impersonal humanity for deliverance "in the day of trouble"? What we need, then, is a Father, and a Father to whom we may go as freely as our children come to us, and into whose fatherly heart we may unburden all our grief, sure that His sympathy and love will not send us unheard away. So long as man is man, and is "born unto trouble as the sparks fly upward," so long will this verse and verses like it touch a deeper chord in his heart than either pantheism or materialism can ever reach. Above and beyond all law and force there is a Father in heaven, and a Father who speaks to every sorrowing child throughout the world in words like these: "Call upon Me in the day of trouble and I will deliver thee."

III. Last of all, let us never forget the individuality of God's love and care for us in our trouble. In this verse God speaks to the world as if there were but one child in it, and that child was ourself; and as if there were but one trouble in it, and that trouble was our own. It has been said that "the most precious thing in the promises of God is that they are addressed not to the many, but to the one; not to the indefinite 'you,' but to the personal and individual 'thee;'" and we may apply this here. The lowliest and humblest of God's children may say, "I sought the Lord, and He heard me, and delivered me from all my fears."

G. S. B.

LXV. Penitence. Ps. li. 16, 17. "*For Thou desirest not sacrifice, else would I give it; Thou delightest not in burnt offering. The sacrifices of God are a broken spirit; a broken and a contrite heart, O God, Thou wilt not despise.*"

THE occasion of this psalm is supposed to be the mourning of David under the searching rebuke of Nathan the prophet, for his sin in the matter of Uriah the Hittite. There are two facts in the psalm; the fact of sin, which is the basis of the confession and of the entreaty, and the fact of David's penitential sorrow. And as this existence of sin is a universal fact, so this feeling of penitence must be a universal experience, ere that sin can be purged away. There is a disposition in some modern teaching to ignore the necessity for such repentance, or to treat it as a subsidiary or accidental thing. But Christ is "exalted as a Prince and a Saviour," first "to give repentance unto Israel," and then "forgiveness of sins." We dare not make the Gospel offer freer than God Himself has made it. "Except ye repent, ye shall all likewise perish." There is a sorrow which worketh death, and semblances of contrition that are not only unavailing, but pernicious. There is a dark spectre of remorse that flits avengingly before the conscience even of the stoutest sinner; he may tremble at the thought of death, and may relent in his perverseness and vow reformation; and yet with all this there may be an utter want of one solitary element of true contrition. There are various qualities of genuine repentance noticed in this psalm.

I. The first verse brings before us the true penitent's hope in God's mercy. There is a remembrance in the heart's deepest sorrow of a loving kindness which compassionates, and of a multitude of mercies which delights to blot out transgressions.

II. The true penitent's intense loathing of sin.

III. The true penitent's full confession.

IV. The true penitent recognises the fact that he has sinned against God.

V. He recognises the original taint which is the source of all this evil.

VI. Recognising the intense spirituality of the law, he sees the absolute necessity for the gift of the Holy Spirit, in order to work the penitence of the mind.

VII. The penitent's willingness to endure all, to part with all, if only his sins may be forgiven.

These are some of the characteristics of true repentance. Are they yours?

W. M. P.

LXVI. God's Salvation. Ps. lxvi. 16. *"Come and hear, all ye that fear God, and I will declare what He hath done for my soul."*

It is possible the psalmist refers in these words only to some great deliverance from temporal trouble he had experienced, rather than to the spiritual blessings he had found in God and His salvation. But this need not hinder us from taking this verse in its fullest and widest meaning. We may read it—we ought to read it—with the light of the New Testament shining upon it, and learn the lessons it should teach us. They seem to be two.

I. First, it teaches us the true idea of salvation. It is "what God hath done for our soul." Now it is in this one point the Gospel of the Lord Jesus Christ differs fundamentally from all the false religions and from all the systems of moral reformation the world has ever known. All of these begin their message to man by telling him *what he is to do* to secure the favour of Heaven, or to amend his evil life. The Gospel, on the other hand, begins by declaring *what God has done to save man.* Instead of telling him to save himself, it invites him to "be saved." It comes to him, not as a new code of moral duties he needs to learn, but as a "free gift" he is welcome to receive. Every other religion had said to the world "Do this, and live." The Gospel reversed the message and proclaimed, "Live, and do this." And this is the reason for its constant appeal to belief, or faith, or trust as the one condition of its saving man. If it had been an elaborate scheme of morals, it could have dispensed with trust, for it would have been sufficient for it to have given new light and clearness to the conscience, and a new impulse to the will; but since it is vitally and essentially a work God is willing to do for man, it is clear everything must depend—if man be free, and the Gospel never ceases to recognise and respect the freedom of man—on man's willingness to allow God to save him, and this is really determined by his "faith." The connection between belief, in this high moral sense of the word, and salvation is simply inevitable.

It is clear, also, if this be salvation, why so many who seem to be in earnest fail to attain it. They begin with a fatal mistake,—the mistake of endeavouring to save themselves, instead of trusting in the Lord Jesus Christ to save them. And they find it very sad and weary work. The burden and responsibility of trying to save their own souls grow unbearable, as they become increasingly in earnest and make the bitter discovery that the more they strive to save themselves, the further off salvation seems. Only those who, like Luther, have passed through an experience like this, who have known the hopelessness of the struggle, can tell the blessed light and peace that broke upon the soul when God's way of salvation suddenly became clear before them. It was worth having lived through all the weary struggles of former days to hear the voice of Jesus say, "Come unto me all ye that labour and are heavy laden, and I will give you rest."

II. But the text teaches us another lesson as well, and it is this, that when God has saved our souls we are to confess it before men. It was not enough for the psalmist to know "what God had done for his soul;" he invites others to come and hear, that he may declare it to them. Now the confession of God's salvation, so far at any rate as confession is made with the lip, is one of those Christian duties in which most of us constantly and grievously fail. We find it easy to talk about politics, or literature, or art, but we are generally silent about our religious life and faith. It would excite considerable astonishment, even among a company of Christian people, if at the close of an interesting conversation on miscellaneous subjects, some one were to say, "Now listen to me, and I will tell you what God has done for my soul." The Lord Jesus Christ and the greatness and glory of the salvation He has accomplished are the only subjects about which it is forbidden to speak.

Perhaps it may be said, in answer to this, that there is a danger of too much freedom in talking of sacred subjects, or that the soul has its modesty as well as the body, and resents exposure quite as keenly, and that this is why it shrinks from uncovering the secrets of its spiritual history to others. All this is perfectly true, and fully justifies us in not speaking too freely or indiscriminately of "what God hath done for our soul," but the question is, Does it justify us in never speaking at all ? Or if it be urged that after all the life is the great thing, and if that be a witness to the truth, it can matter very little if we do not speak in words about it, again we answer, Be it so. But did the witness of the life satisfy Christ? None of us can pretend to bear such a confession of the truth in our lives as Christ did in His, and yet He was more than an Example for men, He was a Voice to them as well; He was "the Word" as well as "the Life," and if we follow Him, we shall find there are times when the silent influence of an example does not satisfy us, and when we shall be compelled to say, in the words of the Apostles, "We cannot but speak those things which we have seen and heard."

III. The truth is, some confession of our faith is as much needed for the sake of our own faith as it is for that of others. Confession is to conviction what air is to flame. To compel faith to live a silent and secluded life within the soul is to endanger the very life of faith; it needs the light and the air for its own health and growth. Besides which, no man really knows how much or how little he believes until he tries to utter his faith with his lips. It is quite possible some of us never confess our faith before men, because we have no faith to confess.

G. S. B.

LXVII. The Cry of the Aged. Ps. lxxi. 9. *"Cast me not off in the time of old age; forsake me not when my strength faileth."*

THIS is the cry of trembling, tottering age, to man, as well as to God. Among the very saddest of human experiences is the decay which is the harbinger of death.

I. The phenomena of human decay. At both ends of life, man is the most helpless and the weakest of the creatures. Man grows slowly and toilsomely to his prime, and as slowly and painfully decays.

II. The reasons of this law of physical decay:

(1) To drive home the lessons which God is ever seeking to teach us about sin. Death is not translation nor is it intended to be such. It is a curse which sin has inflicted on the world.

(2) To develop the noblest qualities of the human spirit by the ministries which sickness, suffering and decay call forth. The stern law grows beautiful, as it calls forth tender and unselfish ministry.

(3) That He may strengthen faith and hope in immortality. The destroyer is suffered to ravage, that the deliverer may be welcomed and blessed.

III. The duties which spring out of these facts.

(1) The tender care of the old.

(2) To press on their hearts the Gospel, which brings to light, life and immortality.

"Now when I am old and grey-headed, O God, forsake me not."

J. B. B.

LXVIII. Thoughts of God. Ps. lxxvii. 3. "*I remembered God, and was troubled.*"

PERHAPS more than any argument that is possible to us these words set forth, by gloomy but most positive inference, the solemn and pathetic doctrine of human depravity. It is unnatural that the creature should think of the Creator and be troubled : there is something behind a confession of this sort. So when Asaph says "I remembered God and was troubled," we feel at once that Asaph had been doing something wrong, that a very tormenting memory is now asserting its authority over him, and that his recollection is like a sting piercing and poisoning his whole life. It is just the same the world over; if we have fear in thinking about God we have been doing something ungodly. If God as a thought and as a reference be our supreme joy, that is the measure of our obedience.

I. This text appeals to every one of us. How is it when we think about God? If the answer is "He is our greatest joy," then blessed are we. If contrariwise we say, "Talk about something else, it is too ghostly a subject," then it indicates a state of the utterest corruption of the heart. We call for what we like, and if we never call for God it is because we do not like to retain God in our knowledge. Do not put me off with the notion that you are too religious to talk about religion. They that fear God talk often one to another.

II. The remembrance of God must always be an intellectual trouble. There is not room enough in our mind to entertain God in all His majesty. He could have but a mean lodgement even in the most capacious mind. Sir William Hamilton said, " A God that could be understood is not a God." We cannot make any intellectual advances towards the conquest of the ideal God. The world is no nearer intellectually the true conception of God than it was five thousand years ago.

III. The remembrance of God is a trouble and fear to the conscience. Conscience says, " Let me go where He is not; let me flee from His presence. His questions will be judgments, His glances will be fires penal, for I have no answer to any tittle of His law." Do not discourage this operation of conscience—it is a kind of worship. When a man thinks himself too bad to pray, he is within the mystic lines of worship—the man is not lost. If thou hast in thee any torment of conscience, and swift upbraiding of recollection, thou art not lost; the Good Shepherd comes after thee, even the wounded Christ, all blood, blood on the feet, on the head, on either hand, in the wounded side, all blood, He comes to thine all sin, God's great answer to thy crime and need. Do not discourage the operations of an upbraiding conscience; they are a kind of social salvation, because they are a terror to evil doers. There are some of us who cannot be reached by other instruments than fear, apprehension and the like, and the true minister of God will not forget this fact, but will, on occasion, knowing the terror of the law, make use of them for the persuasion of the obstinate and the hard-hearted.

IV. If sinners come penitently to Christ their trouble will be turned into joy. If they come intellectually only they will find sore trouble of mind. One man came to Christ saying, "God be merciful to me, a sinner," and He sent him down to his house justified. One woman could not speak to Him except with her tears, and He said to her, " Thy sins are all forgiven thee," and the great clouds went up and the great light shone, heaven-full.

V. Sooner or later the thought of God will need to be faced. Do not be led away because you have seen some one who has succeeded in the miracle of forgetting God: it is no miracle. The recollection will come, and the mighty man who has forgotten God and lived upon the memory of a wrecked divinity will remember when God has forgotten him. Either God will be your greatest trouble or He will be your supremest joy.

J. P.

LXIX. Is Life Worth Living? Ps. lxxix. 13. "*So we Thy people and sheep of Thy pasture will give Thee thanks for ever: we will show forth Thy praise to all generations.*"

SINCE this question is now being deliberately discussed, Is life worth living? we are not, as Christians, to pass it quite lightly by without consideration. It is not desirable that we should separate the pulpit from the thoughts of the week-day world, or avoid the questions which men who scorn religion discuss among themselves. Our faith should be no mere exotic, covered with a glass lest the winds of heaven should visit it too roughly; but rather it should be like the green blade of corn, on which the rain may descend, and the snows lie, and the scorching sun shine, and the winds blow, but which, because God's sun does shine upon it, and as a result of that, has a vital power; then, not in spite of, but because of these influences, should still grow up to the tiny blade, the tender ear, and to the ripened corn. Is this life worth living? life as regarded by itself; life on this earth, life apart from God; life considered under its purely earthly aspects and relationships. Let us look at life steadily and as a whole.

It is not all darkness; it has its crimson glows and its golden sunsets. It is not all clouds; and even those we have have their silver linings. It is not all winter; it has its summer days on which it is a luxury to breathe the breath of life. Life has its May when all is glorious. Then the woods are vocal, the winds breathe music, the very breeze has mirth in it.

Though darkness comes alike to all, yet we all have such periods—call them intervals, at least—between storm and storm, interspaces of sunlight between the breadths of the gloom, until over every one of us the night at last sweeps down.

Let us acknowledge, let us cherish, let us be grateful for these natural pleasures, these innocent and simple and holy joys!

Let us admit, too, that God is very good to us, and that the lesser evils of our lives are often only in anticipation, or of our own making, not of God's. The Christian is no pessimist to encourage in himself a view of life needlessly discouraging; no ascetic thinking that God cares for pain and sorrow for sorrow's sake; no optimist dwelling in the groves of myrtle. Yet if we ask if these coloured threads are strong enough to weave the warp or the woof of life, we think we know what your answer must be. Let us grant that childhood, keen as are its little trials, can hardly be otherwise than happy; and that its tears are dried as soon as the dew upon the rose. Let us grant that boyhood is generally happy.

But how is it with us when youth merges into manhood, and the golden gates close silently behind us, and we step forth into the thorny wilderness?

We will not take the great crimes of life into account, though which of us can say he is quite safe from them. But we will take the common cares of life, its daily fevers, its necessary trials. Our sorrows are quite different sorrows; but which of us, be he rich or poor, be he senator or shop-boy, is exempt from them? Take pain: is there one of us who has not known the throbbing head, the aching nerve, the sleepless night? Take health: are there not some who rarely know what perfect health is? Take reputation: have you not been in anguish when cruel and untrue things have been said of you? Take households: is there no household whose "graves are scattered far and wide"? Is there no father who has seen the dust sprinkled over the head of his bright, happy child?

A man may bear up bravely against sorrow; he may think it no great matter whether he be happy or unhappy; and if life be bitter, and not sweet, he may find it still to be borne, and if he be a true Christian he may say, " I have received a cross at His hands, and I will bear it even to the death." But when to these sorrows sin is added, when calamity meets an accusing conscience, when a man has a sense of wasted opportunities, the shame of forsaken ideals and the sting of evil memories, is there no sorrow or anguish in thoughts like these, apart from all deeper or darker errors?

If you ask whether life without God in the world and no

hope beyond the grave is worth living, we say, "no," and all the best and wisest of mankind echo it.

Over the volumes of human history is written "Vanity of vanities," and the knell of lamentation, mourning, and woe; and the very Scriptures are the record of human sorrow. There are those who would rob us of our human hopes: who would take our Lord out of the sepulchre and not tell us where they had laid him: who would change our God into a stream of perplexing tendencies. But if they want to take our fine gold from us we do not want their dross or tinfoil in its place. We, some of us, will cling to duty though it be lost of sanctions, and to virtue though she have lost her oracle; but we do not need sham gods or mock eternities. And as for the world, if atheism reign, it will go on its way picking and stealing till the pit swallow it up. If there be no God, no heavens unseen, if there be no atonement for intolerable wrongs, if praying nations lift up their hands in vain, if hollow echoes are all the answer which follows Christ's words upon the cross, then life is a make-believe which nothing can save from intolerable weariness.

But let one sound from God's voice thrill through the deafened ears, let but one ray flash upon the blinded eyes, and how is all changed? How can we then thank God 'for our creation, preservation, and all the blessings of this life"? Ask the Christian "Is life worth living?" and he will say, "Yes"; "for me to live is Christ, and to die is gain." Death is the veil which they who live call life; we sleep, and it is lifted!

F. W. F.

LXX. The Joyful Sound. Ps. lxxxix. 15. "*Blessed is the people that know the joyful sound; they shall walk, O Lord, in the light of Thy countenance.*"

I. WHAT are we to understand by the blessedness here mentioned? Blessedness is something more than happiness, and it was a mistake to translate: "the glorious gospel of the blessed God," by the words: "the glorious gospel of the happy God." A bee may be happy when it dips into the flower, the fish are happy as they flash in the sun-lit rill, and the bird is happy as it rains music from the morning cloud, and the deer are happy as you see them moving in the forest and bounding over the fen down to the water. Everything in the Indian or Australian forests at times suggests happiness. We are not now, however, having our attention called to the meaning of the word "happy." The great God by His great Spirit working in the psalmist had a meaning far greater than that. To be blessed is more than to be happy, happier than the deer in the dingle, happier than the parrot in the forest can ever be. Blessedness is more than the happiness of animalism even when the will is excited.

Blessedness is God's happiness. There must be an infinity in this kind of happiness, happiness beyond happiness that merely mortal man can know without having a new life. This blessedness may exist even with the most painful surroundings. The most blessed of our race are those who have had such surroundings—when they were strained on the rack or when they endured the fire. Jesus in the Sermon on the Mount speaks of the persecuted for His sake as *blessed*; "Blessed are they which are persecuted for righteousness sake ; for their's is the kingdom of heaven. Blessed are ye when men shall revile you and persecute you, and say all manner of evil against you falsely for My sake. Rejoice and be exceeding glad : for great is your reward in heaven ; for so persecuted they the prophets which were before you." When any spirit renewed by the Spirit of God has this happiness, which we call blessedness, although the surroundings may be painful, such a spirit will in God's time come right out of what now cramps and stifles it, it will come right out of darkness, it will come out of sorrow, out of fear, stainless out of slander, and will share the very happiness of God Himself, and will know from its own experience something of God's purity.

II. What does the "joyful sound" spoken of in the verse mean ? What is it ? We read "Blessed is the people that know the joyful sound ; they shall walk, O Lord, in the light of Thy countenance." Take the whole phrase—what are we to understand by the "joyful sound"? The "joyful sound" is a phrase that had original reference to the sound of the trumpet which was then used to summon the people to service, to sound for service as the bell is used in more modern times. You have the commandment in the tenth chapter of the Book of Numbers. It begins thus— "And the Lord spake unto Moses, saying, Make thee two trumpets of silver; of a whole piece shalt thou make them: that thou mayest use them for the calling of the assembly, and for the journeying of the camps. And when they shall blow with them, all the assembly shall assemble themselves to thee at the door of the tabernacle of the congregation." To the mind of the Jew there was the very soul of joy in the sound of the trumpet. It suggested jubilee day; on the morning of the jubilee day there was the offering of the atonement, and the first sound of the jubilee trumpet notified that the sacrifice had been paid. "In the day of your gladness," it was said, "and in your solemn days, and in the beginnings of your months, ye shall blow with the trumpets over your burnt offerings, and over the sacrifices of your peace offerings." The sound of the trumpet signified the finish. When the priest had completed the atonement there was a blast from the trumpet. A "joyful sound" it was, and then the trumpeter posted further on, took up the strain, and it went on from man to man till all the land was alive with this joyful sound.

III. Do we know what this joyful sound is? It is not "blessed are the people who hear," but the people who *know*. It must be the people who know what the joyful sound proclaims—the knowledge which brings with it flashes of realization. Do we know really, know in our hearts, what this meant typically. If we do know that, that on the day of the Atonement it was done for us, then we have the blessedness of the people who know the joyful sound. O brethren, do you know that Jesus Christ has done all that is necessary to be done as the basis of your life everlasting? I am not speaking about intellectual knowledge, not about the knowledge of theory, but the knowledge I have just briefly explained—do you know that? Do you know the words of the man who said "What shall I do, that I may inherit eternal life?" Do you from the depths of your own consciousness know that it *is* done for you, done for ever? Do you know that as the man once sentenced to death knows the pardon when he has the Queen's letter giving the pardon placed in his hand? Do you know that as the slave knows the land of the free, when, hearing the dogs and the lash behind him, he reaches it?

Let us look for a moment at David's standard when he uttered these words. He had in his mind perhaps some jubilee day. He had heard, perhaps in memory, the sound of the jubilee trumpet. He saw a man in yonder field when he heard that sound at once drop his tools; he had entered into rest. Oh, happy was that man, for he knew the joyful sound; and there was another man whom the note of the trumpet told that he was free instead of being a bondman; and there was another man who had lost his property, but who, hearing the trumpet note, knew he had got it again. But David could not have limited his meaning to the mere material type. I do not mean to say that he knew all about the fulfilment of prophecy, but I do mean to say that his face was fixed on the great Saviour who was to fulfil prophecy and to fulfil this type; and now, in this day, we have the fulfilment of this ancient typical figure. The Gospel proclaims the fact that the jubilee is now ours, that we may if we will have rest and go free and be delivered from our debts. Do we know this, do we know this joyful sound from our own comprehension? Do we grasp the things which this sound notifies, do we rejoice in the liberty of this sound to-night? It is our own privilege and if we do not take it as such we cannot say we know the joyful sound.

IV. "Blessed is the *people* that know the joyful sound." The people redeemed, the people, especially, typified as God's. This trumpet sound was nothing to other people; the Philistine robber would have heard it, but it was nothing to him—to him there was no joyful sound in it; and the Amalekite and the Egyptian would have heard it, but without the joyful sound. Perhaps there may be some here to-night who do not know the joy of this sound, who hear the Gospel but to whom there is no joyful sound therein.

V. We are led on to another section of the phrase, "Blessed is the people that know the joyful sound; they shall walk, O Lord, in the light of Thy countenance." This is an advance from the first-named thought. It is a favour-

K

ite expression of poetry. Do we understand it? Some expressions have become so familiar that I think we have lost the sense of their brightness. "The light of the countenance," I think you understand that. You look into some countenance and you see a shadow, a frown, and in that countenance you see a light at some especial times. There is surely light in the father's countenance when he sees his son has stood the test of some temptation or has got through with honour some college examinations. You have seen the dying face, you have seen the face with the shadow of the grave upon it, and you have thought perhaps there was no more expression to be lighted up; but there is a light in that countenance when some loved one comes into the room. Only think of this: there is light in the countenance of God at the thought of those who have believed in Jesus Christ! If you have come back after your wandering and look up to His face you will see a light in His countenance. If you feel you are not speaking to empty space but to a living, loving Father, you will realize by faith that there is a light in His countenance when you come to His throne.

The elements of wonder belong to the Redemption. The more we know about that the more we wonder. We are told that wonder is an element of ignorance. But what a wonderful thing it is to have God as our friend, to know more than the prophets, to have a right to the privilege of His love. It is joyful beyond our power of expression, and if we were not so taken up with self that we did not understand what we have to make us happy, when we realize that the joyful sound is ours we should with feelings of deepest thankfulness accept an inheritance that fadeth not away. But I am speaking to Christians and yet a cold shadow comes over me—not a mere passing shadow, but something that is a damp on happy feelings and hopes—that friends whom I love do not care for the things I love, that they cannot know this joyful sound. You know about the arts, you know about science, you know these things; but some of you do not yet know the joyful sound, the one thing needful which you must know or die without putting the matter to a test.

What do you say now? Jesus Christ is proclaimed, and the statement is made to you that if you will by trusting

Christ have freedom from your spiritual debts, if you will have liberty from your spiritual bondage, you can have it. Accept God's offering. Now what will you do? Is it "yes," or "no"? The question would never balance between yes, or no, if men weary were offered rest, if men were offered freedom from material debts, if men were offered wealth instead of poverty; if men were offered material freedom instead of slavery there would be no question as to yes, or no. Would any person say, "I do not want rest, I will keep my poverty, I will keep my debt"? Would any one say that? But when this question is put to you about spiritual things there is a disposition to wait and to say "I will think about it. I will turn it over in my mind. I shall come to your terms, but not now." I know that some of you are inwardly saying that; but if so, you cannot know the joyful sound, and walk in the light of God's countenance. And now may God by the Holy Spirit make you to see the truth and believe the truth as it is in Jesus, and make you willing to accept that which is offered to you in the name of the Lord now.

C. S.

LXXI. Religion and Science. Ps. xc. 2. *"From everlasting to everlasting, Thou art God."*

THAT true religion and true science are essentially one in aim and spirit there should be no doubt. But it is equally beyond doubt that through faults and mistakes in their votaries, though not in themselves, they find themselves upon a battle-ground, eyeing each other with jealous looks, instead of together, like two sisters, raising a wistful eye towards heaven and deriving a common love-light from the fountain of common truth. The men of science say "we don't say there is no God; but we have not weighed and analysed Him yet, so we have nothing to do with Him, and have no name to give or homage to present to Him." We say, "we don't say that matter is not life, but we do say that God is the life of matter and the author of law, and the source and manager of all phenomena, and light alike of science and religion, and we believe in Him." The search in the one case is for the dead-cold "It is"; in the other for the living and eternal "I am."

There are certain germ-truths which a finite mind must accept upon some authority or other before it can reason at all. And this germ-truth surely must be an intelligent and wise First Cause behind all the laws and the life which we experience and behold. There is but one key-word by which the sentry at the Eden-gate of knowledge may be challenged and the door of hope flung open, and that word is "faith." When man ceased to trust in his desire to know, what was it that he discovered? Just what our learned men fling at us as a novelty to-day—Materialism. He saw the dust of which he was made and knew that he was naked. And the effect of the knowledge was to cover him with shame. It is only a return to the simplicity of faith that can hide his shame behind a righteousness Divine. It is contrary to the whole genius of Christianity to suggest restrictions to the researches of man or to put any superstitious or arbitrary check on the independence of the mind. Every stipulation which He makes is founded in a deeper philosophy than the schools have ever yet set forth. It is not the hysteric of emotion or the sob of sentiment, but the fiat of a common sense which insists that there must be faith before thought can have a basis, and that before man can be taught he must have a living teacher.

Search the world as God's world and the God who made it shall reveal its mysteries. Fool and fanatic! shouts the wisdom of the world; but still I stand beside the cross and say the nursery creed, as the creed also of my death-bed at the end: "I believe in God the Father Almighty, Maker of heaven and earth, and in Jesus Christ, His only Son, my Lord."

A. Mu.

LXXII. The Extension of the Kingdom. Ps. cii. 15. *"So the heathen shall fear the name of the Lord, and all the kings of the earth Thy glory."*

A GREAT injustice is often done to the Jewish religion. It is spoken of as if it were a selfish and exclusive religion, never passing beyond the limits of the Jewish people, and providing a law and a worship which not only ignored but positively excluded all the myriads of the human race not descended from Israel. Even Jehovah Himself is spoken of as "the God of the Jewish people" in as local and as limited a sense as Jupiter or Zeus was the god of Rome or of Greece. The text is a sufficient refutation of this utter misconception of the true spirit and genius of Judaism. Here is the psalmist—whom we know not—suddenly breaking away from the load of trouble and of care that was oppressing him, and rising to the sublime thought of the unchangeable mercy and goodness of God. And as he dwells on the greatness of this truth, he sees in it a pledge and a prophecy that, in spite of all the desolations and grief which now afflict God's people, a time of blessing and of prosperity is at hand. Because God changes not, therefore His promises to His people cannot be broken. "Thou shalt arise," the psalmist sings, "and have mercy upon Zion; for the time to favour her, yea, the set time, is come." The complete forgetfulness of his own affliction; its absorption in the thought of the coming day of Zion, is not the most remarkable thing here: it is the way in which the writer of the psalm goes on to declare the true purpose and meaning of this restoration of Zion that is most astonishing: "So the heathen shall fear the name of Jehovah, and all the kings of the earth Thy glory." All that is greatest and best in the missionary spirit of the Gospel itself could hardly be expressed in fuller or more emphatic words.

I. This world-wide extension of the kingdom and mercy of God fills the thought of the psalmist as he sings. Not his own chosen nation alone, but "the people which shall be created shall praise the Lord;" not his own personal griefs alone, but "the earth" hath Jehovah beheld, "to hear the groaning of the prisoner, to loose those that are appointed to death." And finally, when the "name of Jehovah" is declared "in Zion, and His praise in Jerusalem," then shall "the people be gathered together, and the kingdoms to serve Jehovah."

Now this psalm, or this text, is by no means singular in the Jewish Scriptures. Those who have never read them, with this thought in view, would be astonished to find how repeated and copious are the references to the coming of a time when even Judaism itself shall pass away, and be absorbed into the vaster kingdom that the Lord God should set up in the earth. Here are two passages taken from a multitude of others like them : " The earth shall be full of the knowledge of the Lord, as the waters cover the sea ; and in that day there shall be a root of Jesse, which shall stand for an ensign to the people ; to it shall the Gentiles seek ; and his rest shall be glorious " (Isa. xi. 9, 10) ; and this : " All the earth shall worship Thee, and shall sing unto Thee ; they shall sing to Thy name " (Ps. lxvi. 4). It is hardly fair, after this, to speak of the narrowness and exclusiveness of the Jewish religion ; that is, if we may judge at all from what its authorised expounders, both psalmists and prophets, have told us about it.

II. But it is also worthy of notice that wherever this extension of the kingdom of God to all the earth is referred to in the Old Testament, it is spoken of as springing from the new glory and prosperity to be given to Jerusalem itself. It is so in the psalm from which the text is taken, as we have seen ; when " Zion " is favoured, then " the heathen shall fear the name of Jehovah, and all the kings of the earth Thy glory ; " and it is so all through ; Jerusalem is to be made " a praise in the earth," and " salvation " is to be " of the Jews."

III. These are the watchwords of Old Testament prophecy, and they have a double lesson for us. First of all, as a matter of fact, Christianity itself was born in Judæa ; Christ was, " according to the flesh," an Israelite ; Christ's first apostles were all Israelites ; and Christ's first Church was set up on Jewish soil, with Jewish disciples as its members. So far, then, these ancient predictions have vindicated themselves, but there is yet another and a still richer fulfilment which they are to have. The Church of Christ has inherited both the glories and the responsibilities of the Jewish Church ; the Jerusalem which is from above has taken the place of the Jerusalem which was below, and therefore all the increase of the kingdom of God, which has been declared to depend on the prosperity of Zion, now depends on the prosperity of the Church. This is the true lesson those who are in Christ's Church need to lay to heart. Whether Israel will ever be restored to its ancient glory in its own land or not, may be a question admitting of different answers. But of this there is no doubt whatsoever, that for us the progress of Christianity among men depends on the spiritual life and energy of the Church of Christ. Where there is a dead Church the missionary spirit will be dead too, and the moment it begins to live its missionary enterprise will return.

Parents and teachers could hardly do their children a greater service than by making them feel, even from their earliest years, that the life and glory of Christianity depend on the missionary work it is doing in the world.

G. S. B.

LXXIII. Prayer for a Complete Life and its Plea. Ps. cii. 24. "*I said, O my God, take me not away in the midst of my days: Thy years are throughout all generations.*"

THIS is a prayer which springs from the bosom of the Old Testament, and it bears the impress of its time. Life and immortality had not yet been brought to light, and long life in the land which the Lord their God had given them, was a special promise made to these ancient saints.

The prayer looks to that promise. It is a request for a complete life. The wish is submitted to the will of God; for the man is a believer, and is ready to accept life in the form in which God orders it. He feels that there can be no real life without God, but that with Him it is certain to have a perfect and happy issue. In such a prayer, then, a future and eternal life is implied.

When the Gospel comes and shows us eternal life in Jesus, it merely unfolds into flower and fruit the germ which is already contained here.

I. When is it that a life may be said to be complete? While length of life in this world is not the chief blessing of the New Testament, there is nothing wrong in desiring it. The love of life is natural, and length of days is a gift to be employed in God's service,—the woof on which a good man may weave valuable material and many rich and fair colours. But even in the Old Testament there is the lesson that a complete life does not need to be a prolonged one; the very first death recorded, that of Abel the righteous, was sudden and premature.

(1) The first thing needed to gain a complete life is that

a man should have secured God's favour. Whensoever a man dies without this he is taken away in the midst of his days, hurried out of existence before he has secured its one grand prize. If God's favour has been gained he can rejoice in the blessed equality of all who reach it. "The child dies an hundred years old," the youth comes to his grave "in a full age, like as a shock of corn cometh in in his season."

(2) A complete life has this in it, that it has done God and His world some service. We are here not merely to find God's favour, but to do God's work. Therefore there are degrees of completeness even in Christian lives. They all reach the haven, but some of them with fuller sail and richer freight. The salvation in the great day will be to all God's people of free grace, and yet we must believe that its rest will be sweeter to the wearied labourer and the enjoyment greater to him who brings home sheaves which are the fruit of tears and toil.

(3) A complete life should close with submission to the call of God; warm hearts and active natures are sometimes so interested in the friends and work around them that it is hard to find an open place for parting. The speaker in this psalm felt it so. This submission may be gained through the long experience of the Christian life; it may be witnessed also in those who close their eyes on a beautiful dawn or bright noon day as unrepiningly as if they had seen all God's goodness in the land of the living. There is a dew of youth that exhales in sunlight, and there is a dew of nightfall that waits for the morning. It comes like God's dew, always from a clear sky, and tells of His completed work.

(4) A complete life looks forward to a continued life with God. There are many bitter farewells in our world but we can bear them all if we do not need to bid farewell to God. Our night taper lasts long enough if it lets in the eternal day.

II. The plea for a complete life which this prayer contains. The psalmist contrasts his days with God's years, his being cut off in the midst of his days with those years that are throughout all generations. There is deep pathos in it; a sense of his own frailty and evanescence, and yet in the heart of it there is faith and hope.

(1) The eternal life of God suggests the thought of His power to grant this request.

(2) It suggests the thought of His immutability, to secure the request. The unchangeableness of God in the midst of all life's changes is a deep source of comfort. Those ancient saints dwelt upon it and were made strong by this thought.

(3) It suggests His Divine consistency as an encouragement to this request. He has done so much that we may infer He will do still more. Will not the Being who formed me capable of conceiving of all immortality, grant me the immortality which is the indispensable requisite to the unity and completeness of my being?

(4) It is a plea for this request because it suggests the Divine compassion for us. Those men who think they exalt God by making Him indifferent to humanity are as far wrong in their philosophy as in their divinity. Great natures are made not more limited by their greatness, but more comprehensive; and the eternity of God does not shut out the thoughts and trials of human lives, but brings them more within His merciful regard.

In conclusion, let me ask myself, can I say that death shall find my life thus complete? There is but one way of assurance. It is through laying hold of that Saviour of whom it is said "ye are complete in Him," who offers Himself freely to our acceptance with the words, "He that findeth Me, findeth life, and shall obtain favour of the Lord?"

J. K.

LXXIV. God's Benefits. Ps. ciii. 2. "*Bless the Lord, O my soul, and forget not all His benefits.*"

THERE is a sense in which we can forget nothing. No fact seems more certainly established by modern biological science, than that each event as it happened to us in the past has left its own record behind, a permanent memorial of itself graven into the very substance of the brain. The path of life we have trodden has not been like the path of a ship crossing the sea, the marks of which are obliterated as soon as they are made, but it is rather like the path of a traveller over a field of newly-fallen snow, on which every footstep has left its print. So our past, each step of the way, the thoughts and words and deeds which have made up our life, the mercies and the sins, have all left their own separate footprints behind, and memory is only the soul turning for a little while to gaze on the footmarks we have thus left behind us. In this sense we can forget nothing. The way is always there. But the light may have faded from the path and it be hidden in darkness, or we may be so occupied with pressing on the path that lies before us as to have no leisure to turn and ponder the past, and in this sense we may forget it. And it is one of the sad perversities of our human nature that we forget most quickly the things we ought to remember, and remember longest the things we ought to forget. How easily, for instance, we have forgotten the special mercies we have received from God, and how readily we can recall the ills we may have suffered. Let any one look back on the year that is gone, and he will find that the things which rise up prominently in the past are not the ceaseless mercies God has shown to him, mercies which have come with the regularity and gentleness of the morning light, "blessings unasked, unsought," that have entered his door; but the disappointments, the sufferings, the injuries, it may be, he has endured. One week's illness is far fresher in our memory than fifty-one weeks of unbroken health. We do not "write our injuries in the sand, and our kindnesses on the marble;" we write our mercies on the sand, and to-morrow's tide obliterates the record, whilst too often we grave our misfortunes, as with a pen of iron, on the rock.

I. Now one result of this melancholy perversity of memory in remembering what it ought to forget, and in forgetting what it ought to remember, is seen in the prevalence of the sin of ingratitude to God. We lose all recollection of the mercies of God almost as soon as they have been enjoyed, and our gratitude is as short-lived as our memory. We do not "bless the Lord," simply because we forget all his benefits.

II. And yet, common as this sin of ingratitude unhappily is, there is no sin we more unsparingly condemn *in other people* than the want of a grateful spirit, or more indignantly resent when the ingratitude happens to be shown to ourselves. Even when we confer a kindness upon a friend who is an equal in social position, we look for some recognition of our kindness as a matter of course, and the warmth of our friendship undergoes a sensible chill if we fail to find it. Still more keenly do we resent ingratitude when the favour is conferred on an inferior who has no special claims on us, but who nevertheless receives our kindnesses with complete indifference, as if he were entitled to them. We are apt to express our astonishment at such conduct in strong language, and to resolve, inwardly at any rate, we will attempt no more kindnesses in that direction. But if we would see indignation or ingratitude at white heat, we must look for it when it witnesses the ingratitude of our enemy. If at the cost of considerable moral effort we have succeeded in quenching our natural hatred of some one who has deliberately injured us; if, instead of returning evil for evil, we have done him an act of real and undeserved kindness, and if, in spite of everything, he receives a kindness with supercilious indifference, manifesting neither gratitude nor appreciation of what we have done, then our disgust and indignation know no bounds. Such ingratitude is not a fault—it is a crime. It is worse than brutal, for even the dogs lick the hand that fondles them—it is devilish. It warrants the conclusion, so we say, that neither heart nor conscience is left in such a man ; both are turned to stone.

III. All possibly true, but how seldom we pause to think that in thus condemning another we may be really condemning ourselves. The mercies God has shown to us have been mercies bestowed not on an equal, not simply on a creature infinitely inferior to Him, but on those who once at least were "enemies by reason of wicked works." The very first "benefit" the Psalmist reminds himself he has received is this, " Who forgiveth all thine iniquities ; " and it is this fact, that all through the year God has been ceaselessly blessing us who have as ceaselessly been sinning against Him that makes His mercy and our ingratitude so wonderful. If we take this one thought with us in our review of a year, and remember, not only "all God's benefits," but how sadly unworthy of them all we have been, perhaps we shall begin to "bless" Him for them as we have never yet done.

IV. Only let us remember there will be no gratitude so long as we look only at our own unworthiness. The old story of the statue of Memnon in the desert may teach us a lesson. All through the hours of the night it sat there motionless and dumb, but as soon as the light of the rising sun smote upon it, and it felt the warmth of his rays, its stony lips began to move and it broke into music. Just so our lips and our heart are dumb whilst the darkness of our own sin surrounds us, but the moment the light of God's great love falls upon them, they begin to utter his praise. The Hebrew words for praise and for light are very nearly connected. We sing "Hallelujah" only as the bright shining of the mercy of God breaks upon us.

G. S. B.

LXXV. The Spread of Christianity. Ps. cv. 24.

"He increased His people greatly, and made them stronger than their enemies."

THE children of Israel went down into Egypt numbering "seventy souls;" they left Egypt, according to exodus xii. 37, numbering "600,000 on foot that were men," and if we add to this number the women and children, there must have been more than two millions who made the exodus under Moses. A second account in the Book of Numbers (chap. i. 46), which states that at the numbering of the people at Sinai there were 603,550 males of twenty years old and upwards, substantially confirms this enormous increase. Now it is well known that this extraordinary multiplication of the original "seventy souls" during the stay of Israel in Egypt—whether we reckon that stay at the longer period of 430 years, or, as seems most probable, only allow them 215 years for their residence there—has long been one of the standing difficulties of the Old Testament history. Without discussing the trustworthiness of the numbers, or the explanations which have been given to account for them, it is sufficient to say that they are accepted as correct, and defended by Ewald himself, the greatest authority in the modern rationalistic school of criticism in Germany, and may therefore be taken as at any rate not so indefensible as objectors generally assume.

It is worthy of notice also, that the history itself emphasises the multiplication of Israel in Egypt as an unusual and extraordinary fact, and provides for it a special cause, the peculiar promise made, not once, but over and over again, to Abraham, that God would "multiply his seed as the stars of heaven, and as the sand which is upon the seashore" (Gen. xxii. 17); for it is a distinctive feature of the Divine reasonableness of the Bible history, that it never asks us to believe in a supernatural wonder, without at the same time justifying its appearance by an adequate cause.

I. The lesson that we may learn from the text is independent altogether of the results of modern criticism. Whatever deductions may be made from the numbers of the Book of Exodus by the most hostile critic, the fact still remains to be accounted for, that a small and obscure tribe not only rapidly multiplied into a great nation, but became one of the mightiest powers, if not the mightiest, in the education and development of the human race. A great German Emperor once asked his chaplain for a short proof of the inspiration of the Bible. "The Jews, your Majesty," was the chaplain's answer; and he was right. Not only is the continued existence of the Jewish people, dispersed throughout the world, in it, and yet in a sense not of it; "present in every country, and with a home in none, intermixed and yet separated," one of the standing miracles of history, and a fact to which there is no parallel in the history of the world; but the influence which Jewish thought, and especially Jewish religious thought, has had upon mankind is at this moment the chief factor in the moral life of the world. Nor is it the least remarkable peculiarity of the Jewish people that their own religious leaders, their psalmists and prophets, have from the very first attributed all the wonderful growth and power of the nation, not to themselves, but to God. No other people, in the authoritative documents of its history, has ever so completely renounced all ordinary human explanations of its prosperity, as the Jews have done. From first to last they have given but one reason for the position they held in the world, that they had received a supernatural revelation from God, and had been chosen from all the nations to be His peculiar people. The inspiration of the greatest psalms in the Jewish psalter may be traced back to this conviction as its spring, and however the song may vary, it recurs again and again to this faith as its fundamental note.

II. We believe the Christian Church has now inherited both the glory and the responsibilities of the Jewish people, and if the whole of the past history of Israel was a type of the future history of the Church, the multiplication of the children of Israel, and their influence upon the world, are but a prophecy of the vaster triumphs of that Kingdom which is now set up, not in one nation alone, but in the whole earth.

III. The true ground of our confidence in the ultimate spread of Christianity is simply this, that God is on its side and therefore it must finally overcome every foe to its progress. Truth will finally prevail, however long it may seem to be worsted in the struggle with unbelief, but it will prevail, not because truth by itself is stronger than error, but because behind all truth there is the arm of the Eternal God, from whom truth springs, pledged to win for it the victory. And when its last triumph has been won, and "all nations, and kindreds, and peoples, and tongues," stand before the throne, the new song which they shall sing shall but take up and transfigure the ancient song of the Jewish Church, "He increased His people, and made them stronger than their enemies."

G. S. B.

LXXVI. Deliverance from Bondage. Ps. cvii. 14.

"*He brought them out of darkness and the shadow of death, and brake their bands in sunder.*"

THE deliverance of Israel from Egypt has long been regarded by the Christian Church as the pregnant and suggestive image, if not actually the prophecy, of its own redemption from the power and thraldom of sin. In the language of its poetry and of its devotion, Canaan and Egypt have become types—the one of the bondage, the other of the liberty, of the children of God.

I. The words of our text, although primarily referring to the exodus from Egypt, may therefore be taken, without doing any violence to their meaning, as suggesting the deliverance the Lord Jesus Christ accomplishes for the soul. The darkness and the slavery and the death which Egypt was to Israel, sin is to man, and it is from these Christ has come to redeem us.

From darkness, first of all. For sin is darkness as well as defilement. The soul alienated from God is also alienated from the truth. The head as well as the heart suffers. It is not that the man only *feels* wrong about God, or about himself, or about his relations to his fellow-men; he *thinks* wrong also about all these things. "The truth is not in him." Now the redemption Christ accomplishes has for its object the whole man, not a part of him only. It has a mission to his intellect as well as to his conscience and his heart. It comes to put his thoughts, quite as much as his actions, right. Christ Himself promised His disciples that they "should know the truth," and He declared Himself to be "the Light" as well as "the Life" of men.

It follows from this that for any man, however learned or able he may be, to turn away from Christ is to turn away from what is true in thought as well as from what is supernatural in its influence on the life. But this is too often denied in the present day. Indeed, it is frequently assumed that the rejection of Christianity is sufficiently accounted for by the progress of intellectual enlightenment, whereas the exact contrary is the fact. To turn away from Christ, and to refuse to admit His claims, is a sign, not of the strength, but of the weakness of the reason—is the result, not of its light, but of its darkness. The highest homage of the intellect, as well as the truest love of the heart, is due to Christ, and to refuse to render either to Him is to dishonour ourselves as well as Christ. In the teaching of the young, and especially of young men, we cannot be too careful to insist on this fact, that whatever be the criminality of unbelief—and of this God alone is the judge—however it may mean moral, it must mean intellectual darkness. On the side of Him who was the Eternal Word, the Uncreated Reason, all truth must be. On the other hand, it is equally true, as we have said, that where Christ is received the "darkness is past, and the true light now shineth." Coleridge once said that the intellectual and the spiritual would ultimately be found to be one; and the Gospel of St. John seems to hint the same truth, when it declares of Christ "in Him was life, and the life was the light of men."

II. Then, too, Christ delivers us from bondage. For sin means slavery of one kind or another. No one doubts this in the case of the "sins of the flesh," where we may sometimes see the wretched slave of vice delivered body and soul to its power; but it is just as true of the sins of the heart and of the intellect as it is of sins of the flesh. One man, for example, may be as much the slave of gold, chained hand and foot to his cursed passion for money, as another man is of lust. Or it may be as difficult and, humanly speaking, as impossible for him to break away from the chronic ungodliness of the heart as it is for another to rid himself of the miserable thraldom of drink. The same thing is true of sins of the intellect. A vicious habit of thought may become as incurable as a vicious habit of life, and with precisely the same result, that of fettering the freedom of the soul, and at last bringing it into bondage to itself.

Now, from the slavery and tyranny of sin in all its forms, the "bondage of corruption," as St. Paul emphatically calls it, Christ comes to set us free. And He sets us free by reuniting the soul to God. He removes the guilt which had hitherto haunted the conscience as the shadow cast by its sin, and had turned God into an object of dread instead of love; He delivers the will from the alien and evil power that had usurped it and held it in bondage, and in place of self, He enthrones God as the Lord and centre of the life of the soul. And the moment the will becomes the servant of God, it enters into the "glorious liberty of the children of God."

Perhaps it may be asked, if this liberty "wherewith Christ makes us free" is so great and glorious, why is it all who are slaves of sin do not at once gladly avail themselves of it. The answer is not far to seek. Even a slave will not abandon his slavery if he loves it. When the law for the abolition of slavery came into force in America, there were some plantations where the slaves actually begged their masters not to free them; they had learned to love their chains; and in the same way, those who love their sin rather than God will refuse even the liberty Christ offers them. But there were other plantations where the slaves had long tasted the bitterness and degradation of slavery, and there they wept for joy on hearing the good news of their emancipation, and were ready to kiss the name of Abraham Lincoln which was at the foot of the proclamation of their freedom. And so wherever the misery of this more bitter slavery of sin has been felt, the soul will welcome the Lord Jesus as He comes to "break its bands in sunder," and will be ready to fall down at His feet, covering them with tears of gratitude, as it cries, " Lord, I am Thy servant, I am Thy servant ; Thou hast loosed my bonds!"

III. Last of all, Christ delivers us from death. The Bible never conceals from us the tremendous reality of the peril to which sin exposes us. It tells us, plainly enough, that the "end of those things is death:" "Sin, when it is finished, bringeth forth death." And in our teaching we shall make a fatal mistake if, in order to conciliate, as we think, the opposition of some to the Gospel, we try to minimise the danger and the evil from which it comes to deliver us. It is the greatness of the danger that necessitated and justified the greatness of the interposition God has made in Christ to save the world ; and the more profoundly that danger is realized the deeper will be our gratitude to Him who, instead of paying us "the wages of sin," which we have deserved, offers to us as "the gift of God" eternal life, "which is in Christ Jesus our Lord."

G. S. B.

LXXVII. The Day which the Lord hath made.

Ps. cxviii. 24   " *This is the day which the Lord hath made; we will rejoice and be glad in it.*"

WHAT is the exact day to which the author of the psalm refers ? Possibly it was the day on which the new Temple was consecrated to God, or perhaps it was the Feast of Tabernacles. In any case, it was a great historical occasion, or a festival of the first importance.

The whole of the 118th Psalm applies to Jesus the Messiah, and so we ask, what was the day in His life which He made His own beyond all others? The day of days in Christ's life was the day of the Resurrection. " This is the day which the Lord hath made ; we will rejoice and be glad in it." The Resurrection should provoke a joy in Christian hearts greater than any event in their private lives, greater than any in the world's public history, greater than any other event in the life of our Lord.

I. The joy of the Resurrection is the joy of a great reaction from anxiety and sorrow. The apostles had been crushed by the sufferings and death of the Master. When He was in His grave all seemed over; and when He appeared first to one and then to another on the day of His resurrection, they could not keep their feelings of welcome and delight within bounds. "Then were the disciples glad when they saw the Lord."

II. It is the joy of a great certainty. The Resurrection of our Saviour is the fact which makes an intelligent Christian certain of the truth of his creed. Christianity without the Resurrection would be a failure. "If Christ be not risen, our preaching is vain, your faith is also vain."

III. It is the joy of a great hope. The Resurrection sets before us the completeness of our life after death. Hope and joy are twin sisters. Hope best enters the human soul when she is leaning on the arm of joy. As the apostle says, "We rejoice in the hope of the glory of God." The Resurrection of Christ has quickened our perceptions of the unseen and of the future. The hope of meeting those whom we have loved and lost—the hope above all of seeing and being welcomed by Him, their Lord and ours, who, in His human body is set at God's right hand—this glorious, this most inspiring hope, springs directly from the Resurrection morn, and we may exclaim that God has "begotten us again to a lively hope, through the Resurrection of Jesus Christ from the dead," and that "This is the day which the Lord hath made; we will rejoice and be glad in it."

H. P. L.

LXXVIII. Time for Thee to Work. Ps. cxix. 126-8.

"It is time for Thee, Lord, to work: for they have made void Thy law. Therefore I love Thy commandments above gold; yea above fine gold. Therefore I esteem all Thy precepts concerning all things to be right; and I hate every false way."

THE psalmist was surrounded, as would appear, by widespread defection from God's law. Instead of trembling as if the sun were about to expire, he turns himself to God, and in fellowship with Him sees in all the antagonism but the premonition that He is about to act for the vindication of His own work. That confidence finds expression in the sublime invocation of our text.

Then with another movement of thought—the contemplation of the departures makes him tighten his own hold on the law of the Lord, and the contempt of the gainsayers quickens his love: "Therefore I love Thy commandments above gold." And as must needs be the case, that love is the measure of his abhorrence of the opposite, and because God's commandments are so dear to him therefore he recoils with healthy hatred from false ways.

We have a fourfold representation here of our true attitude in the face of existing antagonism.

I. Calm confidence that times of antagonism evoke God's work for His word. This confidence rests upon our belief in a Divine providence that governs the world, and on the observed laws of its working. It is ever His method to send His succour after the evil has been developed and before it has triumphed. Had it come sooner, the priceless benefits of struggle, the new perceptions won in controversy of the many sided meaning and value of His truth, the vigour from conflict, the wholesome sense of our weakness, had all been lost. Had it come later, it had come too late.

We are no judges of the time. Our impatience is ever outrunning His calm deliberation. If He does not "work" it is because the time is not ripe. Nor can we forecast the manner of His working. He can call forth from the solitary sheepfolds the defenders of His word, as has ever been His wont, raising the man when the hour had come, even as He sent His Son in the fulness of time. Therefore we wait for His working, expecting no miracle, prescribing no time, avoiding no task of defence or confession; but knowing that, unhasting and unresting, He will arise when the storm is loudest—and somehow will say, "Peace, be still."

Then they who had not cast away their confidence will rejoice as they sing, "Lo, this is our God: we have waited for Him, and He will save us."

II. Earnest prayer which brings that Divine energy.

The confidence that God *will* work underlies and gives energy to the prayer that God would work.

The prayers of Christian men do condition and regulate the outflow of the Divine energy. The actual power wherewith God works for His word remains ever the same, but there are variations in the intensity of its operations and effects in the world. Wherefore? Surely because of the variations in the human recipients and organs of the power. Our faith, our earnestness of desire, our ardour and confidence of prayer, our faithfulness of stewardship and strenuousness of use, measure the amount of the unmeasured grace which we can receive. The true antidote to a widespread scepticism is a quickened Church. If our own souls were gleaming with the glory of God, men would believe that we had met more than the shadow of our own personality in the secret place.

III. We have here, thirdly, a love to God's word made more fervid by antagonism. The hostility of others evokes warmer love. Love has a place in the defence of truth. It gives weight to blows, and wings to the arrows. It makes arguments to be wrought in fire rather than in frost. There are causes in which an unimpassioned advocacy is worse than silence, and this is one of them. Such increase of affection because of gainsayers is the natural instinct of loyal and chivalrous love. Again, it is the fitting end and main blessing of the controversy which is being waged. No truth is established till it has been denied and has survived. Such increase of attachment to the word of God because of gainsayers is the instinct of self-preservation. The tendencies to which they have yielded operate on us too, and our only strength is "Hold Thou me up and I shall be safe."

IV. We have here a healthy opposition to the ways which make void the word of the Lord.

The correlative of a hearty love for any principle or belief is a healthy hatred for its denial and contradiction. Much popular teaching as to Christian truth appears to ignore this plain principle and to be working harm especially among the young, whom it charms by an appearance of liberality which in their view contrasts very favourably with the narrowness of sectarians. "These things are written, that ye might believe that Jesus is the

Christ the Son of God, and that believing ye might have life through His name." Wheresoever that record is accepted, that Divine name confessed, that faith exercised, and that life possessed, there will all diversities own a brother. Wheresoever these things are not, loyalty to your Lord demands that the strength of your love for His word should be manifested in the strength of your recoil from that which makes it void.

A. M.

LXXIX. Out of the Depths. Ps. cxxx. 1-3. "*Out of the depths have I cried unto Thee, O Lord. Lord, hear my voice: let Thine ears be attentive to the voice of my supplications. If Thou, Lord, shouldest mark iniquities, O Lord, who shall stand!*"

THIS psalm is the sixth of seven traditional Penitential Psalms. It has always been a favourite in the Church, and is well known under the name of the De Profundis. The general character of the psalm is that of a prayer for the forgiveness of sin, with accompanying reflections upon God's hatred of sin, and God's forgiving love, and with an exhortation to the people of Israel to hope in God's mercy. We find in these verses a personal experience developed into a theology.

This is the right order. A true theology is bound up with experience, and elaborated in living.

I. In this psalm we see a man under the deep conviction of his own sinfulness. He represents the case to us figuratively by the picture of a shipwrecked sailor struggling with the waves. The waves go over his head. Out of the depths he lifts up his voice and cries for help. He has been long among the floods. The words "have I cried," mark a long experience continued up to the present. This troubled soul not only cries for help, but meditates while it waits for help. And all its meditations turn on the attitude of God toward sin. His minute cognizance of sin, the inability of man to sustain the test applied by His immaculate holiness, and withal His tolerance, His forgiving love and the plenteousness of His redemption from sin.

II. Perception of God's holiness goes to create a deep sense of sin in the man to whom it is revealed. The revelation of God's holiness in Jesus Christ is adapted to awaken in men the same sense of sin which the vision of the Temple created in Isaiah; and he who can look upon Jesus Christ and not be dismayed at the contrast with his own character, but rather meets the revelation with a heart of unbelief, is a sinner indeed. "If Thou, Lord, shouldest mark iniquity." If Thou, Lord, shouldest look for iniquity with all the eagerness that the watchman waits for the morning, who would escape!

Here, therefore, we have a soul passing through the experience of conviction of sin, conviction wrought by the perception of God's holiness, and the fearful contrast presented by its own character.

III. The cry for help.

The result of this conviction of sin is not a struggle to justify itself, not a defiance of the billows, but a call on Divine mercy and succour. "Lord, hear my voice, let Thine ears be attentive to the voice of my supplication." In the fourth verse there is a gleam of light, "there is forgiveness with Thee;" and in the seventh verse the light breaks full and strong, and the cry of distress is exchanged for the language of hope. We see the man come to shore. His face is that of one who has brought a treasure with him out of the waves. He can think of others now beside himself. In his mouth is a word of joyful exhortation. O Israel, God hath forgiven me, hope ye in Him. O Israel, hope in Jehovah, for with Jehovah is loving kindness and with Him is plenteous redemption, and He will redeem Israel from all his iniquities. The Gospel corresponds with this psalm in emphasizing this first element of Christian theology, the great sinfulness of the sinner. It treats sin as a deep seated malady which none but God can cure. It treats it in the very spirit of this psalm, as a "depth" out of which man must cry to God, "Lord, hear my voice, let Thine ears be attentive to the voice of my supplications."

The Gospel even improves upon this psalm in its emphasis upon the second element of Christian theology—God's forgiveness. The New Testament states no truth which is not here in the psalm, only it states it differently;

incarnating the truth which the psalm states in words, the truth that God loves man, and loved him from all eternity; that it is God who redeems him; that plenteous redemption is with Him, and that He shall redeem His Israel out of all his iniquities. With Him is the forgiveness which takes away all sin, the loving kindness which satisfies all wants and comforts all sorrows, the plenteous redemption which saves from all iniquities.

M. R. V.

LXXX. The Dew of Hermon. Ps. cxxxiii. 3. *"As the dew of Hermon, and as the dew that descended upon the mountains of Zion; for these the Lord commanded the blessing, even life for evermore."*

THE first verse of the psalm tells us what it is that is like the dew. "Behold, how good and how pleasant it is for brethren to dwell together in unity." Dew is a unity which represents the unity of soul in which dwells God's full "blessing—Life for evermore." This little psalm is a very heavenly one. It sings about brothers and sisters, for God's sons and daughters are of course brothers and sisters, united and harmonious brothers and sisters. How have they got to be so happy? A man is made happy by getting all selfishness under his feet, and then, being emptied of all self, God sees to it that he is filled with Himself. This psalm sings of how good and delightful it will be to come again to the brothers and sisters who have gone before, for God will never divide you from those who belong to you. All these heavenly brothers and sisters know well that the unity is not of their making; they know that it is nothing but the Lord's love in them all. To help us to get some insight into this unity we have here the beautiful illustration of dew. Dew is water that has been liberated from the earth and disenchanted of earthliness. Perhaps it has been caught up from the stagnant ditch, and now there is nothing impure about it. Does the mud go through my soul as the mud goes through the ditch water, or has my soul been purified? Man's soul going up in prayer is met by the truth and the love of God, and these blend together harmoniously; and thus the soul, chastened and purged of earth's muddiness, at length becomes clear, a glass for God's purity to look through. "Blessed are the pure in heart, for they shall see God." They shall be dew-drops prepared by God's grace to mirror the perfect One. If you want confirmation that God's end is to purify your souls, think what God has done to do it. Think of the birth of the Lord Jesus in your nature, and think of His pains and sufferings in your nature. By the power and light of the Holy Spirit may His own purity be wrought in you, that you, being God's prepared dew-drops, after you have passed through death's valley, the golden sun of eternity may rise upon you and reproduce itself in the centre of your spirit, and gladden and lift up all your powers for evermore.

J. Pu.

LXXXI. The Fulfilment of the Promise. Ps. cxxxviii. 8. *"The Lord will perfect that which concerneth me; Thy mercy, O Lord, endureth for ever. Forsake not the works of Thine own hands."*

WE do not know who wrote this psalm, but whoever he was, the circumstances under which it was drawn from the singer's heart are plainly enough expressed in it. There had been some great promise from God to him, the fulfilment of which had begun but was only partially accomplished; for he says in one part of it, "Thou hast magnified Thy word—the word of Thy promise—above all Thy name,"—all the rest of Thy revealed character—"in the day when I cried Thou answeredst me, and strengthenedst me with strength in my soul," yet, "though I walk in the midst of trouble, Thou wilt revive me, Thou shalt stretch forth Thy hand against the wrath of mine enemies." So the circumstances are these: the great word of promise that was beginning to work in the man's experience and life, and which had not yet so come to its fulfilment as to conquer these difficulties and these pains, needed to be grasped by a very firm hand of faith, or else all its preciousness and sweetness would go. And so standing in the middle of an unfinished work, with a partial and progressive fulfilment historically realizing itself round about him, he looks forward to the end and says, " The broken and incomplete shall be completed, the circle will round itself over, and the sphere will be perfect, there shall be nothing lacking of all that He has said, the Lord will complete that which concerneth me," and then having thus said—as a man might do from a cliff—makes a spring to catch the rope that held him up, he shakes it to see is it firm at the top there, his confidence begins to give account of itself to itself and to tell why it believes itself to be so relying, " as the old psalm reads that I have heard many a time in the Temple—Thy mercy endureth for ever." And then having shown himself that it is not a gleam, or a mere ghost of momentary rapture without a good sound bottom of reality, he turns his preface into a prayer which appropriates the perfecting help of God, and says, " Forsake not the works of Thine own hands." And in that puts, not only a petition but a plea, " the works of thine own hands."

I. And so look at these three phases of thought: The Lord will perfect that which concerneth Him. Look to begin with, how of set purpose he picks out a vague expression—vague as to the region in which this Divine power is to work; and vague too about the manner in which it is to work. " I know not what Thy purposes with me may be ; this I know, Thou wilt complete them," that which concerneth him, everything which lies around him. " I cannot take upon myself to specialize the things which I want, I would not if I could ; enough for me that everything which interests me, interests Thee—everything which affects my well-being really is an object for Thy hand lavishly and sedulously to labour at till it is all finished—that which concerneth me in the outward life, in the bread which perisheth, in the relationships of life, the loves and friendships whose sweetnesses are so dear, whose losses are so bitter ; in all the trials and cares, in all the hopes that go to water, all the wishes that are fulfilled proved to be bitter, in all this incomplete and partial consecration, of half-hearted love of which I am conscious ; in all the limitations of the understanding of Thy great will, and my reluctant submission to the sweetness and power of that will ; everything that belongs to this, everything that belongs to the other; the two hemispheres of this life, I dare not prescribe, I would not prescribe, I believe in Thy perfecting of it. Though I know not how that shall be, yet I believe in thy perfecting of it, though I know not yet what that may include. And so, notice all the circumstances in which this large and quiet confidence comes. It is to a man that has got half a loaf and not a whole one; who though he has got a great promise there in the horizon to rest upon, in the nearer distance are a great many troubles, a great many imperfections certainly. There is the great, shining, starlike pointed sky there, but here upon this poor plane of earth there is plenty of sorrow, care, and busy enemies, and the words before my text tell us the condition of the man that spoke it: Though I walk in the midst of trouble, behind me, round about me, above me, there is the circle. What am I to do? I cannot break through this circle. No, but I can rise above it! When I feel most the sorrow and perplexity and weariness, how many things in my earthly career, judged by any worldly point of view, have been miserable failures, half success, broken and perturbed; and when I feel how much in my own heart is dwarfed and stunted as compared with what it ought to be, let me take that great assurance and shake it in the face of my enemies and in the face of my sins, and say, "Lord, Lord, perfect that which concerneth me; they compass me about like bees, and in the name of the Lord will I destroy them."

Then notice that this is no saying of Paul's about our perseverance. Men have no right to say, "Sovereign grace, Irresistible power will make it right for me." Yes, but on conditions. If you will let Him. Not else. It is no use for a man to fold his hands and say, "Thou wilt work it." Yes, but on the other hand, "Work out your salvation with fear and trembling;" then down on your knees and say, "O Lord, forsake not Thou the work of Thine own hands."

II. Look then at the next phase: the Psalmist seems, as it were, to say to himself, "How do you know that God will perfect what concerneth you? What business have you to cherish such an expectation as that? You have not perfected anything in your life." And then he flings himself out of himself altogether. "Thy mercy endureth for ever." It seems here as if he were quoting snatches of hymns, a bit of a great song that he had heard. There is one great psalm of which you know the chorus of each verse is "For his mercy endureth for ever," and the psalmist goes through all the regions of God's work and appends to each verse, "His mercy endureth for ever." And so the psalmist here quotes the refrain of the old Temple song, and sustains himself by saying, "Thy mercy, O Lord, endureth for ever." That is to say: God's loving kindness. "The mountains may depart, and the hills may be removed, but my kindness shall not depart from thee." The loving kindness that changes by no change on His part; the mercy that endureth for ever; after all its communication of itself to the whole Universe. Philosophers tell us now that the central sun is only a great furnace that is fed by bodies falling into it, the impact of which induces heat, which certainly will also be exhausted some day. But this great Sun that stands in the midst of the Universe and round which all creatures gathers is none the less powerful to warm and give heat for all the years past and all the eternity to come.

III. But there is a deeper and a more practical thought than that for us all. Unexhausted by all Thy gifts, unchanged by any change in me, and incapable of being provoked unto cessation by anything in me:

> "Though I have most unthankful been
> Of all that here Thy grace received,
> A thousand times Thy goodness seen,
> A thousand times Thy goodness grieved."

Yes! "the Lord will perfect that which concerneth me; Thy mercy endureth for ever." And so having filled his heart with that great thought of God's unlimited and endless mercy, the psalmist leaves his investigation into the *basis* of the confidence and turns it into a prayer, "Forsake not the works of thine own hands." As good John Newton says:

> "By prayer let me wrestle
> And He will perform."

And the word that is translated here "perfect," is the word which in another psalm is rendered as "perform." "I will sing unto the Lord that performeth all things for me." There is the condition of our receiving that perfecting help, and it is that we come with the petition, "Leave not, neither forsake me, O God of my salvation." Ah! how beautifully the psalmist puts his prayer, making not only a petition of it, but also a plea of it, "the works of Thine own hands." Thou art not going to leave Thy work half done. Thou art not a man that Thou shouldst repent. Is it to be said of Thee, as people go down the street of the universe and see it filled with temples to Thy praise: this man began to build and was not able to finish it? Beginning, Thou hast bound Thyself to complete. Or, as one of the later books of Scripture has it, "Commit the keeping of your souls as unto a faithful Creator," who recognises the obligations of His creative work, and who thereby binds Himself with observing the conditions, to fulfil and to complete the work He has undertaken. "Faithful is He that calleth you, who also will do it, knowing that He which hath begun the good work will perform it unto the end in Jesus Christ."

So, in all the strange and terrible incompleteness of Christian character under which so many of us consciously groan, let us look to that one great thought—God's inexhaustible mercy, and God's equally inexhaustible quickening Spirit and power, and the as inexhaustible energies that are stored in His great heart. All these are worthy of Him and their appropriate end is nothing short of absolute perfection. Let us come with this prayer, "Forsake not the works of Thine own hands," and we shall get the old blessing, "I will not leave thee until I have done to Thee that which I have spoken.

A. M.

LXXXII. Humility. Prov. ii. 10, 11. "*When wisdom entereth into thine heart, and knowledge is pleasant unto thy soul; discretion shall preserve thee, understanding shall keep thee.*"

HUMILITY has been described as the first sought and the last won of the Christian graces. Humility is not the effervescence of momentary abasement, but the sum total of modest thought. It is not to be gained by lowly speech, or demure looks, or submissive gaits ; but by the gradual moulding of the heart, in the wholesome experience of trials, defeats, progress, and blessings, and in the increasing knowledge of God and the Lord Jesus Christ. So it is that this grace resides upon the highest pinnacle of the Christian edifice.

I. Humility presupposes a soaring spirit: as obedience implies the capability of disobeying, as faith is brightest when inducements to unbelief are spread around ; so, and even in a higher degree, humility only exists when the soul is uplifted to high and lofty things. Our Lord places humility in the very front of His teaching : "Blessed are the poor in spirit," there is the abasement—"for theirs is the kingdom of Heaven," there is the soul set upon uplifted aims.

II. Self-repression is another element of humility. Repentance must begin with humility. St. Chrysostom says, "As the moon appears smaller when she approaches the sun, so does the soul become less in her own sight as she draws nearer to God."

III. Reverence is another element of humility. He who is uniformly reverent to Almighty God will most naturally and easily pay proper respect to men ; and the man who is deferential in all relations of life will readily venerate the triune Majesty on high.

Does not our Blessed Lord teach us in His own example to raise high our aspirations, to refrain our souls and keep them low, to devote our attention to what is before us, and to cultivate the reverent life ? On the hill Calvary, at the foot of that cross which is set up towards heaven, drawing all men unto it, we may come to learn what we can learn nowhere else—how to lower our pride, and to foster humility in our souls, before the wondrous sacrifice of the Son of God.

E. M.

LXXXIII. Mockers at Sin. Prov. xiv. 9. "*Fools make a mock at sin.*"

THE word "sin" is here used in its general sense, for all moral evil or anything hurtful ; and the wise man calls all men "fools," who either treat it or think of it as a small matter.

Let us inquire—

I. Who are those who make a mock of sin?

(1) Most manifestly every man does this who openly glories in his own wickedness; all who pride themselves in evil exploits and successes.

(2) Any man who winks at or smiles graciously on the evil deeds of other men, in business, politics, social life, who either condones it or excuses it, because of any partiality for, or participation with, its perpetrators.

(3) Those who mock at its reprovers, or despitefully use them who labour for its reformation.

(4) Those who either lead others into sin or encourage them to abide in it.

In short, every man "makes a mock at sin," who either in his religious creed, or by his daily conduct, shows that he regards sin as a trifle.

Consider what sin really is. It is an immense moral evil. As Theology defines it: "Sin is any want of conformity unto, or transgression of, the law of God." "There can be no little sin, because there is no little God," is a true saying. Even the smallest sin is a violation of the whole stupendous law of God.

But if you would understand why God denounces it as something so terrible and monstrous, you must observe its awful consequences, inquiring not merely what sin is, but what sin has done and will do.

Every form of evil and suffering in God's universe is a consequence of sin.

All physical evil we see in the world is only symptomatic of the deadly ailment of the higher life of the soul made in God's image. Down into the springs of the spiritual life goes the malign influence of sin, and the consequence is spiritual death.

As you look on Calvary's cross you see the outworkings of sin, and surely there is needing no other argument to prove that sin is an evil, demanding awful punishment; and no further illustration of the truth of the text, that fools, and only fools, make a mock at sin.

II. Consider why such mockers are fools?

We have indeed been answering this question in what

has gone before. To make a mock at a thing is, in any way, either to treat it or regard it as of little moment ; and if the thing is very mighty or great, either in itself or its influence, such mockery must be foolish.

Either to speak of sin or to think of sin lightly shows a want of understanding, and just because a man thereby puts in jeopardy ineffable good, or hazards immeasurable evil, does this simple making a mock of sin prove the man a fool, Beware of making light of sin. Beware of the wine-cup. Beware of bad books. Beware of the theatre. Beware of evil and infidel companions. Beware of the profane man. Beware of the Sabbath breaker. Beware of the untruthful man ; the dishonest man.

III. Beware, as for your life, of these beginnings of evil. Bring your heart to Jesus, for that heart is already sinful, and He alone can purify and save it ; and just to do this He came into the world.

He was revealed among men, that He might destroy all the works of the devil. " He came travelling in the greatness of His strength, mighty to save."

This was the end of His Divine mission, that He might nail a crucified sin to His own cross, and bury a dead death in His own grave. He brought gloriously to pass that blessed saying, " I will ransom thee from the power of the grave ; I will redeem thee from death. O death, I will be thy plagues ! O grave, I will be thy destruction !"

And the redeemed of the Lord can now lift up the triumphal cry, " O death ! where is thy sting ? O grave ! where is thy victory ?" Yes, the only sting of death is sin, and Christ both tears away the sting and destroys the monster for ever.

Come then to Jesus. He is a Saviour from sin. However mighty the sinful fetters that are on you, He will break them ! However terrible the monster be whose hot breath is on you, whose gleaming fangs are over you, Christ is stronger than he.

Take Christ to be your Saviour, and then you will know how wise a thing it is to have heaven for a home, and will never know all the tremendous meaning of the text's solemn truth, " That they that make a mock of sin are fools."

C. W.

LXXXIV. The Best Friend. Prov. xviii. 22. "*There is a friend that sticketh closer than a brother.*"

Man was not made for solitude. He has a craving for fellowship and sympathy which can be satisfied only in the conscious possession of the affection of another. A true friend, therefore, is one of the best of blessings. And when the human bond is sanctified and strengthened by Christian communion, the blessing is correspondingly increased.

When Solomon wrote these words of the text, it is but probable he made direct reference to the Messiah. But however that may be, the text in its highest sense is applicable to the Lord Jesus, for let our earthly brother be the best and noblest possible, it will still hold good that in Jesus we have a friend that "sticketh closer than a brother."

I. The surpassing excellence of the friendship of Jesus is seen in the sacrifice which He has made for us.

He who had the riches of Divine glory as His own, stooped to the depths of human poverty for us, and humbled Himself to the death of the cross that we might be forgiven. Think of His humble birth, His lowly life, His privation, His weariness, His sorrow, His agony, His crucifixion: then contrast all these with the uncreated light in which eternally He dwelt, and you will have some idea of the magnitude of the sacrifice which He made for us. Truly looking at Calvary's cross we may well exclaim, "There is a friend that sticketh closer than a brother."

II. It is seen in the sympathy He feels for us.

Friendship is based on sympathy, and the nearer the experience of one comes to that of another, the closer is the intimacy between them. This is the reason why the friendship of a brother is especially referred to here. When strangers cannot understand the actions and expressions of a man, they are commonly quite plain to his brother. But there is a limit even to a brother's sympathy. Influences may come into operation which may raise a barrier between them, or another love may come between them and interrupt the free, unfettered interchange of sympathy. It can never be so with us and Jesus. For as God He is always acquainted with our inmost feelings, and as man He knows our human limitations and struggles. His love is stronger than death, stronger than to be broken even by our folly and our falls.

III. It is seen by the constancy which He manifests.

The friends of earth too often worship prosperity, and come fluttering round us in our summer gladness, as the swallows come twittering about the house eaves in "the leafy month of June"; but like them too they disappear when winter's cold sets in, and the chill of adversity is upon us. But Jesus is true to us all times, and most especially in our hour of need. He is a very present help in trouble.

IV. It is seen in His faithfulness.

A flattering friend is in the end the most dangerous of enemies, but faithful are the wounds inflicted by a friend, and he is our truest adviser who will rather hurt our self-conceit than suffer our self-conceit to injure us. Our very trials, therefore, are evidences of the superiority of Christ's friendship in the matter of faithfulness.

They are the incisions of that pruning-knife wherewith He cuts off all superfluous affluence of growth, and fits us to bring forth much fruit.

V. It is seen in His tenderness.

Too frequently in the attempt to become faithful we become unfeeling, or in the wish to be gentle we become unfaithful. But Jesus is both tender and faithful. The bruised reed shall He not break and the smoking flax shall He not quench.

VI. It is seen in its perpetuity.

Other friendships are interrupted by death, but this love is stronger than death. Yea, is strong in death. Death, that breaks all human ties, only knits more closely to Jesus, and never till we close our eyes on sublunary scenes and gaze on the King in His beauty shall we know fully the depth and ardour of the love of Him who is a "Friend that sticketh closer than a brother."

VII. The superiority of this friendship is apparent when you consider the resources which He commands.

Many earthly friends have the will to help us, but lack the ability, but in Him the power and the will are united.

He never fails, never disappoints, never deceives. His

power, His goodness, His wisdom are yours, and when your faith takes all that in, you will be able to sing "God is our refuge and strength, a very present help in trouble."

W. M. T.

LXXXV. Vanity of Vanities. Eccl. i. 2, 3. "*Vanity of vanities, saith the Preacher, vanity of vanities; all is vanity. What profit hath a man of all his labour which he taketh under the sun?*"

The general drift of this book of Ecclesiastes is peculiar to itself. It gives us an estimate of life which, to a certain extent, reappears in our Lord's teaching, but which is generally speaking in the background throughout the Old Testament. Our text is the keynote of the book. The word "vanity" occurs thirty-seven times in it, and it means properly speaking a breath of wind; and thus it comes to mean something fictitious and unsubstantial. The vanity of life, and of that which encompasses it, has been brooded over by the human mind under the influences of very different moods of thought. But it was neither subtle pride, nor weary disgust, nor a refined mysticism that prompted this language of Solomon.

The Preacher does not ignore the circumstances and duties of this life, while he insists that this life does not really satisfy. The true lesson of the text before us is that this earthly life cannot possibly satisfy a being like man if it be lived apart from God. The reason is threefold.

I. All that belongs to created life has on it the mark of failure. Man is conscious of this. The warp and weakness of his will, the tyranny of circumstance, the fatal inclination downwards, of which he is constantly conscious, tell a tale of some past catastrophe from which human life has suffered deeply. And nature too, with its weird mysteries of waste and pain, speaks of some great failure.

II. Life and nature are finite. The human soul, itself finite, is made for the infinite. God has set eternity in the human heart, and man, as man, has a profound mistrust of his splendid destiny.

III. All that belongs to created life has on it the mark of approaching dissolution. This is a common-place, but common-places are apt to be forgotten from their very truth and obviousness. Personality survives with its moral history intact, all else goes and is forgotten. What profit hath a man of all his labour? The answer is, no profit at all, if he is working only for himself; but most abundant profit if he is working for God and eternity. Christ has passed His pierced hands in blessing over human life in all its aspects. He has washed and invigorated not merely the souls, but the activities of men, in His own cleansing blood. When death is near we read this verse with new eyes, and realize that this is a world of shadows, that the real and abiding is beyond.

H. P. L.

LXXXVI. Regarding the Clouds. Eccl. xi. 4.
"*He that regardeth the clouds shall not reap.*"

THE drift of this saying is plain enough if we look at the context. Solomon is enforcing the duties of charity and hospitality, and he advises his readers to do their best, considering the uncertainty of all human affairs. All is uncertainty. All depends on causes beyond human control, causes which defy human resistance. But, he says, it is unpractical to give too much thought to what we cannot influence. The man who does so will never get through his appointed duties in life. "He that observeth the wind shall not sow: he that regardeth the clouds shall not reap." By the "clouds" in this passage are meant those sources of danger or misfortune which are out of our reach, which we cannot control.

We of the modern world have been taught by a living writer to admire the clouds for their own sake, as in themselves objects of exceeding beauty. But this æsthetic admiration of the clouds is a thing of modern growth. In the Bible the clouds are generally symbols—symbols of some facts or characteristics of the spiritual, the moral, the human world. He that regardeth the clouds, in the language of Solomon, is not an artist who is entranced with their beauty; he is, more probably, a farmer who wants to harvest his crops, and who sees in the clouds sources of too possible disaster.

Here we have at the hands of this great master of life and conduct a rule or principle which corresponds with, but which is much more important than, the rules of good farming. We are not to spend the brief day of life in wistfully surveying those awful conditions or those solemnities which surround our existence. We are to do the utmost in, and to make the best of, that circle of duties, that state of life, to which it has pleased God to call us.

If we suppose a man to be placed in this world without the light of revelation, how is he likely to look upon his existence? Is existence a happiness or a misery, a blessing or a curse? This question will probably be answered in accordance with deep-seated tendencies; but these tendencies, when emphasized, become systems of doctrine, and so it is that there are two main ways of looking at human life.

I. There is what is called optimism—the product of a temper which refuses to see in life anything but sunshine. It draws a veil over the importunities of poverty and pain; it draws its curtains, it pokes up its fire. It whispers to itself, "Soul, thou hast much goods laid up for thyself for many years, take thine ease: eat, drink, and be merry!" and perhaps it fancies that it has got hold of the true meaning of Solomon, and that it is obeying him in not regarding the clouds. This optimism of nature knows nothing of a redemption, because it knows nothing of a lapse from original righteousness and peace—because it closes its eyes to all from which we have to be redeemed. The objection to this theory is that it is inconsistent with hard facts. It is not well to play the fiddle like the emperor of old, while Rome is burning, or to dance upon the deck of a sinking ship.

II. There is also what is called pessimism. We have all met with people who make a point of looking at everything on the darkest side. For them the sun never shines, the flowers never open, the face of man never smiles. Yet this must be said for pessimism, that when Christianity is unknown it has a larger basis of fact than optimism.

III. Let us see how Christianity bears itself towards these opposing estimates of human life.

The religion of Christ is by turns pessimist and optimist. Christianity quarrels not with the principles of these ways of looking at life, but with their misapplication.

St. Paul is pessimist enough in his description of the state and prospects of the heathen world in the beginning of his epistle to the Romans. But who more optimist than he? With human nature left to itself he can hope for nothing. With human nature redeemed and invigorated by Jesus Christ, he can despair of nothing. "I know that in me dwelleth no good thing." "I can do all things through Christ that strengtheneth me."

Thus we see now the birth of our Divine Lord into the human world was the consecration of optimism and the condemnation of pessimism. Pessimism in a Christian is disloyalty to Christ. Optimism in a Christian is mere common sense. Let us not regard the clouds; let us leave them to God. Life is too short, and its real business too urgent. God bids us remember that He is Lord of the darkest clouds, and that to trust Him, instead of regarding them too anxiously, is to reap sooner or later the eternal harvest.

H. P. L.

LXXXVII. The Two Returns. Eccl. xii. 7. "*Then shall the dust return to the earth as it was; and the spirit shall return unto God who gave it.*"

THE Book of Ecclesiastes has been described as the "confession of a man of wide experience, looking back upon his past life, and looking out upon the disorders and calamities which surround him." The subject of the paragraph is the wisdom of remembering God in youth. A lively picture is drawn of the infirmities and incapacities of old age, as the best of reasons why the great "remembering" should not be deferred till that part of life. Let us consider the great end which is before each of us—an end in which each must be alone—an end which is also a beginning. The fact of death, the corporeal fact, is full of significance, and should never be frowned away. If this fact were pondered over, if it even were rehearsed to ourselves morning by morning, it would cause some alterations in the habits which we allow, and in the lives which we live. It is however the other half of the text which gives the chief solemnity even to this. If the whole of dying were just the getting rid of the mortal then there would be no positive "sting" in death. But "the spirit must return unto God who gave it." It is commonly said that the Old Testament has no revelation of immortality. What can we say of the text? Is it consistent with the dream of extinction, of absorption, of annihilation? Why not say then at once, dust and spirit together shall return to earth as they were? This we say—that no saint of God from first days till latest was ever left destitute of the instinct of immortality.

I. The spirit. It is one half of us. It contains the "willing" of which the body does the "running." This spirit is God's gift. Angel, I must be, or else devil, in virtue of this gift.

II. The return. The spirit has to go back to its Giver. It was not for Solomon to enter into niceties and subtleties such as those of the intermediate state, the Hades, between death and resurrection. Enough for him to see the "return."

III. The receiver. "To God who gave it." That spirit as it came from God's hand was not necessitated to evil. In what state, of what colour does it return? Oh, to think of carrying all this filth into heaven! to think of going back to the Father of Spirits with that lie, with that lust black and hideous upon thee! It is this which frightens and confounds us? The Gospel of our Lord does not leave us in despair: "Come unto Me," I will save, My rod and staff shall support.

C. J. V.

LXXXVIII. The Strength of Love. SONG OF SOL. viii. 6. "*For love is strong as death.*"

THERE can be no doubt whose "love" it is of whom Solomon is speaking. It is the Church's language to Christ pleading to be riveted to Christ's heart, and Christ's arm ; and the heart and the arm are brought together and love is strength. "Set me as a seal upon thine heart, as a seal upon thine arm : for love is strong as death." It is very much to be questioned whether it could be said of any other love excepting Divine love that it has this strength, outmatching mortality. Though we cannot allow it to natural affection, yet we extend it to the Christian, and we pronounce of all holy love, whether as that love flows down from God to the believer or as that love flows back again from the believer to God—" Love is strong as death."

We are all conscious of the exceeding strength of "death." It is the great dividing power. The essence of death is that it separates. The natural death separates the soul from the body and man from his fellows. The spiritual death separates the creature from the light and favour of its Creator. The second, or eternal death, separates the whole man from the presence of God for ever. Now let us turn from the strong to the stronger one. We see Him out of His love for souls, saying "Lo, I come," for love is strong as death. And after a life all dying, there came to Christ the last dread struggle, and death arrayed itself in all its terrors. In the midst of that last conflict, there was seen a strength in the dying Saviour's love which "many waters could not quench." His voice of prayer was heard for His murderers, His look of tenderness was upon His mother, His word of promise sent a joy into the dying penitent's soul. And now the gulf that separated God from the sinner is filled up and the soul can draw nigh to God. Thanks be to God, many have borne witness that even in these poor hearts, when touched by God's grace, there is a power in love which death itself can never match. The martyrs witness that "love is strong as death."

If you have to do with dead souls, recollect that love is the most powerful instrument to grapple with. "Love is strong as death." And in considering the approach of death, take the same truth in your hand, that Christ's love is enough for you, then "Love is strong as death."

J. V.

LXXXIX. The Light of the Lord. ISA. ii. 5. "*O house of Jacob, come ye, and let us walk in the light of the Lord.*"

THIS invitation was uttered at a very critical epoch in the history of the kingdom of Judah; either towards the close of the reign of Uzziah or during that of his son Jotham. That kingdom had reached a higher point of prosperity and splendour than at any previous date since the fatal division of the nation under Rehoboam. From the prophecies of Isaiah we discern that the temper of his countrymen was just such as their great prosperity would be likely to produce. They had the strength, the presumption of an overweening confidence—confidence in the government, in the future and in themselves. Every prosperous civilization has a tendency to throw off from its own feverish activity a phosphoric glare, and then imagine that this glare is the shining of the sun in the heavens. Now it was to a generation fascinated by an ignis fatuus of this sort that Isaiah dared to cry, "Let us walk in the light of the Lord." There was the irony of a profound contrast in the very expression. The light in which Judah was walking was certainly not the Lord's light.

I. What did the "light of the Lord" mean for the Judah of Isaiah's day?

(1) It meant a true estimate of what the descendants of Jacob were intended to be in the mind of God. This high and glorious ideal had been revealed to them but had been lost sight of. Israel was to have a place in the spiritual empire of the world, a place unique and unapproachable, and for this she was to prepare, with this no earthly ambition ought to have interfered. To have forgotten this destiny was, in Isaiah's judgment, to walk in the darkness. "Come," he cries to his wandering countrymen, "let us walk in the light of the Lord."

(2) It meant a true appreciation by the Jewish people of their own moral and spiritual condition. "The land is filled with idols," the prophet indignantly cries, " come, let there be a truce to our long self-deception, and let us look at things as they are in the light of the Lord."

(3) It meant an assurance of coming judgment. This third ray of Divine light falling on the national conscience was practically inseparable from the preceding. With Judah's ideal of its capacity for true greatness—with Judah's deep degradations scarce shrouded by what met the eye—it could not be that no penal visitation, no judgment was impending. "While it is not yet too late, come, let us walk in the light of the Lord."

II. What meaning have the prophet's words for modern people—for ourselves.

(1) The light of the Lord teaches every soul upon which it falls that it has an ideal of what it might be, fully formed in the mind of God, more or less set before it in the providences and by the teachings of life.

(2) This light shows the soul its load of secret sin.

(3) It teaches the necessity and certainty of a coming judgment. This revelation of judgment would be too much for our aching heads and sinking hearts, did we not know that in our judge Himself we may, if we will, find and claim our Saviour. The hand which at last will guide the angels on their errands of justice is the hand which was pierced of old for the redemption of the lost.

H. P. L.

XC. Isaiah's Call. ISA. vi. 8. "*Also I heard the voice of the Lord, saying, Whom shall I send, and who will go for us? Then said I, Here am I; send me.*"

THESE words come out of that wonderful vision by which the prophet Isaiah gets his charge and commission. I need not remind you of the previous portion of it; how in the year that the king died the prophet sees the true King of Israel sitting upon the empty throne in the Temple there, with a train which draped Him royally about, and around Him those strange forms with the triple power of wings, swift to serve, humble to adore, lowly in self-depreciation, covering their feet. And there comes the great solemn service of praise, with alternate responses one to the other, "Holy, Holy, Holy, Lord God of Hosts." And at that apocalypse of the Divine glory the prophet is smitten with a sense of his own sinfulness and evil, and says, "Oh! woe is me, for I am a man of unclean lips, myself a sinful soul, and dwelling in the community of such, mine eyes did see the Eternal King, of whom the mortal king that has been laid in his grave is only a shadow; mine eyes have seen the King, the Lord of Hosts." And then comes one of the Seraphim, who touches his lips with a live coal from the altar, and that purges and takes away his sin. And then after that, *after that*, after the vision of God and the cleansing from evil, there comes this strange word of the text, "I heard the voice of the Lord saying, Whom shall I send, and who will go for us?" *For us.* Now notice these points; this form of question, and the Divine help. It does not express hesitation, doubt, or ignorance, but it expresses I think the same thing which is put more distinctly by the double form of the question, "Whom shall I send, and who will go?" viz., that God's commission is offered for the acceptance of hearts that are smitten by His love, and that He calls for volunteers, not for pressed men; not saying to any man who is unwilling and reluctant, "Go"; but saying, "Who will come and grasp the prize of being sent by me?" "Whom shall I send?"—appointment, selection, commission—"but no reluctant messenger will go about my errand." "Who will go for us?" And then there is another very remarkable point. What is the meaning of that strange *us?* It belongs to those heavenly forms that the prophet in his rapture sees worshipping before God, and are, as it were, taken into the Divine counsels, are of one desire and one interest with God Himself. So that the message which the prophet is to carry is a thing in which God is interested, about which God is solicitous, the doing and speaking of which is a thing very near to the Divine Heart. So that the man that does this errand does it for God's behoof, and on behalf and behoof of all the pure and good spirits that cluster about Him, and, with Him, long that His glory should be spread through the earth. So there are three things which come out of this first great question of my text, "Whom shall I send, and who will go for us?"

I. (1) God's commission to every one of us. All we Christian people have got that voice ringing in our ears as truly as ever Isaiah had in the Temple at Jerusalem. Though no special prophecy may be entrusted to you and me, we have the task as certainly as any other person. God's voice sounds to me by the very possession of God's Truth, and by all the faculties that I have for the communicating of it, if I have got it and if I can do anything to spread it, there is the obligation. If I myself see the light, I am bound to try to show it to other people. Whatever I have is my brother's. Most of all, if I have Christ for my Saviour, that makes it a crime in me if I do not carry Him, somehow, to other people. I don't care about how. I don't so much care about to whom. If your ears were purged, and if the noise of the voices of earth, the whispering of worldly consciousness, and the rush of worldly traffic, were once a little hushed, you would hear the voice of the Lord, "Whom shall I send, and who will go for us?"

(2) The next point is: God wants no pressed men. "Who will go for us?" It must be volunteers that do this work. Unless with the consent and assent of their own wills and desires, the service is nothing. Moses, when the charge was laid upon him, was reluctant, and he could not be taken as God's messenger till his will had been brought right. And here at the very beginning comes out the great thought: all the work that has to be done for God and Christ in the world must be done by men actuated by motives above the low level of duty, and who have got up to the lofty level of inclination and choice; and unless with our whole heart and will we do it, we shall not do it at all.

(3) Look at that lovely and profound thought, that the men who hear God's voice and accept the charge that He gives them, are in some sense—I was going to say —helping and delighting and representing God in the world. "Who shall go for us?" "for My behoof"— that means when we speak about one another—"in order to further my desires." And may we not transfer that to God and our relationship to Him? As the Apostle said long ago: "Now, then, we are ambassadors for Christ." That is to say: if you will go and try to speak to some little child; or to some outcast; or to some English heathen, you may gladden and strengthen yourself with the thought that you are doing the thing on which God's heart is set; that you are working to realize His wishes; helping Christ to come nearer the travail of His soul and the satisfaction therein; that you are labouring in the line in which the Divine longing runs; and that you are His instruments and means of effecting the purpose that is nearer His heart than any other—that men should know His love, and in the knowledge should be pure and good.

II. (1) Let us now bring out the thought of this second

part of my text; the great answer that is here given: "Then said I, Here am I, send me." Swift, almost instinctive, and with a very unmistakable tone of gladness, the man's heart leaps up to meet the honour. He rejoices that the commission is laid upon him, and, willingly, as one that has received a great distinction and a high preferment, says, "Take me, take me!" and steps out into the front, a volunteer—if it be for a forlorn hope, never mind—"take me." And so I want to dwell upon this: that there must be a joyful acceptance of this charge. "Collections! collections! collections! nothing but collections! always begging for money! Work! work! work! always telling us to do this, that, and the other. What a weight it is. How much of our ease, how much of our wealth, how much of our effort we are asked to tithe for His service." You grudge it often. I do not know that any of us have ever come to the height of right joyful acceptance of the charge, feeling it rather to be a blessing than a burden, rather a gladness than a mere duty to be done in the spirit of a slave. "Unto me is this grace given, that I should preach among the Gentiles the unsearchable riches of Christ." No lovelier, tenderer sign of regard and confidence could be given us from God than taking us to be the signatures of His name and the savour of His love to the folk round about us. But, I think, if Jesus Christ had never said, "Go ye out into all the world"; or had He withdrawn that injunction, or taken away the permission to speak a word in His name, we should very soon have begged Him with tears in our eyes to give it us back again, and yet our reluctance should teach our conscience that it is a burden to give our money, our interest, and our work—to say, "Here am I, send me."

(2) Look how complete this surrender is in quantity and in quality. As for quantity, extending over all the regions of life. That is the true dignity of a man's life, and the highest bliss of it too, when in all regions, and about everything, he feels, I am His servant—and does all the common things of life, the daily duties of our trade or calling or profession; does them all in this spirit: "Here am I, take me and breathe Thy Spirit and Thy Grace through me, and make me like one of those organ pipes, vocal with the mighty rush of the storm-wind that comes

from Thyself—the might that makes life sweet, serene, noble, pure, strong." But then apart from that, look at these other points which I only name. How in this there is nothing left but complete surrender of will, so as that I do not go picking and choosing amongst my work, and saying, "I will do this," and "I won't do that," but how I say, "Here am I, use me for anything, use me for anywhere, do what Thou wilt with me; I am Thine." As Loyola used to say, like the stick in the blind man's hand, take me and do anything that Thou wilt with me, and set me down anywhere; send me, Lord, I will follow Thee, *but, but,* suffer me first to—to something or other! That is the style of the most of us: "certainly I recognise the obligation and I mean to discharge it, but—" Take these two, the one, alas! the type of the imperfect consecration of the mass of professing Christians of to-day; and the other the example of what we ought to be.

(3) And then there is another point, and that is, the intensely personal nature of this joyful and complete responsibility. A man brings nought as his possession but himself, and lays himself down there on the altar. That is to say, the greater of course includes the less. If a man yield up himself he will yield up his capacity, his relationships, his money, and everything else he has got, for the service. If he has not yielded up himself, it is not at all likely that he has in any of these. But mind you don't get rid of your responsiblity by hiring a substitute, as they used to do in the old militia days; you can't buy yourself out of the army, by putting down the money that is needful to put another man in the ranks. And now, dear brethren, is there no young man; no student or other young person who ought to be a minister of Christ? Is there none who ought to go away and be a missionary? Are there any of you young men here that have felt the stirrings of that duty and have stifled them? Take care. Is there no young woman with culture and with leisure and with many facilities, who might go down into some of the back slums of the city and do some good somewhere? Are there no parents here who have children given to their charge to train and mature for Christ, and who have partially neglected that duty? It is all very well to send your children to Sunday

School that you may get a quiet Sunday afternoon. That is not doing your duty. Let us bring down the thing to the folks that are nearer to us. Is there not a man here above the lower classes who might with unpurchased service go in unto these people and speak about Christ? Depend upon it, it is not the paid men that will convert the world. It is not professional ministers, it must be you, who cannot be supposed to have a selfish motive to serve; you are the men as much as us to whom this charge is entrusted.

(4) Notice how this glad responsibility, that comes from my text, how it is all rooted in a vision of God and an experience of forgiveness. It was because the coal of fire touched his lips that the prophet was ready to say, "Here am I, send me." That is to say, no surrender of the soul that I have been speaking about is possible except we have been drawn to the vision, and there said, "Lo, I am undone," and then had the coal from the altar of sacrifice laid upon our lips and our hearts, that our iniquity may be taken away and our sins purged. And sure I am that the measure of my sense of forgiveness will be the measure of my consecration to Christ; and that in regard to work, and in regard to giving, and in regard to self-surrender, the principle will be true: "To whomsoever little is forgiven the same loveth little." I am afraid that the reason why so many professing Christian people never speak one word for their Master, and grudge their gifts for His cause, and are so sparing in their efforts, and are so reluctant to be pressed, is because they have not felt His pardoning mercy; and I pray you to look very diligently in your own hearts, and to see whether the sense of forgiveness has not waxed dim, and the vision of God pale and unreal, and so the consciousness of obligation become poor and faint, and the consecration to His service wavering and reluctant.

A. M.

XCI. The Prince of Peace. Isa. ix. 6. "*The Prince of Peace.*"

THIS is the climax of the titles which were to belong to the mysterious Child, who in the course of time was to be born to Israel. For us, the children of men, He is the author of one of the best blessings which a fallen and distracted race can know: He is "The Prince of Peace."

The bearer of this title was not simply Himself to reign in a sphere of peace. He was to enlarge and carry forward the range of its blessings.

Peace is not the first effort of the work of Christ, but its flower and crown. Let us enquire how far the Prince of Peace has made good His title.

I. What is the sphere wherein is displayed the peace of Christ? Is it the world at large? Undoubtedly to establish peace in this sphere is our blessed Master's ultimate aim—peace between families, between nations—peace not at any price, but at the price of mutual self-sacrifice. But He takes His time. The Prince of Peace works in the centuries. He can afford to wait. As in the days of His flesh, so in history, He teaches men only as they are able to bear His teaching. If He delays this work this is no proof that He will not complete it and that the world will not be subject to the Prince of Peace.

II. Is the Christian Church the sphere in which we may contemplate the peace of Christ? This is not an unreasonable expectation, and here again prophecy has drawn a picture which might encourage it, and which haunts the conscience of a divided Christendom. "The wolf also shall dwell with the lamb, and the leopard shall lie down with the kid, and the calf and the young lion, and a little child shall lead them." The secret of this union of the unlike is to be found in Him who is the common attraction of all. "And in that day there shall be a root of Jesse, which shall stand for an ensign of the people." The nearer the separated Churches draw to Christ, the nearer do they draw to each other.

III. Is the life of the individual Christian the sphere in which we may look for the peace of Christ? Here it is that the Prince of Peace, from the first and until now, has set up His standard and established His empire. His reign in a single soul depends only upon the loyal disposition of a single will; whereas His reign in the Church and in the world depends upon the dispositions of millions of wills. From this peace of Christ in the Christian soul, peace gradually radiates into the world at large and leavens the mass around. All can contribute something to His work if he will.

H. P. L.

XCII. The Wells of Salvation. Isa. xii. 3. "*Therefore with joy shall ye draw water out of the wells of salvation.*"

THERE are two events far separated from each other, which have a bearing upon this prophecy. The one supplied the occasion for its utterance; the other claimed to be its interpretation and its fulfilment.

The first of them is that scene familiar to us all, when the Israelites in the wilderness, murmuring for water, and the lawgiver being at his wits' end what to do with his troublesome subjects, took his anxieties to God, and got for an answer the command to take with him the elders of Israel and his miracle-working rod and to go to the rock, "and the Lord shall stand upon the rock before thee, and the water shall flow forth." It was not the rock, nor the rod, nor Moses and the elders, but the presence of God that brought the refreshing draught. And that that incident was in Isaiah's mind when he wrote this text is clear to anybody who will observe that it occurs in the middle of a song of praise, which corresponds to the Israelites' song at the Red Sea, and is part of a great prophecy, in which he describes God's future blessings and mercies under images constantly drawn from the Egyptian bondage and the exodus in the desert. Now that interpretation, or application, of the text was very familiar to the Jews long before the New Testament was thought about. For there came in the course of time a number of ceremonies added to the Feast of Tabernacles. Amongst them there was this one—that on each of the days of the feast the priests went down from the Temple, winding down the rocky path, to the Pool of Siloam, and there in their golden vases they drew the cool sparkling water, which they bore up, and amidst the blare of trumpets poured it upon the altar, whilst the people chanted, "With joy shall ye draw water out of the wells of salvation." That ceremonial had been going on for eight hundred years from Isaiah's time, and once more the period came round when it was to be performed, and on the six days of the feast the same ceremonial went on. On the last great day, just as the last notes of the chant of our text were dying on the ears, there was a little stir amidst the crowd, and a youngish man of mean appearance and rustic dress stepped forward, and there before the gathered multitudes and the priests, standing with their empty urns, symbol of the impotence of their system, Jesus stood and cried, "If any man thirst, let him come unto Me and drink."

Let us consider:

I. The well of salvation. The idea of the words here is not that which we attach to a well, but that which we attach to a spring. It does not describe the source of salvation as being a mere reservoir, still less as being a created thing, but there lies in it the deep idea of a source from which the water wells up by its own inward energy.

Who is the well-spring of this salvation? The first answer, and the last, is God. The possession of God is salvation, that and nothing else. And because it comes unmotived, uncaused, self-originated, springing up from the depths of His own heart; because it is all effected by His own mighty work, who has trodden the winepress alone and single-handed, has wrought the salvation of the race, and because its essence and loving heart is the communication of God Himself, and the bestowing upon us the participation in a Divine nature, therefore the depths of the thought, God Himself is the well-fountain of salvation.

Let us try and figure to ourselves the significance and the strangeness of that moment when a man stood up in the Temple court, and with distinct allusion to the whole of the series of Old Testament sayings, in which God and the communication of God's own energy were represented as being the fountain of salvation, and the salvation from the fountain, said, "If any man thirst, let Him come unto Me." "Who art Thou that dost thus plant Thyself opposite the race; sure that Thou hast no needs like them, but contrariwise, must refresh and satiate the thirsty lips of them all?" And these words crossed the lips of Him who, in almost the same breath said, "I am meek and lowly of heart." Strange lowliness! Singular meekness! Who is He that steps into the place that God fills, and says, "I can do it all. If any man thirst, let him come unto Me and drink"? May every one of us be able to answer,

N

"Thou art the King of Glory, O Christ; Thou art the everlasting Son of the Father. With Thee is the fountain of life; Thou Thyself art the living water." The cross of Christ is the realization of the Divine intention, and then He who from everlasting was the strength and song of all the strong and the songful, is become the salvation of all the lost, and the fountain is "opened for sin and for uncleanness."

II. The act of drawing the water. This metaphor without any further explanation might naturally suggest more idea of human effort than in reality belongs to it. The question is, how am I to bring myself into contact with this water, and there has been nothing but a great jangling of empty buckets, and aching of wearied elbows, and what the woman said to Christ has been true all round: "Sir, Thou hast nothing to draw with, and the well is deep." Thank God it is deep, and if we let our Lord be His own interpreter, you have only to put together three sayings to find the true meaning of this matter. Hear His voice. "If thou knewest the gift of God, and who it is that saith to thee, give Me to drink, thou wouldest have asked of Him, and He would have given thee living water." So then drawing is asking. Again, "If any man thirst, let him come unto Me and drink." So then drawing, or asking, or coming, are all equivalent. Again, "He that cometh unto Me shall never hunger, and he that believeth on Me shall never thirst." So then all melt into the one simple word, trust in Him, and thou hast come, hast asked, hast drawn, dost possess.

III. The gladness of the water drawers. It is a pretty picture in our text, full of the atmosphere and spirit of Eastern life; the cheery talk and the ringing laughter round the village well, where the shepherds with their flocks linger, and the maidens from their tents came.

So we have this joy. The Gospel of Jesus is meant for something better than to make us glad, but it is meant to make us glad too, and He is but a very poor Christian who has not found that it is the joy and rejoicing of his heart. There is the gladness of forgiven sin and a quieted conscience. There is the joy of a conscious possession of good. There is the joy of fellowship and communion with Jesus. There is the joy of willing obedience. There is the joy of a bright hope of an inheritance "incorruptible." And there is the joy which is independent of circumstances, and can say, "Although the fig-tree shall not blossom, neither shall fruit be in the vines, yet I will rejoice in the Lord."

There is an old prophecy in this book of Isaiah: "Ho, every one that thirsteth, come ye to the waters." That was the voice of Christ in prophecy. There is a saying spoken in Temple courts, "If any man thirst, let him come unto Me and drink;" that was the voice of the Christ upon earth. There is a saying at the end of Scripture, "Whosoever will, let him take of the water of life freely;" that was the voice of the Christ from the throne. And the triple invitation comes to every soul of man in the world, and to thee, and thee, and thee my brother. Answer! Answer! "Sir, give me this water, that I thirst not, neither come hither of broken cisterns any more to draw."

A. M.

XCIII. A Worldly Life. ISA. xvii. 10, 11. "*Because thou hast forgotten the God of thy salvation, and hast not been mindful of the Rock of thy strength, therefore shalt thou plant pleasant plants, and shalt set it with strange slips; in the day shalt thou make thy plant to grow, and in the morning shalt thou make thy seed to flourish; but the harvest shall be a heap in the day of grief and of desperate sorrow.*"

THE thing that led to the utterance of the prophet here, and the thing that is referred to in the utterances, is the alliance which was made between the king of Israel and the heathen king of Damascus. A very small affair, you say, to be spoken about in such language. But then it is to be remembered that the very secret of the being of that kingdom both of Israel and of Judah was to be living and trusting in God. And so, when they saw out there on the northern horizon, the gathering and the threatenings of that Assyrian invasion, it indicated an utter departure from their true strength that they should go about seeking political alliances. And the prophet being dead against such entangling alliances, is here describing the reason why they had been formed, and the pains which they had taken to foster them, and the miserable end to which it was all going to come. "Slips," by which he means the cultivation of that dangerous, entangling alliance with a strange people, that brought in a relaxation of the austere morals of the nation, and led to sensuousness and idolatry. And then there comes the bitter contemptuous description of two things—the extraordinary rapidity with which this plant of theirs was growing "in the day thou makest thy plant to grow, and in the morning the seed has flourished." Ill weeds grow apace; the thing that I have planted, and cared for, and tended, has sprung up very fast in all conscience; there has been no time wasted, and you have got the thing immediately. Yes, and while, like Jonah and his gourd, you are rejoicing in the quick growth of this plant you have planted, the prophet with his clear eye sees it ripening for the harvest, and sees that all its bravery and greenery, all its beauty and florescence, all its swift growth and apparent success, is going to come to waste. A little heap of a dry bit of green there in the day of grief and desperate sorrow, or in the day of pain and *incurable sickness,* and so tells them, pointing first of all to the secret of all worldly life, pointing next to the pains that men take to secure their ends in worldly things and the apparent success which often attends their efforts, and pointing lastly to the end of it all.

I. I begin with that indictment "Because thou hast forgotten the God of thy salvation, and hast not been mindful of the Rock of thy strength." Now notice the accuracy and moderation of the language here, and how precisely it fits to the fact of the condition of most of the people—up and down and round about us—that yet call themselves religious people. There is no overstrained charge, which men do not respond to, of hating God; there is no exaggeration of either crime or breach of discipline. He does not say a word about anything positive. He confines himself to the plain fact, and that a negative fact—"thou hast forgotten"—that is all. "I don't say you have blasphemed; I don't say you have rebelled against Him, or risen up and declared your unbelief in Him; that you are sceptics, agnostics, atheists; that you are profligate men; not that you are living in open rebellion against Him. But you have forgotten Him. No more;

"not so wide as a church door," but it will serve. The life's blood will ebb out at that wound. Take to-day, which I suppose will be likely to have in it more religious glances in our minds and hearts than most days,—how much of our clear conscious meditation and thought has it seen? how many waves of thought have brought down with them this golden sand? how much has been forgetfulness of Him. And when you go to business to-morrow morning, what about it there? How many things do you think you will do to-morrow, or refrain from doing, because of that thought, which ought to be the living and the happy thought, of that Great Friend in the heaven there. About a great many this will be true: "God is not in all their thoughts." I do not charge you with being bad men. I do not want you to shield your consciences with searching for faults that you have not committed. I am fearful of overstraining any word which I want to get a response to in your own consciences; and so I come and say "thou hast forgotten the God of thy salvation, and hast not been mindful of the Rock of thy strength." The prophet not only with precise accuracy puts his finger upon the real condition of the great bulk of men who are not thoroughly and out and out religious people; but that he suggests rather than expresses two things. First: what a wrong thing that oblivion is. And then, what an intensely stupid thing it is. "Thou hast forgotten the God of thy salvation, thou hast not been mindful of the Rock of thy strength."

What a profound piece of wicked ingratitude it is that you and I, drawing from Him all our strength, who is the basis upon which our very lives are built, and who is He with which all our minds are enlarged,—that we should thus, day by day, go on forgetting and neglecting and shutting our hearts and thoughts against Him. And again, what an immensely, unspeakably stupid thing it is; you cannot get any metaphor that will adequately express the absurdity of a man turning his back upon God—turning his face and opening his heart to the world. The prophet here seems to have a metaphor hidden in his language, which is a very striking one. He says to them in effect, "why, what unwisdom it is of you to come down from the Munitions of Rocks where your fortress is, down on to the flat where there is no defence and no security for you. To barter gold for tinsel, and precious stones for glass. To give up realities in order to get dreams. To abandon a treasure and grasp at the shadow. To leave a safe defence and to trust yourself in the open. All these things are reasonable, and sane, and wise, and good investments as compared with the folly of which a man is guilty that turns away his love and desire from God and fixes them upon anything besides. The maddest thing that a man or a woman can do is "to forget the God of his Salvation and the Rock of his strength." There is only one thing that can come of it, and the prophet goes on to tell us what that one thing is.

II. That is to say there is a second thought which forces itself upon the prophet's mind here, which is also as susceptible of a far wider application, namely, the appearance made of apparent success, for a time, of a life that is built upon this forgetfulness of God. Look how very striking that *because* of our text is. "*Because* thou hast forgotten," therefore thou shalt plant, &c. Now notice in vivid, clear picturesque language this thought: If I lose my hold upon God, if I have not Him to set myself upon, I am driven necessarily to all sorts of painful efforts to make up the loss. The men's hearts were empty, and so they went and scrambled for anything to fill them. They had lost their confidence in the God of their salvation, so they needed to get this bit of ground and plant it to grow something on it to feed them and sustain them, which being translated, is just this: the secret of the feverish activity with which so many of you are living that your inner life has lost, or never had, its hold upon God; and so conscious of a great void, and restless because you have not Him to repose upon, you try all sorts of things in order to fill up the gap. That is why some of you work so hard as you do at your business. That is the reason why some of you don't care to cultivate the habit of solitary thought. That is why it is a relief to a great many of us to have something to do that will help us to turn away our eyes from the unrest that is within. And restless, unsatisfied you know you are, and you keep that down as well as you can, and it is no delight to talk about it. But sometimes the grim thing pushes itself up in spite of all, and I suppose that I touch in many a man's innermost experience when I say, "Because thou hast forgotten the God of thy salvation," therefore thou hast planted these pleasant plants.

And then I want you to notice how too there comes out of this text the other thought: that it is far harder work to get the satisfaction out of the other things, than to remember the "God of your salvation." There had to be a planting of pleasant plants, and a setting out of strange slips, and making plants to grow, and so on. God puts us, every one of us, into an Eden—for life with Him is always an Eden—and says to us, thou shalt dress it, and till it, and when it is done it shall smile back to thee with harvest, and thou shalt eat the fruit of thy labour. There is nothing in this world that is so wearying as doing what this text says: planting plants of pleasure; and when a man once gets that into his head as the thing that he is to try for, it is all over with him. Plants of pleasure. Plants of duty, these are the things which it is easier to grow after all. They are like the flowers and corn that spring up everywhere; and the plants of pleasure are like the greenhouse plants, that take no end of cockering and glass and care, and after all are scentless and perishable as well as gaudy. I do not think there is anything in this world so wearisome as taking upon ourselves, and making in any of its forms, pleasure, instead of God, the end and duty of our lives. It is a far easier thing after all to cultivate duty than delight, and men have to take a great deal more pains to please themselves than they need to take to save themselves. God is given away; but the world's law is nothing for nothing.

So there comes out of these vigorous words another thought, and that is: that hard as the work is which a God-forgetting life brings, it is brightened very often with a very quick and apparent success. The profits may be small, but the returns are very often quick. If a man lays himself out for some mere shoddy vulgar kind of delight, he can generally get it. If a man makes these things the object of his life, the more easy he is swiftly to get them. One day he plants, and in the morning there is the blossom. And then people chuckle and say, "Ah, you Christian men, look here, who are living for a very far-off future, is not our life wise, we who live for the things we can put our hands on?" It is like Jonah's gourd, it springs up in the night, and so, I may get pleasure, sensual pleasures—the narrower advantages of worldly lives you may get very marked and very thoroughly.

III. But while you are standing there looking at the beanstalk that has grown up since the morning, and thinking what a wise man you have been to plant it, there it is green and grey, grown up quickly, and bending down with its clusters of fruit—they will not be very refined in their taste, it may be rather a vulgar kind of fruit—but there it is, you have got it—there is no denying that—but it is all going yellow, it is ripening, and that means it is getting ready for the harvest, and when the harvest day comes, of all that towering mass, there will be nothing left but just that little heap in the corner of the threshing floor, into which all vegetation and luxuriant verdure of a life is somehow shrivelled and shrunk up. Well that may mean, as a very solemn and true thing, of how a life that is built upon the 'forgetfulness of God carries away no fruit that lasts. I wonder how many giant oaks of the forest in the carboniferous period went to make a seam of coal as thick as a sixpence! That is the way that pressure is put upon it as it were. The lives of godless men go into such smallness. There is nothing in it, my dear brother, "so much and you will bring home little"; all our care, our effort, the strivings, the creepings, the tortuosities, the lies, the tricks, the struggles of seventy years, they all drop out of the empty hands, and the man goes away, in all points as he came so shall he go, "their glory shall not descend to them," the harvest shall be only a little. And then I need not remind you of how the prophet here in reference to a very small matter touches upon a great solemn thought that no words of mine can do anything to but vulgarise, so I merely name it and leave it with you. That all my life and actions, and all yours, is but the outcome of an issue which is best described by that great figure of the harvest. "If t'were done, t'were well it were done quickly" for many of us. But it is not well for many of us. I durst not dwell upon that great thought. I fear to weaken the impression, but I gather it into one word: "Be not deceived! God is not mocked, whatsoever a man soweth, that, *that* shall he also reap," himself the reaper, himself the sower. And if we sow to self, the issue will be destruction for us and for our work. If we take Christ for our Saviour and sow to the Spirit, then we shall come with gladness, bringing our sheaves with us, and the harvest shall be an abundance in the day of gladness and joy unspeakable. Oh, dear brother, may you and I find ourselves there, when the Lord of the harvest shall come.

A. M.

XCIV. Waiting for God. ISA. xxv. 9. "*And it shall be said in that day, Lo, this is our God; we have waited for Him, and He will save us.*"

HERE we have the great ceaseless song of Christendom rejoicing beneath the throne of Christ, congratulating Him on His triumphs, on His glorious presence and power—looking back to the ages which preceded His advent—looking forward to the completeness of His salvation yet to be revealed. Let us try to enter even ever so little into the words of this song, in which we ought to be joining.

I. It begins with a discovery: "Lo, this is our God,"—not simply "God," but "our God,"—just as Christ is not simply "the Lord," but "our Lord." He belongs to us; we may have a share in Him; we may presume that He will befriend us. A devout Jew on his conversion felt that he had found in Christ the warrant and verification of the religion of his ancestors. The religion of Moses had been a schoolmaster to bring him down to the school of Christ. When He came, the true Israel did recognise Him as the heir of the promises, and it was natural to say, if not in words, yet in spirit, as they welcomed Him, "Lo, this is our God; we have waited for Him." If the Christian sense is alive within us, our hearts, too, sometimes must bound with joy at the sense of possessing the eternal Christ. A good half of Christian worship is but an expression of this pure, deep joy. Such worship has no meaning for those who do not share what it expresses.

II. "We have waited for Him." We have here the necessary, the precious, discipline by which souls reach truth. Truth is not given, once for all, to the self-willed, to the impatient, to those who would make conditions with the Giver, and bid Him hasten His hand.

Man had to wait from Abraham to Moses, from Moses to David, from David to Isaiah, from Isaiah to Malachi, from Malachi to the Baptist; fulfilment was continuously postponed. "Though it tarry, wait for it." But at last, He, so long anticipated, came, and there was an outburst of joy from thankful hearts. The exulting chant, "Lo, this is our God," is permitted to those who can add, "we have waited for Him."

III. "He will come and save us." This conviction is the climax of the Christian's joy. The salvation is begun, it is not completed here. "It doth not yet appear what we shall be."

H. P. L.

XCV. The Lord coming out of His place.

ISA. xxvi. 20, 21. "*Come, My people, enter thou into thy chambers, and shut thy doors about thee: hide thyself as it were for a little moment, until the indignation be overpast. For, behold, the Lord cometh out of His place to punish the inhabitants of the earth for their iniquity.*"

THIS vivid expression of the prophet, "the Lord cometh out of His place," is an accommodation of the language which we should use naturally in speaking of finite beings like ourselves, to describe the actions of the infinite Being. Without ceasing God makes His arm felt in human history. He goes forth as it were out of His place, equipped for judgment, by extraordinary providences, to visit the iniquity of the inhabitants of the earth. All these judgments are a call to religious reflection, to solitude and to prayer.

The language of the invitation here is based upon the record of the flood. Just as Noah was hidden in the ark while the waters of God's judgment poured down, so, when judgments are in the earth, it is natural for His servants to withdraw into deeper prayer. "Come, My people, enter into thy closet."

What is the object of the retirement which is thus recommended to Israel?

I. Israel will see that God is the author of the great judgment on the nations. One of the faults of this people, which haunted it from age to age, was that it did not see God in history—in its own history, in the history of the world. "The ox knoweth his owner, but Israel doth not know."

II. Israel in retirement may learn something of God's purposes in judgment.

III. Israel in retirement may have power with God in judgment. The Israel of Isaiah's day could do little or nothing directly, but the prophet would say that Israel in his chambers might yet do more for the future of the world than if David still ruled. Prayers are distinct powers which contribute to influence the course of events one way or another.

We ought now and then, every one of us, to come apart into a desert place with Christ, and rest awhile—to enter into our chambers, to shut our doors, to hide ourselves a little moment. All prayer is but a preparation for the supreme moment of death—for that sight of Him before whom heaven and earth shall pass away.

H. P. L.

XCVI. Perfect Peace. ISA. xxvi. 3. *"Thou wilt keep him in perfect peace, whose mind is stayed on thee: because he trusteth in thee."*

THE Scriptures are full of priceless secrets, and here is one of them—the secret of trust in God to us Christians—of trust in God as revealed to us in His Son Jesus Christ, as the sole method and means of that peace which we all desire. The original expresses it still more forcibly in its Semitic simplicity, "Thou shalt keep him in peace—peace—whose mind is stayed on Thee." It is not a promise of freedom from sorrow; it is not a promise of success or prosperity on earth; but it is a promise of that inward peace, of that heart's-ease in the breast, with which sorrow itself is a tolerable burden, and without which prosperity itself is a questionable boon. If we be God's true children then we are in possession of this peace. But there is also a false peace. There is the simulated contentment of a hard indifference. There is the cynical self-complacency of a moral blindness. There is the dull stupefaction of an obstinate despair. Such is the peace of a guilty life, but such is not the peace of God. "There is no peace, saith my God, to the wicked." Let us look at these words of the text by the light of our own circumstances.

I. The Christian proves their truth amid personal anxieties. Though we are the children of God, yet the cares of life come to us which come to all. They are the necessary incentive to our efforts. But how differently do they happen to the Christian and to the sinner. How far more bitter is the gnawing restless, faithless misery of the one who has no hope and is without God in the world, and the chastened troubles of the other, who daily uplifts a holy heart in prayer to his Father in heaven.

II. The Christian has this peace in midst of the agitation and unrest of the world, of the perils of institutions which they are devoted, of the perplexities of nations which they love. The issues of all these things we must leave humbly, calmly, trustfully with God. The earth is not ours nor the inhabiters of it; neither do we hold up the pillars of it. Let us not think much of our own importance. Not one of us is in the smallest degree necessary either to the world or to the Church, and if God wants champions for His truth, so little need has He of us that He could at one word summon twelve legions of angels. It is indeed our honour and duty to array ourselves in what we believe to be the great cause of God; but we must not let it dishearten us if God has seemed to decree that for our punishment His best truths shall be darkened. Troubled was the life of David, yet he could say, calmly and humbly, "God sitteth above the water-floods, and God remaineth a King for ever." And fierce armies girdled the city of of Isaiah; yet he could thus sing with the sweet iteration of unshaken confidence, "Thou shalt keep him in peace—peace—whose mind is stayed on Thee."

III. The Christian may have "perfect peace" amid the strife of tongues. The cleverness of the world, as evinced by its daily outpourings, is turbid and bitter, angry, full of malice and evil words; and whether in a public or in a private capacity, from such enmity we all of us have to suffer. It is easy enough, if we desire it, to win the praise of men; but there are battles in which we ought to fight, and not only to draw the sword but even to fling away the scabbard. And when we do this there are plenty of voices which will bellow against us in the shade. When we have done right we need never quail, but remember Him who pronounced the high beatitude on the persecuted, and remember that His peace differs from that which the world gives, in this, that its prime essential is not ease, but strife, not self-indulgence, but self-sacrifice.

IV. There is yet another, the heaviest of all life's troubles, in which this promise of peace comes to us like music heard over stormy waters. It is when we are most overwhelmed with shame and sorrow for the past. Even from sin, even from the self-destruction of an evil life, God can deliver you if you will come and trust in Him; and for you here is, in all its fulness, the perfect promise, "Thou shalt keep him in peace—peace—whose mind is stayed on Thee, and because he trusteth in Thee."

F. W. F.

XCVII. Gradual Revelation. ISA. xxviii. 10, 13.
"*Here a little, and there a little.*"

THIS text expresses with extraordinary exactness a prominent way of God towards man. Have you considered the manner of God's revelation of His will to His people in the olden times? Have you considered with what marvellous patience and consideration it was conducted? The will of God has not flashed, as in a moment, upon the minds of His people, but unfolded by degrees, as they were able to receive it. And when through unbelief and disobedience they lost it, it was brought back to them by fresh messengers from God. Warnings were repeated, precepts were repeated. The Old Testament is full of various and gracious repetition. God allowed for Israel's slowness to receive, and their slackness to retain, instruction. So He gave them line upon line, precept upon precept, here a little and there a little. The same principle runs through the

New Testament also; Jesus Christ did not deliver His message or doctrine once for all, in a studied manner. He spoke to His followers as they were able to bear it. He used parables and illustrations, which half concealed, half disclosed His meaning. He encouraged men to ask questions, and gave them unexpected answers that reached beyond into deeper truth. He recurred to His great themes again and again, and embedded His doctrine as no other teacher has ever embedded doctrine in human minds and hearts, and fastened it into the memories of men by line upon line, precept upon precept. The apostolic discourses are full of the same kind of wisdom, and so the perfection of the Holy Bible is built up. It is perfect for the purpose which the divine Author of the Bible intends. We must study the balancings of the Book, and we must enter into the progressive character of the teaching in the Bible, as advancing line upon line towards its grand consummation in the now revealed truth as it is in Jesus.

This principle of God runs through all His works and through all His training of His people. Omnipotence makes no haste. It is impotence that is in a hurry. The earth on which we dwell was not built up suddenly. Again, look at man; how is a man built? of body and mind and heart and character. Is it not by little and little that he grows from the beginning? Take the question of moral culture, and also that of spiritual advancement, and no otherwise than on this principle can they be attained.

How is a Christian made? By a process to which these words "here a little and there a little," may be very well applied.

I. How does a Christian receive the truth by the faith of which he is purified? Not by one lesson, but by many. He sees his sin. He will never see much to profit till he sees his sin. Then the Holy Spirit shows him the way of pardon and peace through the blood of Jesus crucified for his sin. He gets a glimpse and yet another and another. He begins to perceive more of the beauty and all-sufficiency of his Saviour. Further truth is revealed, and thus he grows in grace and in the knowledge of the Lord Jesus. The Christian is helped very variously—a little here, a little there, as God sees best.

II. How does a Christian get rid of indwelling sin?

The promise to the redeemed nation Israel was, "Jehovah thy God will put out these nations before thee by little and little." So it is with the redeemed people now; it is the Lord who drives out the Canaanites from their land. He will not do it while you are sleeping; you must be awake to it. He will do it through your effort. He will do it by degrees. The warfare is much checkered but the Lord gives recovery from and deliverance from evil, and He will preserve His people unto the end. He will drive out before your face foul thoughts, evil desires and all things that defile the hearts of His people, and they shall be holy and without blemish.

III. How does a Christian learn wisdom and sobriety of mind? It is not a miraculous infusion into him of another mind than his own. It is his own mind that must be made wise, and a man can never be made wise but by repeated exposures of his folly. God who gives wisdom liberally gives it upon this which is His great principle of working— this principle of deliberation. He does not put it into you, as it were a foreign substance poured into you. He makes it your own. He gives it you so as to work it into your mind, so that you cannot lose it again.

IV. How does a Christian gain likeness to Jesus? There is a progressive assimilation of the Christian to Christ as by line upon line, touch upon touch. Half-finished portraits are poor things to look at. So Christians in their present state of progress are but poor objects to look at. You can scarce discern in such Christians as we are, real lineaments of Jesus. But the spirit of the Lord knows how to perfect that which concerns us and patiently conform us all to the image of the Son of God.

D. F.

XCVIII. The Sealed Book. ISA. xxix. 11, 12. "*And the vision of all is become unto you as the words of a book that is sealed, which men deliver to one that is learned, saying, Read this, I pray thee: and he saith, I cannot; for it is sealed: And the book is delivered to him that is not learned, saying, Read this, I pray thee: and he saith, I am not learned.*"

HERE you have the learned and the unlearned man, and they are both in the same predicament. Both are quite helpless to understand or explain the Divine revelation, but not from the same causes. Sealed or unsealed, the book could mean nothing to the one, for he could not read; to the other it is a simple matter—only a seal that keeps the contents from him. But his learning cannot break the seal. There are many seals which learning cannot break. Poetry is a sealed book to many. Art and music are a closed world to hosts.

The vision given by God to Isaiah is a type, one of the wonderful series of revelations, all of them travelling in the direction of the Gospel of Jesus Christ, and culminating therein. Masters in this or that field of knowledge, leaders in many important respects—it has no signification to them. The Gospel is to them a sealed thing.

What is the explanation of this? Of course there is an easy explanation in this chapter if you take the words literally in the chapter; but literal explanations of Scripture are very often false. It forgets to ask the question— What an intelligent man in the time of the revelation would have understood by it? This is an explanation, "The Lord has poured out upon you a spirit of deep sleep and has closed your eyes."

Now every one knows that the working out of natural laws is often spoken of in Scripture as the action of God. For instance, to take a familiar instance, God is said to have hardened Pharaoh's heart. Now we know that Pharaoh hardened his own heart. It would be impossible to respect and worship God if you could believe it was possible for God to harden a man's heart; but let any one go on as Pharaoh did, resisting all reasoning, making promises, and when the danger passed, breaking them; fly into a panic when the punishments of God overtook him, and then forget God when the punishments were withdrawn—let any one do this and his heart will be hardened. Let a man deal after a certain fashion with the Gospel of Jesus Christ, let him form certain habits and persist in them, and he will become blind and deaf to this matter. A deep sleep will fall upon him and you cannot wake him out of his sleep.

But there is no mystery in it. A man's nature, life and habits are the simple outcome of his own acts.

Let us try to penetrate a very little into this. It is a

vision of God in the first place. In brief it is this: God is love, God is light, God is our Father which is in heaven. The Bible may be compressed into these three formulas. The old mythologists are full of stories of individuals being suddenly surprised by visions, and of every one thus surprised walking ever after in a path by himself. Sometimes the vision half intoxicated him and kept him prisoner all his life long, and he could not walk in the paths of men any more. But the vision never came again.

On the contrary, we have seen God in Jesus Christ, and I want to tell you Christian people what it is you believe about God. First, "Our *Father*"—in the vocabulary of human speech that is the only word which speaks of the love and tenderness of the union between us. It expresses the divinity of God and the humanity of man. God is the light, purity, holiness, the enemy of evil, which kills the unclean thing by shining upon it as the light of the sun purifies the atmosphere. God is love, abundant in forgiveness, bearing with our waywardness, unconquerable in His desire to give us His best gift. That is the Christian God, and the thought of that God is to me perfect rapture. But the Gospel with all its wonder and splendour is a closed book to many. It is like a seal placed in the hands of a learned man.

Now consider this for a moment in this way. First of all there are those to whom the whole subject is strange. They have never learned the alphabet of it. These people are intelligent in every other respect. But you cannot wedge a thought of this into them; they are impervious, their minds present to you the face of a rock. There is a law which plays a very important part in natural philosophy—it is called the "inertia of matter," you may call it the stubbornness of matter. The law is quite true of the mind; there is a mental inertia, and there is nothing more difficult to overcome. It defies you to make it think of that which it is not in the habit of thinking. If you doubt this, take the subject which interests you most in the world, the subject you can get most enthusiastic about. You try to interest in that subject a person who is entirely ignorant of this particular subject of yours. You begin. What excuses you make for disturbing him. You may do your best to show him that it is an important subject. It

O

requires great strategy to get inside a man who has never even thought of the subject which you wish to introduce. Suppose you have seen some fresh disclosure of God's love. God has repeated to you the words which once conquered your heart and which conquers your heart again—the old covenant with God is renewed—you go and speak of it. You need not go into that part of London which is called "Heathen London." I will take you five minutes from here and you shall talk to that man or woman about this vision of God. They have not a glimmering notion of what you mean; you are talking in a language they do not understand. I have been again and again called to read to the dying. I have tried to do it. I have repeated the words, that can never be repeated without emotion, and the look in the poor face out of which life is ebbing, and the eyes into which the darkness of death is coming, says, "What is he talking about?" My very best Gospel, the veritable Gospel of the merciful God, is dark to them and has never touched them. It was giving a book to a man who could not read.

Well, this one other thing. There are those, again, who are well qualified, whom we would expect to understand much above others; yet the Gospel is a sealed book to them. It is to-day the strangest phenomena in the world. You will find this everywhere. Great men are after all only the crystallisation of great thoughts in the era—intelligent and earnest-minded men, and, what is a greater wonder, women who study the highest and most solemn subjects, who take more trouble about them than nine-tenths do. John Stuart Mill wrote down calmly and exactly his idea about religion (I wonder how many of you have done this?)—these want to know the truth, they do not want to deceive themselves or others. Now, this book, whatever you make of it, is the most remarkable book in the world. These people see what you see—God encompassing every life, this marvellous providence over all and training every one. The striving to get at us, condescending to bear our nature so as to save us. They see this. It is only a strange and incredible thing to them, one of the grotesque things which men have invented.

The glorious Gospel of Jesus Christ, which makes you strong and happy, to these people it is only a sealed book.

How comes it about? Amongst many other things is this. The *temporary* fascination—I emphasize the word "temporary"—of one or two great ideas which belong particularly to this generation. This generation has had its vision, and this is it: it has seen the universe growing out of a germ—like a tree from a seed. This is called evolution. There has never been any diminution of this energy. There is no place in it for prayer or the interference of personal wishes. Our prayers can change nothing. This vision has seen a universe travelling surely towards its destination, which our joys or sorrows can neither hasten nor arrest. Our wars or tumults or convulsions *cannot* affect this. Our generation cannot take its eye away from this idea, and our God, who listened to the prayer of your little child this morning—that God is not to be compared with the grand conception, this infinitely complete and perfect nature linked together by links which are never broken. There is some truth in the heart of this idea, and it is no wonder that it hides the glories of the Gospel. You have stood on a bridge and looked down upon the river, and you have felt that you and the bridge were going into the river. You can look long enough into the stream to fall into the stream. It is a thing which the best intellects in England have done. They have repeated and repeated their talk about "evolution," and "the conservation of energy"—they have looked into the stream until they have fallen into the stream, and they have been carried in the direction of the stream.

Again, the Gospel is a vision of God and a vision of the life possible to man; and surely it is a vision of immortality. This is the crowning vision, and perhaps it is the more misunderstood of anything else. I do not mean the difficulty of proving to a man the existence of an unseen world. The controversy does not end when we have finished that argument for the existence of the other world. We cannot get our opponents to *admit the possibility*. It is a sealed book to them. Mr. Matthew Arnold writes as if most people had got their hopes fixed upon rewards yonder and says that this idea is positive selfishness! Is that your idea, brethren? Of course, these men are in earnest, and I think it must arise from this, that they cannot understand that our hope of immortality springs from our belief in Jesus Christ *here*. I zealously guard the resurrection of Jesus Christ. Paul said his hope of immortal life would be wrecked if he did not believe in the Resurrection. But perhaps he rose higher when he said: "Christ in us is the hope of glory." Oh, the life that I have known, poor and miserable and imperfect disciple of Jesus Christ that I have been! Oh, the joy of prayer. Oh, His love has taken possession of my soul, and it is thus I have tasted of Christ here. This is to me the truth of immortality—what I have tasted and known. I know what heaven is because I have been there. And if any one calls that selfish or degrading I cannot find it in me to make an apology for this. Our relations with Jesus have been the putting down of evil and the striving after good. The best things we have done have been in the strength of Christ. Not some great Valhallah, not an eternal lying down upon couches and singing hymns is our heaven, but eternal striving after what is higher and higher still. This is our immortality, and this is the vision we have seen.

There are other things, to be sure. Don't beg anybody's pardon, you poor mother, because your heart goes continually after your child who is gone. Your life has become very poor, and very lonely, and there is not the same zest. We are looking, Oh yes, yes, to the father, mother, child, brother, sister, we shall claim yet at God's hands.

But these are only things by the way. The hope, the conviction, the proof, is the life that we now live in Christ. Christ in us is the hope of glory.

W. M. J.

XCIX. Fears. Isa. xxxv. 4. "*Say to them that are of a fearful heart, Fear not.*"

These words occur in the midst of a prediction which describes in the sublimest fashion, the nature and results of the Gospel dispensation. We understand them as setting before us the fact, the Lord has a consoling "fear not" for all the trepidations of the fearful heart.

I. There are fears that rise in the heart at the thought of God. An horror of great darkness creeps over us when first the truth takes possession of us, that we shall stand naked and open before the eyes of Jehovah. Now, the root of this fear is our guilt. In all the cases in the Bible in which God is represented as coming to talk with men, He begins with the words, "Fear not." He therefore says that we have a wrong idea concerning Him. We regard Him as an enemy, whereas He is our best friend. The cross was God's great "fear not," spoken to the trembling heart of humanity, and with that before us, we say to every sinner running away from God, you are mistaken.

II. There are fears which arise in the heart as we think of our fellow-men. We have often been hampered in our discharge of duty by our regard to those around us. " The fear of man bringeth a snare." We are afraid of the opposition of our fellows. The Gospel come to us with its "fear not," for this ensnaring trepidation. It does not guarantee immunity from trouble, but it is God's word of re-assurance to His tempted, tried people, and when it is heard in faith, the timid one becomes courageous, and takes his place among the heroes of humanity.

III. There are fears about the future. Whenever we permit ourselves to think of the future except in the light of the Gospel, we become despondent and sad. Some have fears about their temporal concerns, others about their spiritual safety, then again about their loved ones. Each has his own dread, but see how with its consoling "fear not," the Gospel hushes the heart of each to peace. The root of fear is unbelief. The cure of fear is faith. Trust in Christ is peace, and peace is power.

W. M. T.

C. A Message of Comfort. ISA. xl. i. "*Comfort ye, comfort ye, My people, saith your God.*"

THIS famous chapter marks the point of a great change in the strain of prediction. The great river of prophetic narrative here takes a bend. Before this, the river, wide sometimes and dark, seems to work its way between steep rocks and difficulties and amid shadows, but from this time it becomes clear and tranquil and sunlit—a river of God full of refreshing waters.

Before this we meet with messages of gloom and reproof, but from this time, as a rule, the messages are messages of hope and mercy and consolation, in which we learn much about Christ, His sufferings, and the joys of His people that out of those sufferings spring.

This verse strikes the keynote of the chapter, and in it God summons His servants to convey to His people consolation. We must see this chapter in a Christian light and interpret it with a Christian key. It all leads up to the consolation of Israel, and we find its full completion in Jesus.

I. Let us identify the people spoken of: "Comfort ye, my people." There was a first reference to the people of the Jews, who all through were the people that shadowed forth every people. So the people who are to be comforted are pre-eminently the people of God. No matter in what age they live, they are those who are identified with Christ, who have Christ for their righteousness, and the Spirit for their strength, grace for their life, God for their Father, and heaven for their home. As the people of God they must pass through affliction; they must have the trials that make life sweet, that give new power to prayer. Theirs must be the sorrow that comes of ungenial occupations, from fear of the future, and from the discordance that exists in this imperfectly sanctified nature.

II. Notice the messengers through whom the comfort is to be given. God says to each present now, God is asking you, my brother, to comfort some sorrowful child of God. Look out for some one who is suffering from some stroke, and carry to such the celestial message of consolation from God. He is our Comforter. All our music begins in Him, all our joy begins in Him. He is ready to comfort you through your life, not only in speech but in deed. God is going to carry through you messages of consolation to those who are dying for it. You say, "How can I comfort God's people?" God says, "Through Christ. Love Me and My people, and you will comfort them. I call on you to love them."

III. I would seek to make some remarks on the comfort you are to convey. You find, if you look through the chapter, that my heads of remark are supplied by the chapter itself, but I wish to convey the original meaning in an evangelical sense.

(1) "Comfort by reminding them that I am their God."

All this chapter is a remembrance that God is the Father of His people. God, who knows your frame, seems to be saying to me, "Go to that child of Mine; he has forgotten Me. Remind him of what he has forgotten. Tell him I am his resting-place, and so give him comfort."

(2) We are to remind the people of God that the time of their captivity in this world is nearly over, and that they will soon be home. Some Jews loved Babylon, but the spiritual people longed to get back to their temple; and so they fretted and chafed. And now came the message that the day of restoration was at hand; but it was a poor return theirs, and for a short time. Ours is not going back to a temple in ruins; ours is going to that place which Christ has prepared for us. Do not forget that this is not your rest, and that the rest upon the way is only the rest travellers have upon the oasis. There is a better home beyond the haunts of the robber—a glorious world where we shall see God as He is.

(3) The Saviour is coming to this world, and is on His way to show His glory here. Comfort the people who are disquieted by the sight of the strength arrayed against Christ. Tell them that Christ will overcome these things. Babylon looked as if it could never be overthrown; but the prophet told them that it would fall. The forces of evil seem now to be organising themselves for a fight with God. They speak about overturning Christ, who said, "I will overturn, overturn, overturn." Our Lord is an overturner, and we are not afraid as to the issue of the battle. At the same time, there is war in the air, and we must take some part in it. We live in the midst of disturbance. But there is One who makes those very movements of disturbance contribute to His own grand march. God in Christ would comfort us by cheering us up from these fears that come from our misgivings about our weakness and feebleness.

(4) We sometimes think that we are so little that our way is hid from God; but the prophet reminds us that His very greatness shows itself in noticing littleness; and he gives us comfort in the words, "He calleth them all by names by the greatness of His might." Our God, then, is not a being to be distracted. He is Ruler of everything, little and great. The grandeur of His nature interferes

not with the care of His creatures. He knows every little fear and little thought that make the sum of my life.

But all this comfort is not comfort for you unless you be God's people. God does not say, "Comfort ye that rebel, who will not be one of My people." You must first give yourself up to Christ; and then God says to me, in reference to you, "Comfort ye, comfort ye, my people."

C. S.

CI. Preparing the Way of the Lord. Isa. xl. 3–5.

"*The voice of him that crieth in the wilderness, Prepare ye the way of the Lord, make straight in the desert a highway for our God.*"

God has many messengers, and they have often lifted up their voice in the wilderness. Some speak with a voice of thunder to arouse a sleeping world. The doctrine of others distils as the dew. Ever since man was driven from the beauty of Eden he has been a wanderer in the desert. The imagery of the text appears to be drawn from the journeying of Israel to Canaan.

I. Compare this prophecy with the history of the Exodus. The prophecies of God's word shine both before and behind. They illumine the future and reflect a radiance back on the page of history. In the desert the Gospel was preached to Israel in types and ordinances, and especially by the great act of their redemption out of Egypt; for this was a foreshadowing of the inspired song, "Comfort ye, comfort ye, My people, saith your God." The law was a schoolmaster to bring Israel to Christ. It humbled pride, and so mountains and valleys were levelled, the crooked made straight, and the rough places plain. So in the ordinances given by the dispensation of angels might be heard the voice of one crying in the wilderness, "Prepare ye the way for our God."

II. Isaiah uses it as an illustration of his own ministry. He too felt himself in a spiritual desert, yet by faith he sees afar off, and the seer is himself transported into that bright future.

III. These words as pointing onwards to Gospel times. John the Baptist distinctly announced himself as "The voice of one crying in the wilderness, Prepare ye the way of the Lord." Before this wilderness preacher the mountains of Pharisaic pride were levelled, the valleys of Sadducean unbelief were filled up, the tortuous vices of the courtly Judæan were corrected, and the rude ignorance of the Galilean smoothed and reformed.

IV. The words had the wider signification also of the Gentile world being prepared to see the salvation of God. Providential agencies were then at work preparing Christ's way among the Gentiles. The two most powerful agencies were Greek literature and Roman dominion.

V. Every Christian should be as the voice crying " Prepare ye the way of the Lord." Each true servant of Christ is a successor of prophets and apostles in the highest sense. He is, by word and life, to witness for His Saviour and King.

H. P. L.

CII. Precious Promises. ISA. xli. 10. *"Fear thou not, for I am with thee. Be not dismayed, for I am thy God; I will strengthen thee, I will help thee; yea, I will uphold thee with the right hand of My righteousness."*

THE exuberant repetition of these words strike one. Everything said over twice, and some of them three times. And that is not merely Hebrew poetry; nor is it merely rhetorical amplification; but it suggests two or three very striking considerations. One is, how very hard it is to get people to lay hold of the rest and the strength that there is in confidence in God. How you need to keep hammering in the same thing into people's minds, and repeating it over and over again in all sorts and shapes, before the sluggish heart hears. Line upon line, precept upon precept—one exhortation is not sufficient, two even are not enough, and three are requisite, and they open out into all the rest of the word—" I am thy God," " I will strengthen thee ; " and that is not all, something more may be said yet —" Yea, I will uphold thee with the right hand of My righteousness." And then there is a lovely and most impressive climax in these three words which at first sight seem only synonymous, and I take it in all the expanding of the promises that are wrapped up in the one thought, "I am with thee."

And so, here are three things—a twofold exhortation, resting upon a twofold encouragement which breaks out into a dual repetition, "Fear not, be not dismayed."

Scholars tell us that the meaning of the last two words is a very beautiful one—the first I need not dwell upon—the second of them is very picturesque. The literal rendering of it is, "Don't look"—the paraphrase I mean—"don't look all round about you to see where the thunder-clouds are." Be not afraid, is the one thought, and the other is really, don't be like the hunted creature, or the savage that carries his life in his hand, and is ever keeping his eyes upon the thickets. Don't go through life looking at the places where danger may come; lift your eyes up to something higher. Don't train your eyes to look along the low level of earth, but train your eyes upwards. It would be a very poor affair if all the exhortation that was given us were only the empty one, "Be not afraid." The answer might be Jonah's answer, "Ah, but I do well, being afraid, and it is no use telling me not to be afraid unless you can deal with the facts; you cannot get rid of the fact that there is a large sting in every man's life to make him not only very sad, but very timid." The things that may come—and it is the *may* that gives the thing its sting, the *musts* we can stand—it is the *mays* that give us fear. We think of defeat, and if we have got over the fear of that, we think of possible dangers that may come instead. We think of something in our lives that *we* only know,—some hidden sorrow, some hidden disease, some rottenness that is sure to break out sooner or later—and unless a man can say, "Thou art with me," and "Thou art my help," I think the wisest man is the man that is afraid, and it is only fools that do not know what fear is. So I think there is a very large waste of breath in the well-meaning advice that is sometimes given to people. Yes, but to arrive at this superiority over fear, a man needs something more than fancies to take hold of. I don't think there is anything strong enough to draw away a man's eye from that dark corner yonder where the enemy is, where sits the shadow feared of man, except only the encouragement that is here, "Fear thou not." Yes, but I must. "For I am with thee: don't be gazing into the eyes of thy enemies." Ah, but I can't help it. There is a fascination like the rattlesnake, and I cannot withdraw my eyes from it. "I am thy God: come, child, look up at Me, and that is a better thing than looking at the foes that are round about you."

So look at this twofold encouragement, "I am with thee, and I am thy God," and "I will strengthen thee, and help thee, and uphold thee." Look at the majesty with which the sovereign autocratic *I, I, I*, keeps rolling forth. God puts, as it were, His own great being as a shelter and a breakwater between us and that great sea of danger without there, its billows round in front there. Get behind that great Breakwater—it is quiet riding on the other side of it. *I. I*, My own magnificent personality, that is the only thing that can make you strong. There is only one great antagonist that can master fear, and that is faith. And there is only one Being that can evoke faith, and the old word has it in all its beauty, and in all its simplicity, "I will trust," and so I will not be afraid. If you do not begin with the trust, you will never have come to the not being afraid. It is no use trying to expel the fear with a fork, it will come back again. Only you fill the heart with the other thing, "I will trust." And all we have got to say is, "Stand Thou above, and let me see that it flows out from Thy hand;" all this thing I am afraid of comes out of His hand. And so if I trust I find out the soul of goodness in the thing that is evil, and I cannot be afraid of what He sends me. "I will be with thee, be not dismayed, for I am thy God." And that is beautiful! A single man can lay hold of God, and put out an unpresumptuous hand, and say, "I claim Thee for mine!" That mystery of my possession of God, and God belonging to me! as well as of God owning it! We cannot get to the bottom of it. "He that dwelleth in love dwelleth in God, and God in him."

But the principal use of the thought is, if a man feels that God belongs to him, he need not be afraid of anything that comes to him. That one thought about God will open itself out into the threefold meaning of this great text, which with such tender reiteration and repetition sets this thought before us. "I will strengthen thee." Is that all? No. "Yea, I will help thee." Anything more? Yes. "Yea, I will uphold thee with the right hand of My righteousness." " I will strengthen thee "—that is something done upon me. " I will help thee "—that is something done beside me. In the one case God comes to me and breathes into me courage and power; and in the other case He comes and sits down beside me, and thinks for me. The meaning and the climax between these two things is this, "Strengthened by His Spirit in the inner man;" as Paul says, " I can do all things through Christ who strengthens me." Within, it is something in my heart; but then that is not the whole battle, there must be something else. And God says, " I will be—*I*—at thy side, an inspiration within thee, I will give thee power within thy hand, I will put My hand round about thee; I will strengthen thee within, and working all about thee, in the faith of Providence, and in regard to thine own inmost being, and in regard to external things I will give thee what thou dost need. Don't be afraid of the world in any of its shapes, I will help thee, the Inspirer within, and walk by thy side." " He will cover my head in the day of battle," and also He will teach me to walk.

And so the climax to the last words of this text seem to be plain. It climbs up to be the crown of promise in two ways. First, because it specifies the great means by which man will be upheld—" the right hand of His righteousness," which is the symbol for the power whereby His righteousness works for His children. It is no arbitrary kindness, no whim of a capricious tyrant; it is the love and the power, and the upholding of that great Sovereign righteousness which is full of tenderness to them that trust it, and only shows the side of wrath to them that reject it. Just as the eagle's eye is full of tenderness for the eaglets, so the right hand, the mighty power that is guided by the Divine righteousness, that, and nothing less, is what you and I have to rest upon. So there will be no blunder in our trust.

And then besides that, the climax that comes is not only this distinct statement of the strong foundation on which our hope rests, but it is the picture of the consequence of all this mighty energy of an inspiring Ally. " I will strengthen thee." Yes. " I will help thee." Yes.

And shall I stand, or fall? Thou shalt stand. "*I* will help thee, thou shalt not fail." The Lord is able to make me stand. It shall be no vain help, no inadequate help, no partial, no transitory help. Unlike the vain relieving armies that sometimes go to assist people in extremity, who themselves fall into an ambush, but fail to help their brethren,—where God strengthens there is no failure, and they whom He upholds shall not fall. That we may be able to withstand in the evil day, and having done all, to stand, "I will strengthen thee, I will help thee, I will uphold thee with the right hand of My righteousness."

A. M.

CIII. Sin and Mercy. Isa. xli. 22. "*I have blotted out as a thick cloud thy transgressions, and as a cloud thy sins.*"

THERE are two thoughts in the text.

I. There is the thought of sin. Sin is everywhere broad and deep, the wide world over, for you may trace the fire-written syllables—"As by one man sin entered into the world, and death by sin, so death passed upon all men, in that all have sinned." The Gospel proceeds upon the basis of universal depravity; the Gospel assimilates all varieties of human nature into one common experience of guilt and need and helplessness, and this is just what men do not like about it. The man of honest worldliness, the man of graceful generosity, cannot brook that he should be put with publicans and harlots upon one platform. But the Scriptures recognise only two varieties of condition here, they predict only two varieties of condition yonder, and it is easy to trace, if you only set about it aright, in all characters, from the extreme of murderous atrocity to the extreme of moral blamelessness, the same feature of ungodliness. The ungodly shall not stand in the judgment any more than the sinners in the congregation of the righteous. There is sin—sin as a thick cloud and as a cloud.

II. The thought of mercy : " I have blotted out."

It seems strange, that after the awful declaration of apostasy and impenitence in the beginning of the chapter, the prophet should not have gone away after pronouncing sentence of doom. And yet, when the voice speaks, it is the voice not of vengeance but of mercy. This is the great Bible theme, the mercy of God. Every promise distils it, it is the burden of every prophet's message. Sin is everywhere, but so is grace. As God always put the poison and the antidote together, so when sin came into the world, grace came into the world. Where sin hath abounded, there grace doth much more abound, and like the rich music of some ever present and majestic river, grace goes flowing on past the habitations of every man, never ceasing, never drying up, bearing continually its musical message to the ear of the world. There is pardon and rest for you in Jesus. There, in Jesus, is mercy, mercy for the vilest, and God is waiting that He may say to your consciences, "I have blotted out as a thick cloud thy transgressions, and as a cloud thy sins."

W. M. P.

CIV. God's Servant. ISA. xlii. 1–4. "*Behold My servant, whom I uphold; Mine elect, in whom My soul delighteth; I have put My spirit upon him: he shall bring forth judgment to the Gentiles.*"

THERE is no need to enter into argument as to the reference of this passage to Christ and His great work in the world. We feel instinctively that the words could refer to no other; and it strikes us as a matter of course that they should be quoted by St. Matthew and expressly applied to Jesus. So we may regard the passage as referring to the whole work and government of the Messiah, alike in the humiliation of His incarnate life, in the progress of His gospel through the ages, and in His future enthronement in the universality of His mediatorial kingdom.

I. Consider the need of the world. The need of the world is affirmed in this passage to be the bringing forth or establishment of God's judgment. The word has many senses in the Scripture, but there are three to which we shall refer.

(1) In Psalm cxlvii. and 19th verse, the term "judgments" is used of the precepts of God's law. It is needful, surely, that there should be a bringing in of judgment

as a revelation of God's word and will. Where there is no revelation, there is obscured or distorted vision, and the people perish. If it were possible to conceive of a world without a Bible, and consequently without a standard of authority, in the spectacle which would be presented of wayward and active mind, with no restraint upon its folly or frenzy, there would need no darker conception of hell. But the judgment of the Lord, true and righteous altogether, is revealed unto men. God has spoken, and every cavil may be silenced at His presence.

(2) In Luke xi. and 42nd verse, the term "judgment" evidently stands for righteousness, that which is just and true alike toward man and God, the high moral excellence which is the ideal of character and which a weary world has almost broken its heart in fruitless endeavours to attain. Surely it is needful that there should be a bringing in of judgment as a habit of righteousness. It has been well said that man can neither renounce his sins nor his God. He flees from the deity he worships; he is a slave to the sins which he condemns.

The master want of the world is holiness.

(3) In Psalm cxix. and 20th verse, and in the quotation of the text in Matthew, the term would seem to have reference to the dispensation of grace, the provision of might and mastery for human feebleness and struggle. By unaided effort ignorance cannot acquire saving knowledge nor pollution be cleansed from its stain. There must be a power by which the scales can be taken from the eyes and the warp from the mind and the enfeebled nature become valiant for the truth. Without the revelation of this power all other revelation would be an aggravation of the torture, as the sunlight on the shroud is only a gay mockery of the death it robes. The bringing forth of judgment, which is declared to be to open the blind eyes, is declared also to be to bring out the prisoners from the prison; and the effect of the Saviour's mediatorial work is described as the judgment of this world and the casting out of its prince.

II. The designation of its deliverer.

(1) Christ is called here the servant of the Father. This is only an official servitude in reference to His mediatorial work. He took upon Him the form of a servant, and with

glad heart and willing feet went forth to do a servant's work.

(2) Christ is called the elect or chosen of God in whom His soul delighteth. He was chosen to this work and beloved on account of this work. The Father's love was intensified on account of this, "Therefore doth My Father love Me."

(3) He was the anointed of the Spirit. Although He knew no sin, and therefore needed no renewal, yet even His sinless human nature must have this anointing to enrich it with all suitable qualifications and to make it strong for service or for suffering, as if to show that even in its highest embodiment human nature cannot do without God.

III. The manner and issue of His work.

(1) He works unostentatiously. "He shall not cry, nor lift up, nor cause His voice to be heard in the street."

(2) He works tenderly. "A bruised reed shall He not break."

(3) He works perseveringly and successfully. "He shall not fail nor be discouraged." Against embattled earth, against the gathered forces of the pit, He shall bring forth judgment unto victory, until He rests from His labours, until He gathers His children, until He makes up His jewels, until He wears His crown.

W. M. P.

CV. The Lost Ideal. Isa. xlviii. 18. "*Oh, that thou hadst hearkened to My commandments! then had thy peace been as a river, and thy righteousness as the waves of the sea.*"

EXILE and home-coming, captivity and deliverance, judgment and mercy, these are the things of this chapter. There is in the immediate context an expression of the deepest regret on God's part, that the spirit and behaviour of His own people had been such as to make it necessary to bring on them these heavy judgments, while this text is a tender wish and longing that they had from the first chosen the better way.

I. The first thought implied here is the lost ideal, what might have been; something that in the high and true sense not only might have been, but ought to have been, which God cannot even yet cease to think about and lament over as a thing as yet unrealized. He saw, He who sees all things, who has no illusion, who makes no mistake in His estimate of men or things, saw clearly that there had been a bright and beautiful possibility for them as a nation. He saw that there had been a possibility to individuals as well as to the nation, which they had not attained and which now was unattainable, at least to this extent, that things with them could never be exactly the same as if they had attained it from the first.

So, too, there is to each of us an ideal life that is a bright, pure, perfect course along which we might go from earth into heaven. This is something not barely possible, not abstractly imaginable. The ideal life is the life, the others that come in the place of it are usurpers and pretenders. But it is strange, and to some it may very well be alarming, to think of the difference between what might have been and what has been between themselves, and as they have made themselves, and themselves as God would have made them.

It might not be an unprofitable exercise for any one to try to discover his own ideal and proper life. We are not left altogether without guidance for any inquiry of this kind, because there is a natural outline in every man's life. Sin depraves, but it does not obliterate the organic powers and the natural peculiarities and tendencies of the individual. There is some outline left in each individual of what might have been. The ideal of another person would not be mine nor mine his. There are diversities. Just as we get a glimpse of the sun on a wintry morning, so I have had now and then, in a supreme moment, a glimpse of what I might have been. This lost self is the self that must be found, else happiness cannot be found.

II. The Divine lamentation over this lost ideal. This passage shows that it is no matter of indifference with God how men live. God feels this matter to pain and intensity, to sorrow and regret, to yearning love and great longing. "Oh, that thou hadst hearkened to My commandments! then had thy peace been like a river, and thy righteousness like the waves of the sea."

"Thy peace" means the prosperity, thy welfare "had

been like a river" which fills its banks, spreading fertility in its course. "And thy righteousness," a term here used in its large sense for universal goodness, truth, honour, every virtue, "like the waves of the sea"—a still grander image than that of the river. We see how great and beneficent God would have man's life to be, and how beautiful. Could any one say, that if they had never received God's special gracious help by the Gospel that their life would be anything like God's ideal?

III. The Divine proposal for restoration.

In our text God stands in the first instance as with uplifted hands pathetically lamenting over a great loss and ruin. What means the next verse? If things were all so hopeless would God exhort them to do anything at all? He means evidently by that to declare that He will continue His work and carry it on to ultimate success. It is exactly what God is doing to all discouraged ones, to all hopeless hearts to-day. He is putting before them the great Gospel of good news with Divine strength in it. Begin where you are, do the nearest thing, forsake the sin that is strongest, take the path that is open, make room in your heart for all that God will give you, and especially for the renewing spirit, and in all this look unto Jesus and press towards Him as you look, and you are now a new creature in Him, Eden blooms once more, the dead is alive again, the long-lost self is found.

A. R.

CVI. Spiritual Despondency. ISA. l. 10. "*Who is among you that feareth the Lord, that obeyeth the voice of His servant, that walketh in darkness, and hath no light? let him trust in the name of the Lord, and stay upon his God.*"

IT is not, as you see from these words, a thing unheard of or impossible, that a child of God should "walk in darkness and have no light." And when the sadness of such an experience comes upon the saint it will not be always safe to say that it is the shadow of some special sin.

The case described in the text is that of one who even at the moment "feareth the Lord and obeyeth the voice of His servant," while yet he has lost the radiant happiness of the new life and is bending under the weight of spiritual despondency. The first reference to be drawn from the text is, that a man may be a sincere, devout follower of the Lord Jesus, and yet be "walking in darkness."

I. Look at some of the causes out of which despondency may spring.

(1) It may spring from natural temperament. It is a fact that each of us is born with a certain predisposition to joy or sadness, to irascibility or patience, to quickness of action or deliberateness of conduct, which we call temperament. And it is also true that while conversion may Christianize that temperament, it does not change it.

The Lord takes men as they are, and works in and through their very idiosyncrasies, so as to produce in His Church that unity in variety which is the charm of the physical universe. Do not fret, therefore, over that which is the result of temperament. Keep resisting it, and take to yourself the helping hand which the Lord stretches down to you in the precious injunction of the text.

(2) Spiritual despondency may be caused by disease.

The connection between soul and body is both intimate and mysterious. They act and react upon each other, and a sound body is in all ordinary cases necessary to the sound mind.

(3) Spiritual despondency is often the result of trial.

"Ye are in heaviness through manifold trials." One affliction will not usually becloud our horizon. But when a whole series of distresses comes to us in succession, the effect is terrible. Only those who have passed through a series of afflictions and who can say in the words of the old prophet, "He hath barked my fig tree, and made it clean bare," can tell how much there is in such a history to weigh the spirit down. Nay, the same effect may be produced by the mere monotony of our labour without any special affliction.

(4) Spiritual despondency may be caused by mental perplexity.

We are living in an age when the spirit of inquiry and bold independent criticism is abroad. The old beliefs are once more on their trial, and when a youth reaches the age when he must exchange a traditional piety for a personal conviction, he is plunged for a time into the greater misery. One assails him on the supernatural character of Christ; another on the authority of the scriptures; and others, bolder still, will question even the existence of God to him. And so he is launched on a black and stormy sea over which he toils in rowing, and even when in the fourth watch the Lord appears to him, marching over the waves, he is so broken down that he mistakes the Master for a ghost and is affrighted. When a soul is called to pass through such a trial, it is agony, deep, intense agony. Let those who are thus walking in darkness take to themselves the comfort of the text, and walk on in the full assurance that there is light beyond.

II. The counsels to the desponding which are suggested by the text.

(1) The oppressed spirit must keep on fearing the Lord and obeying the voice of His servant.

(2) The oppressed spirit must keep on trusting God. "Let him trust in the name of the Lord and stay upon his God."

When we cannot see, it is an unspeakable blessing to have some hand to cling to; and when that hand is God's, it is all right. What is that name in which I am to trust? It is "Jehovah, God merciful and gracious; long-suffering; purifying iniquity and sin; and who will by no means clear the guilty." Therefore I need not despair about my guilt, for there is forgiveness with Him. What is that name? It is Jehovah Tsidkenu—the Lord our righteousness; therefore we may in Him have boldness in the day of judgment. It is Jehovah Rophek—the Lord that healeth thee; therefore I may bring all my spiritual maladies to Him for cure. It is Jehovah Jireh—the Lord will provide. It is Jehovah Nissi—the Lord my banner, and as I unfurl that signal I may see in it the symbol of His protection. It is Jehovah Shalom—the Lord of peace, and so beneath His sheltering wing I may be for ever at rest.

Then note the meaning of that word "stay." It does not bid you only take a momentary grasp of God's hand. It encourages you to lean your whole weight upon Him, and to do that continually, and He will not cast you off.

W. M. T.

CVII. The Origin of Christianity. ISA. li. 1.

"*Look to the rock whence ye are hewn, and to the pit whence ye are digged.*"

THE subject before us is the impossibility of accounting for the "origins" of Christianity on purely natural grounds, or, in other words, the impossibility of its being other than a true religion in its simple historic aspect as involving supernatural facts.

I. If Jesus did no superhuman act, how is His character to be explained? He asserts an authority; He demands an obedience to which no mere teacher has a right; He promises what no mere teaching can possibly impart. "He that loveth father or mother more than Me is not worthy of Me." "Ye have heard that it was said to them of old, but I say unto you"—things quite different, contradictory. These are characteristic sayings, bearing the undoubted stamp of genuineness; no Jew could have invented them. Where do such expressions land us in evaluating the character of Jesus, if He were what it is fashionable now to deem Him?

Look again at the strange absence, in every recorded word of Jesus, of the slightest trace of guilt or even of imperfection. The feeling of sinlessness pervades His whole recorded life. Who was ever like Him in this respect? The difficulty created by the inseparable interweaving of the miraculous in the history and character of Jesus is yet unsolved by unbelievers.

II. How came Christ's followers, immediately after His death, to set up a religion professedly derived from Him, but based on so entirely false a conception of what He actually did? Nothing can explain their actions, nothing can explain their success, save their strong belief in the resurrection. In a few years they had persuaded myriads of Jews in Jerusalem and elsewhere to share their belief. The true upshot of all theories which deny the supernatural character of Christianity may be expressed in the pathetic words of a modern sceptical writer, "We know nothing, life is a journey between two long nights. All that we can deem certain is that at intervals a parental smile traverses nature, and reveals to us that an eye looks down on us, and a heart follows us." But once started on the downward road of scepticism, we must go down the incline till we reach the bottom, where no paternal "eye" is felt to watch us, no paternal "heart" to follow us, and we feel that not of one great malefactor only, but of all mankind it may truly be said, "it would have been good for us not to have been born."

C. P. R.

CVIII. A Threefold Appeal. Isa. li. 9, 10. *"Awake! awake! put on strength, O arm of the Lord. Awake, as in the ancient days, in the generations of old! Art thou not it that hath cut Rahab, and wounded the dragon? Art thou not it which hath dried the sea, the waters of the great deep; that hath made the depths of the sea a way for the ransomed to pass over?"*

RAHAB, or pride, is the name for Egypt, given to it on account of its contempt for all foreigners, and its haughty national character. "The dragon" is an old prophecy of the emblem of Pharaoh. Egypt is to be considered as the symbol of the world against which the children of God are pledged to fight. From this life-long struggle it is impossible to escape, save by cowardly desertion into the ranks of Satan. The wise son of God recognises this fact—cherishes a spirit of mingled fear and confidence as he thinks of that spiritual Egypt in which the Lord was crucified. He thinks of it with fear, knowing his own weakness, and the power of the enemy by which he is confronted. He thinks of it with confidence, because he knows that he can never finally be destroyed so long as he fights in the strength of God the Holy Ghost.

How far Isaiah realized the import of his words is a matter of secondary importance. Enough for us that they express exactly the spirit in which we have to address ourselves to this great and glorious battle. The words from part of a threefold appeal to God and the Church. It is a grand appeal—an appeal worthy of that glorious, free Jerusalem into which we have been baptized.

The principle of the warfare that is suggested by the text is the same that is taught in the New Testament, for there is a marvellous continuity in scripture. Those who study it devotionally are almost startled to see the same grand principles underlying the entire volume. It is exactly the principle of the 5th chapter of 1 John. "Whatsoever is born of God overcometh the world; and this is the victory that overcometh the world, even our faith." Faith is the gift of God. It is bestowed by God the Holy Ghost. The habit of faith must be formed; like every other habit alike in the natural and in the spiritual world, we must in this, as in everything else, be fellow-workers with God.

I. God desires that our faith should be centred on the Lord Jesus—as man, to be with us; as God, to help us. We appeal to Him, "Put on thy strength for us, O Christ! Awake, as in the ancient days, in the generations of old. Awake, awake, thou that hast cut Rahab, and wounded the dragon, and destroyed the world, and delivered us from its power."

II. This is the victory that overcomes—confidence that we are united to Christ and made to be partakers of the Divine nature. Do we cry "I am so weak?" Then Christ bids us remember that the same life and the same power has been poured into men and into women as weak and as helpless as ourselves.

III. This is the victory that overcomes—confidence that Jesus Christ is the same yesterday, to-day, and for ever. We are fighting under an invisible but a most mighty Leader. We are fighting as it were in the mist; and oft-times the form of the great General is hidden from us. The mist breaks; we catch for a moment just a sight of that glorious white raiment of the all conquering King, and then the mist gathers round again. But thanks be to God the victory is sure. He gives us the victory through Jesus Christ the Lord.

G. H. W.

CIX. The Care of God. ISA. lii. 12. "*The God of Israel will be your reward.*"

Ps. xxxiii. 6. "*Surely goodness and mercy shall follow me.*"

THESE two passages are the expression by different men in different ages of the same religious confidence; a confidence in an unseen Presence shielding them from harm and injury; confidence in an unseen Presence encompassing the weak, and that might be depended on for protection and support from danger of whatever form; in an unseen Presence covering unguarded points and accompanying unguarded moments. In the psalm, King David speaks, probably as the close of his life was drawing nigh, with a remembrance of a life full of mercies from his earlier days, and with the trust which a life experience had taught him to repose in Jehovah's care and providence. He sings to Him as Shepherd, and, remembering what he had been himself in his youth, the figure had a world of meaning in it. "The Lord is my Shepherd; I shall not want. He maketh me to lie down in green pastures; He leadeth me beside the still waters." He too, like those sheep of Jesse's which were once his charge, was in the hands of One who looked after and guided his steps, who knew how to restore him when he wandered from the right way and went into the wrong path, and who would sustain him when he passed through the dark valley, the Valley of the Shadow of Death, unto which he was drawing nigh. Then he sings of Jehovah again as a host entertaining him at a feast even while difficulties lay thick around him; in the midst of these, in spite of these, the Lord gave him inward peace. He was a traveller in the desert finding a banquet spread for him by the way; the Lord made him glad with His countenance though the outward scene and surroundings were gloomy. And then he winds up his song by representing Jehovah as a solid column of defence between him and the enemies who were pursuing him. They might be following him closely but Jehovah was following him also and much more closely. There were enemies whose secret step was unknown to him, but before them was the Lord, the Lord mighty to save, the pledge of never-failing goodness and mercy; so that however portentous the circumstances, he was living and would be living in safety all his days.

King David is no more, but still his spirit of belief remains, and now far down the century is Isaiah, who in the book of his prophecy repeats the same strain of holy confidence; looking forward to a time of bitter adversity for his nation during which they would be suffering bondage and oppression, he yet anticipates an ultimate glory and deliverance. He sees, beyond the lamentations, the multitude of captives, their chains broken, going forth not in haste as of old, but at their leisure and with thanksgiving ; and he sees that same progress and the successful issue of the march secured by the attendance of an invisible escort, the Lord moving before them and the God of Israel offering a sure protection and guard against all mischief that might come upon them.

These words of Isaiah and David suggest certain reflections.

I. The ugly things that are waiting in the way for us like ambuscades. How sometimes ugly things have lurked in our path, black with sorrow, that could have been so easily avoided had we only known. But we knew not, we suspected not, and went forward lightly as if we were about to receive a boon ; and the calamity comes which the starting of a new idea, a moving aside, might have sufficed to remove. If a hint could have been granted, if something could have happened to guard our movements, just to incline us to caution and watchfulness ; the least thing might have been enough to save us and secure a redemption. If the President of the United States, for instance, had had a presentiment of disaster so as to arrest the act of his murderer, what a difference it would have made. Often have men said, " Oh, why were we not led to hesitate, to shrink back ? Why did no foreboding arise ? Had only something occurred to detain us, to make us lose that train, to relinquish that enterprise."

II. Occasionally, indeed, we are disturbed before misfortune or disaster with some idea or presentiment of evil, and which we have shaken off, and it has seemed to us as if some guardian angel had been seeking to save us. Now and again how remarkably presentiments have come to be effectual in snatching from death. A man has withdrawn a decision in obedience to an impulse which he has been unable to explain. It has proved afterwards the best thing he could have done ; or else he has been hindered from some action, to his extreme annoyance, and that hindrance has saved him.

III. But in the case of each of us, how close we have often been, without perceiving, to calamities from which we have been spared. How many dangers we have been enabled to escape, unknown to ourselves, just by a hair's breadth. Were these displayed before us what a grim and ghastly host would be revealed! We have run along, quite unconsciously, the edge of dark pits. Not seldom would our heart be strangely agitated with wonder and awe and gratitude and love if we could have seen all we have escaped from during our life.

IV. And again, might we not say that goodness and mercy are frequently following us to our salvation from mischief, in our better thoughts that come in the wiser mind that presently awakens and scatters the evil? If all the inward evil promptings we have had were carried out, if we had been abandoned to do all the evil longings and desires we were disposed to do! why what precipices we have been snatched from at the very brink. St. John of the Apocalypse beheld a door opened in Heaven and heard a voice inviting to ascend. Have we not had a door opened from hell, and has it not been suddenly shut, and thus we have been saved? We have seen the possibilities of evil in us that have made us shudder. Goodness and mercy have followed us. Or suppose that in certain moments of passion, of relaxation, opportunity had concurred—it has concurred with others, to their utter undoing, in like moods and moments. The opportunity that might have been our undoing did not concur and we have been rescued. How much of what we call our virtue has arisen from the non-opportunity of what might have been the very opposite. We have been hedged in and guarded. Under certain circumstances and under certain influences something terrible might have happened to us. Can we not say on looking back in such crises, that our God was before us and encompassed us and saved us? What should we have been if we had not been environed by His presence—who can tell what our conduct might have been?

V. How many can give sincere thanks for sorrows and misfortunes which came just in time to ripen and restore them just as they were sinking into doing and going wrong. Do they not recall with gratitude how in some directions in which they were feverishly anxious, disappointment came and turned them from the low flats on which they had found them back to the high levels on which they have built. Oh! what rest this has given them, what peace: it is as if they had been visited by an angel of the Lord sent to save them. In that prosperity they were deteriorating inwardly, gradually losing that fineness of heart which before had distinguished them, and who can say to what it might have grown? But presently there came trouble, disappointment, sorrow, and in these you came out better, and stronger, and nobler, and recovered tone.

VI. And now once more. True as it is that we are constantly, whether for good or for evil, reaping what we have sowed, true as this is, are we not constantly reaping the fruits of a bad past? Have we not felt after enduring the judgment of some grievous mistake or misdeed, that it was not so severe as it might have been? We indulged yesterday, we gave way to passions that were calculated to make us weaker and more distempered. This was succeeded by pangs of repentance, by a feeling of deep contrition. We have been delivered thus from a good deal. It might have seemed to us sometimes that goodness and mercy have followed even our transgressions, for these have not pursued us as they might have done. Have we not often seen the ultimate rescue and shapening of some whom we thought beyond recovery? While the iniquities of the past are laid upon us, we might have said that they have not pursued us to the utmost. There must be a residuum in every evil; but when you endure the severe flagellation of an unwise past, when you appear to be spared nothing, when the strokes seem to fall pitilessly, are we not fain to believe that there is goodness and mercy in them, to give us deliverance and to bring us home through their blows? Unto Thee, O Lord, belongeth mercy, for Thou renderest to every man according to his work.   S. A. T.

CX. Missions in the Light of the Redeemer's Work. ISA. liii. 2. "*He shall see of the travail of His soul, and shall be satisfied.*"

IT has been said that Missionary sermons are not uncommonly preached from Old Testament texts, and it is no wonder that thus it should be; for when we wish to glance afar off, it is natural that we should ascend the highest hill we can find; and just so when we want to take a wide view of God, and His purposes towards mankind, we seek those great mountain ranges called the Prophecies of Isaiah. These prophecies look forward to our own times, to the millennial times, and to the everlasting days.

We shall look at missions in their vital connection with Him who is the one theme of all missions, the one head of every Missionary Society.

I. Let us consider the travail of the Redeemer's soul. We may well pause and inquire what was that soul itself that thus travailed. Who can tell how deep and strong and sensitive was His pure soul? That soul was ever at war with sin. Christ did not go through any make-believe conflict with sin, but while tempted in all things, He never gave way to the temptation. That soul of Jesus travailed. That His body travailed is obvious enough; that His heart suffered, and that He had much to forego for the sake of His work, is also true. But who can describe or conceive what was the travail of His soul? His soul was ever working and suffering. When He was twelve years of age (and that is the one glimpse we have in those thirty years before He began His mission), He said, "Wist ye not that I must be about My Father's business?" And who can tell what experience He went through during these thirty years? We know no more of them than we know of the forty years that Moses spent in the wilderness when God was preparing him for his great work. Surely Christ went through much suffering and conflict and hidden labour, that was needful to prepare Him when the hour had come. The sorrows of His passion when He saw them from afar, troubled Him. "Now is my soul troubled; and what shall I say: Father, save Me from this hour." But saving Himself, He would not have saved us, and therefore He went through to the bitter end.

II. The certainty of Christ seeing of the travail of His soul. Did the Redeemer endure these sufferings for nought? Rather might we believe that a good seed falling into good ground bears no fruit. He is sure to see fruit; He has begun to see it. He began to see it at the very hour when He rose from the dead, and He shall see it on a larger scale, and with a fuller scope, when the day comes, and the words of the prophet shall be fulfilled, "He shall see of the travail of His soul and be satisfied." We sinners are the gift of the Father to the Son, we are the very object of the prayer of Christ, we are the answer of the Father to the Son. "Ask, and I shall give Thee the heathen for thine inheritance, and the uttermost parts of the earth for Thy possession." When we ask that the uttermost parts of the earth shall be given to the Lord, we are simply praying His prayer, and we are sure to be heard by Him who heareth Christ alway.

III. He shall be satisfied. What a word is this "satisfied!" Who is satisfied in this world? What mind or heart can say I am satisfied? Christ shall be satisfied in His Father's grace. He shall be satisfied in the salvation of men; He shall be satisfied, because His love shall have found its response; because His sufferings shall have borne their fruit. There is no stronger incentive than this to missionary zeal and missionary work. Can I not do something and bear something that Christ may be satisfied?

T. M.

CXI. The Silence of Christ. ISA. liii. 7. "*He was oppressed, and He was afflicted, yet He opened not His mouth: He is brought as a lamb to the slaughter, and as a sheep before her shearers is dumb, so He openeth not His mouth.*"

AFTER the trial and condemnation of our Lord by Caiaphas and the Sanhedrin, He was led away to the Procurator or Roman Governor of Judæa, Pontius Pilate, to be tried over again. The reason for this procedure appears to have been that the Jewish Sanhedrin at this time had no power to inflict, although they might pronounce, the punishment of death on criminals; and Christ was therefore arraigned before Pilate to procure Pilate's authority to carry out the capital sentence which had already been pronounced upon Him. It does not, however, appear that Jesus was entirely silent before Pilate, for to Pilate's first question, which was founded on the formal accusation that had been laid against Jesus (Luke xxiii. 2), "Art Thou the King of the Jews?" our Lord answered just as He had answered the High Priest under similar circumstances, "Thou sayest" (compare Mark xiv. 62, with Matt. xvi. 64); and in the Gospel of St. John we find this was followed by those memorable words concerning the true nature of Christ's of human lives, but the words, "The Word was made flesh and dwelt among us, full of grace and truth."

II. But it is the continual wonder of the character of Jesus that though it is so unlike any human character, so far above the highest elevation to which we can attain, yet the contemplation of Christ never disheartens nor discourages us in our endeavour to imitate Him. Some ideals crush all achievement by their very remoteness and elevation; but here is confessedly the highest moral ideal the world has ever seen, and yet to look at it, to linger over it, to ponder it again and again, until we see new wonder and beauty in it, is not to quench all effort to grow like it, but to inspire us with new desire "to follow Him." The greatness of Christ's example is not its only marvel, but that with its greatness we should feel it is an example for us, one we can follow and make our own, is a greater wonder still. "He left us an example that we should follow in His steps;" and those who follow Him most nearly at once see most of the unutterable loveliness and grandeur of His character, and grow likest to it.

III. There are very few of us to whom that single aspect of the character of Christ which is portrayed in our text, His bearing injustice and malignity and false accusation with silence, will not teach a lesson we need to learn. We are so quick to resent injury; so ready to denounce malice, especially when it is directed against ourselves; so vehement in our indignation when we are unjustly accused, that our very indignation may sometimes lead us into sin in defending right against wrong. It is not easy to be silent when the words of passionate protest against iniquity are burning on our tongue, or when we are made to "suffer for righteousness' sake." But there are times when we follow our Lord most closely, and serve His cause best, by quietly and meekly bearing injustice without a word. And nothing will so help us thus to suffer and be silent as the rememberance of Him who "did no sin, neither was guile found in His mouth; who, when He was reviled, reviled not again; when He suffered, threatened not, but committed Himself to Him that judgeth righteously," and the righteousness of whose cause all the years that have gone by since He suffered have only served to vindicate.

G. S. B.

CXII. God's Loving Kindness. ISA. liv. 10. *"For the mountains shall depart, and the hills be removed; but My kindness shall not depart from thee; neither shall the covenant of My peace be removed, saith the Lord that hath mercy upon us."*

THERE is something of music in the flowing sound of these words. The stately march of the grand English translation lends itself with wonderful beauty to the melody of Isaiah's words. But the thought that lies below them, sweeping as it does through the whole creation, and parting all things into the *transient material*, and the *immortal Divine*, is still greater than the music of the words. *These* are removed, *this* abides. And the thing in Gód which abides is that gentle tenderness, that strange love, mightier than all the powers of Divinity besides, and permanent with the permanence of His changeless heart. "The mountains shall depart," the emblems of eternity shall crumble and change and pass, and "the hills shall be removed," but this immaterial, impalpable, and in some minds fantastic and unreal *something*, the thought,—and as some of you think, the dream, that shall outlast them all, "My loving kindness, and the covenant of My peace." And for guarantee of that we have the revelation of the intimate and inmost nature and character of God in its bearings upon me: "saith the Lord that hath mercy upon us."

I. Think, first of all, of that great antithesis that is set before us—what *passes* and what *abides*,—and then draw two or three marked lessons and applications from the thoughts thus suggested. First of all then, we have to deal with the contrast between the apparently enduring which passes, and that which truly abides. The mountains depart, the hills shall be removed, etc. To begin with, a word or two about that first thought: "the mountains shall depart." There they tower over the plain. Lebanon looks down upon the flat valley beneath it, as it did when Isaiah spoke; the strong buttresses of the hills stand, and, to the eye of the fleeting generations that ebb away beneath their silent cliffs, they seem the very emblems of permanence. And yet winter storms and summer heats, and the slow process of decay, which we call "the gnawing tooth of time," is

Q

ever working upon these, chasing them into form, and changing their outlines, and at last they shall pass. Modern science, while it has enlarged all but incalculably our conceptions of the duration of the material universe, emphasises, as faith alone never could, the thought of the the destined perishableness of all the material world. For geology tells us that where rears the mountain there rolled the sea; that across through the cycles of the shaping of the history of the world there have been elevations and depressions, so that the ancient hills in many places are the newest of all things, and the world's forms have changed many and many times since first it circled round its centre sun. The recent researches that carry men's thoughts forwards tell us that as certainly as science can read the past, there will come a time when all matter, by reason of that great law of dispersion and energy, shall be agglomerated into one uniform temperature, when all life, and all that is in it, shall cease to be. And so Peter's word of prophecy is verified by the last bold researches of the most recent science, "the earth and all that therein is shall be burnt up, and the elements shall melt with fervent heat." No man should be able to utter with such profound conviction and certitude these great words of my text, "the mountains shall depart and the hills be removed," as the men that devote themselves to physical science to-day.

But there is something more than that here: there is the emblem of it, a part of it; cursed with transiency, certainly the past shall fade. And you and I stand in midlife, and we look round us and see all this creatural existence,—it is but a ripple upon the surface of the great sea; and those milleniums of ages which may have passed, or may still have to pass, they are but an incident in the great eternal silence of the years,—and so we begin to think that humanity is small and that life is insignificant, and sometimes to feel as if we were orphaned and nothing were left to us. And so we come to the words of my text, "the mountains shall depart, and the hills be removed; but My kindness shall not depart from thee." And to turn for a moment to that other side of the great thought, rising higher—for all that filmy material, which, though it counts its existence by milleniums, is but for an instant,—towers to the eye that sees deep enough and high enough into the realities of things, the Present Spirit who can move all the material things Himself and live undiminished by Creation, and undiminished after Creation is swept out of existence. Let that which may pass, pass; that which can perish, perish; the mountains crumble and the hills melt away; beyond the smoke, and athwart the conflagration, and rising high above the destruction and the chaos, stands the calm throne of God, with a love to us, with a counsel of peace and a purpose of mercy for you and for me, the creatures of a day, that shall live when the days have ceased to be. Look how there come out of those words thoughts of that Divine relationship to us which are meant to strengthen us in the contemplation of that which is perishable, and amid the changing of all that is material.

"My kindness"! That is a wonderful word, so far from the cold adoration of so-called Theism. "My kindness." The tender-heartedness of an infinite love; the bending, yearning favour of the Father of my spirit; His gentle goodness bending down to me, and round all its tremulous tenderness casts the solemnity of eternity. Love never can die wherever it is, but the immortal love is the love of God; and the one thing that lasts in the universe is He, His kindness, and the creatures that receive it. Everything else is for a day, *that* is from everlasting to everlasting. "My kindness"—what a revelation of God! Oh, if only our hearts could open to the right acceptance of that thought, sorrow and care and anxiety, and every other foe to peace and purity, would fade away, and we should be at rest. The infinite, undying, imperishable love of God is mine; older than the mountains, deeper than their roots in the great abyss, wider than the heavens, and stronger than all my sins, is the love that grasps me and keeps me, and will not let me go—that lavishes its tenderness upon me, and beseeches me, and pleads with me, and woos me, and rebukes me, and corrects me, and sent His Son to die for me: "My kindness shall not depart from you."

And then there is the other side to the same thought: the consequence and outcome of that imperishable and unremovable loving kindness is what my calls text "My covenant of peace," or "the covenant of My peace." That is to say, we are to think of this great, tender, changeless love of God, which underlies all things, and towers above all things, which overlaps beyond them all and fills eternity; we are to think of it as being placed under a guarantee, and being under a solemn obligation. God's covenant! It is of course a strong metaphor, a violent one, if you like to call it so, and yet it covers for all that a great truth. God comes into a covenant with you and me, and His covenant is this: "I promise that My love shall never leave thee." He makes, as it were, Himself a constitutional Monarch, so to speak, giving us an articulate word to which we can appeal and come to Him and say: "There, that is the charter given by Thyself indeed, and being given, irrevocable for ever, and I hold Thee to it. Thy covenant is this, fulfil it O Thou God of Truth." "My covenant of peace." Isaiah spoke a deeper thing than he meant when he uttered these words. Let me remind you of the largest possible meaning of them. "Now the God of peace that brought again from the dead the Lord Jesus Christ, that great Shepherd of the sheep, by the blood of the everlasting covenant, make you perfect in every good work, to work His perfect will." God has bound Himself by His promise and by His act, and given you and me the peace that belongs to His own nature; and that covenant is sealed to us in the blood of Jesus Christ upon the cross. And so, we sinful men, with all the burdens of our evil upon us, with all the stings of conscience, with our manifold sense of infirmities and failure, we can turn to Him and say: "Thou hast pledged Thyself to forgive and to accept, and that covenant is made free to me because Thy Son has died, and I come and ask of Thee to fulfil it"; and be sure of this, that no poor creature upon earth who puts out a hand to plead that covenant, can plead in vain. My brother, have you done that? Have you entered into this covenant of peace with God? Peace in believing; peace that rules in the heart; peace that rules between you and God; peace that rules amidst all the perturbations and disturbances of life? Then you may be sure that that covenant will stand for evermore, "though the mountains depart and the hills be removed."

II. So turn to two or three plain practical lessons that we may gather from this great contrast between the imperishable material and the immortal Divine life.

(1) First of all I want to put it in this shape: ought not such a thought as this of my text to wake you and me from our setting our hearts upon these perishable things? What folly it is, looked at from the lowest point of view, for a man to invest his effort and his interest, and to risk his hopes and the strength and joy of his life upon things that crumble and fade, when all the while there is lying before him, open for his entrance and wooing him to come in, the eternal home of his spirit. Here are you and I, living day by day, necessarily planted amidst these material realities, and we are always tempted to think they are the true abiding things, and it needs some power to lift us above this thought. Philosophy tells that *it* helps us to do it, possibly in some ways. Sorrow helps us some way. But there is nothing like the love of Jesus Christ. Then we can see over these little permanencies after all, and know that they are ebbing, ebbing. Look at them, they are changing like the scenery in the sky there, on a summer night, with its cliffs and clouds that change and roll even as we gaze; where there was a mountain there is a valley; where there was a depression has shot up a spire. The world lasts very little longer. It is only a film upon the great surface, it is only a delusion after all, there is no reality after all. It is but a dream and a vision, sliding, sliding, sliding away, and you and I slide, slide, sliding along with it, only we are not going the same road. And so, how foolish, how foolish and obstinate the eagerness with which we cling to that, though even the very grasp of our hand tends to make it pass away. Like the children that one saw these last holidays, coming in from the fields with their little store of buttercups and daisies in their hot hands, withering by the very grasp of the palm that keeps them there. So our position and all that belongs to this fleeting world in the midst of whose enchantments we live for a brief moment, they all perish in the using, and the very having of them is the killing of them. Wilt thou set thy heart upon these things which are but for a moment, when all the while, serene, sweet, waiting and longing to bless and love us stands the eternal God with His unchanging love and the faithful covenant of His perpetual peace. Surely it were wiser, wiser to put it on the lowest grounds, to seek the things that are above, and, knowing as we do,

that the mountains shall depart and the hills be removed, to make our portion the kindness which shall not depart, and seek our share in the peace that shall not be removed.

(2) There is another point that I would put in the same simple fashion. To use thoughts like these of my text in order to stay the soul when—as is the case with everybody—it is sometimes made painfully conscious of the transiency of this present. Meditative hours come to us all, moments when perhaps some strain of music that brings back childhood's days; when perhaps some perfume of a flower, or some touch of a sunset sky, or some words of a book, or some evidence in ourselves, may pour in upon our heart and mind the thought of how everything is past and in the process of dissolution. All have got these thoughts, some of us stifle them, they are not pleasant to many of us; some of us brood over them unwholesomely, and that is not wise; but the meaning is: the mountains pass and the hills are removed; that the covenant may bear us onward into the peaceful region of that other thought, yes, and of something that cannot go. And that is *my* home. If any of us have hearts heavy with earthly loss; are bending under the weight of the law, that everything becomes part and parcel of that dreadful past and goes away from us; if any of us have empty hands, and are saying "they have taken away my gods and what have I more!" Oh let us listen to the better voice that says, "Child, My kindness shall not depart from thee, and so whatever goes thou canst not be desolate."

(3) Then this same thought here may avail to give to us hopes of ourselves immortal as itself. We do not belong to the mountains and the hills that shall depart, and to the order of things to which they belong; there is coming a very solemn day, when, by no mere process of natural decay as I take it, but by the action of God Himself, the Judge, that day of the Lord shall come as a thief in the night, the mountains shall depart and the hills be removed, and the throne of judgment shall be set, and you and I will be there. Lay your hand on that covenant of peace which is made for us all in Christ the Lord.

"Herein is our love made perfect, that we may have boldness before Him in the day of judgment." And, if that kindness shall not depart from us, and God's gentle tenderness is eternal as Himself, then we shall not depart from it either, and we are immortal as the tenderness that encloses us. God's endless love must have undying creatures on whom to pour itself out. And if to-day I possess, as you all may possess, in however feeble a measure, some drops and prelibations of that great flood of love that is in God, I can look unblenched right into the eye of death, and say: Thou hast no power at all over me, and have none over this body of mine unless it is given thee from above. I am eternal because God that loves me is. And since He hath loved me with an everlasting love, and His loving kindness shall not depart from me, therefore, seeing that all these things shall be dissolved, I have a building, I know that I have a house, not made with hands, eternal in the heavens; and because He lives and loves I shall live also, leaving all mortality and lifted above decay and change. The hope that is built upon the eternal love of God in Christ is the true guarantee to me of immortal existence. And it turns upon the one thing—Come into the covenant, come into the covenant, the covenant of peace. God says: I will love thee, I will bless thee, I will cure thee, I will save thee, I will purge thee, I will glorify thee, and there is My bond on that cross, the new covenant of Christ's blood. Come. It takes two to make a covenant. God offers, do you close with the offer, and then life and death and things present and things to come and height and depth and every other creature shall be impotent to separate us from the love of God which is in Christ Jesus our Lord.

A. M.

CXIII. God's Thoughts and Man's Thoughts.

ISA. lv. 8. *"For My thoughts are not your thoughts, neither are your ways My ways, saith the Lord."*

"THOU thoughtest that I was altogether such an one as thyself." Thus, in one of the psalms, is God represented as speaking to the wicked; and His words expose the root of much of the misapprehension prevalent among men regarding Him. This tendency to humanize deity is everywhere apparent. Now for this characteristic of our nature two causes may be assigned. Man being originally created in God's image, has some lingering consciousness of that primal greatness which seeks to assert itself in his disposition to think of God as such an one as himself. The other cause lies in the imperfection of our language, which is primarily adapted to external things.

Let us consider the differences between God's ways and thoughts, and man's.

I. God's ways and thoughts are infinite, while men's are limited. In God we have the telescopic sweep that takes in the farthest outlying dependencies of space, combined with the microscopic exactness that brings out each minutest existence. His thoughts, instead of being confined within narrow limits, range through immensity. His knowledge, instead of being fragmentary, includes a perfect understanding of all things. Space and time hem us in so that we cannot see beyond here and now. This knowledge of God's Infinity should reconcile us to mysteries in revelation and in providence. Mystery is imperfect knowledge; and the more a man knows, he comes at more points into contact with the unknown.

II. God's ways and thoughts are holy; man's are polluted. There can be no happiness for man until he is in thorough harmony with God. Such a spiritual revolution can be wrought out in us only by the power of the Holy Ghost.

III. God's ways and thoughts are merciful; man's are suspicious and implacable. This ought to encourage us to return in penitence to God. God's assurances of mercy are fully to be trusted. He is above suspicion. Trust him even in this, to you, incomprehensible grace, and return to Him who, over the cross of His Son, has solemnly covenanted "to receive you graciously and to love you freely."

W. M. T.

CXIV. God's Word. Isa. lv. 10, 11. *"For as the rain cometh down, and the snow from heaven, and returneth not thither, but watereth the earth, and maketh it bring forth and bud: so shall My word be that goeth forth out of My mouth: it shall not return unto Me void."*

THE subject before us is the success and efficiency of the

Word of God. The comparison between the government of the world of nature and the world of grace is continually applied in the Bible. One of these comparisons is set forth in our text, "As the rain cometh down . . . so shall My word be." God sends His rain with a certain specific object; till that is accomplished it cannot return. It does its work primarily described as nourishing the grain which is to be the food of man. Equally certain is the object and result of His sending forth His Word.

I. Let us see how exactly the two members of this comparison correspond. In the natural world the rain and the snow do not fall in an equalled and measured manner, adjusting themselves to the different wants of the soil. The sandy soil still thirsts, when the deep loam is abundantly satisfied, or the rain, perhaps, expends itself on its parent ocean ere it can reach the crop thirsting for its moisture. This is the way in which the Almighty has dealt with this world as respects the rain and the snow. Will He deal differently with what He sends as the spiritual nourishment of our souls? We discover here, just as with the rain, abundant supplies of His word; vast multitudes perishing without it, there. In all this there is much perplexity. We cannot comprehend these ways of God in nature and in grace; but we can discern the sameness of the hand, and recognise the identity of the author. There is, after all, no waste in that rain which falls so capriciously. That which falls on the ocean but aids to preserve the balance of these vast reservoirs which from age to age water the earth. And may we not well imagine that there is no waste in the Word of God, that none of it is lost?

II. The responsibility which lies upon those to whom the Word of God comes. There should be the solemn reflection, this Word is meant to be the fertilizer of my soul. It is intended to be as the dew of heaven there, causing each grace to flourish, each pure and holy temper to grow. Blessed are those to whom the Word thus comes.

T. P. B.

CXV. The Future. Isa. lvi. 12. "*To-morrow shall be as this day, and much more abundant.*"

THESE words, as they stand, are the call of boon companions to new revelry. They are part of the prophet's picture of a corrupt age, when the men of influence and position had thrown away their sense of duty, and had given themselves over, as aristocracies and plutocracies are ever tempted to do, to mere luxury and good living. They are summoning one another to their coarse orgies. The roystering spender says, "Do not be afraid to drink: the cellar will hold out." He forgets to-morrow's headaches; he forgets that on some to-morrow the wine will be finished; he forgets that the fingers of a hand may write the doom of the rioters on the very walls of the banqueting chamber.

Like a great many other sayings, these words may fit the mouth either of a sot or of a saint. All depends on what the things are which we are thinking about when we use them. There are things about which it is absurd and worse than absurd to say this, and there are things about which it is the soberest truth to say it.

I. This expectation, if directed to any outward things, is an illusion and a dream. These coarse revellers, into whose lips the text is put, only meant by it to brave the future and defy to-morrow in the riot of their drunkenness. They show us the vulgarest, lowest form which the expectation can take. We may note this fact, that to look forward principally to anticipate pleasure or enjoyment is a very poor and unworthy thing. It is weakening and lowering every way, to use our faculty of hope mainly to paint the future as a scene of delights and satisfactions. It is base and foolish to be forecasting our pleasures, the true temper is to be forecasting our work. Let us notice how useless such anticipation, and how mad such confidence as that expressed in the text is, if directed to anything short of God.

We are so constituted, as that we grow into a persuasion that what has been, will be; and yet we can give no sufficient reason to ourselves of why we expect it. "The uniformity of the course of nature" is the corner-stone not only of physical science, but in a more homely form of the wisdom which grows with experience. We all believe that the sun will rise to-morrow because it rose to-day and for all the yesterdays. But there was a to-day which had no yesterday, and there will be a to-day which will have no to-morrow. The uniformity had a beginning and will have an end. So this axiom of thought seems to rest on an insufficient basis. How much more so, as to our own little lives and their surroundings! There the only thing which we may be quite sure of about to-morrow is, that it will not be "as this day." It may be said of each step of our journey, "Ye have not passed this way heretofore."

We know that these breathing-times when "we have no changes," are but pauses in the storm, landing-places in the ascent, the interspaces between the shocks. The least serious spirit, in its most joyous moods, never quite succeeds in forgetting the solemn probabilities, possibilities, and certainties that lodge in the unknown future. There is ever something of dread in Hope's blue eyes.

II. There is a possibility of so using the words as to make them the utterance of a sober certainty which will not be put to shame. When we turn our hope away from earth to God, and fill the future with the light of His presence and the certainty of His truth, the mists and doubts roll away, the future is as certain as the past, and hope as assured of its facts as memory.

(1) We have an unchanging and an inexhaustible God and He is the true guarantee of the future for us. To-day's wealth may be to-morrow's poverty, to-day's health to-morrow's sickness, to-day's happy companionship of love to morrow's aching solitude of heart; but to-day's God will be to-morrow's God, to-day's Christ will be to-morrow's Christ.

If only our hearts be fixed on God and we are feeding our minds and wills on Him, His truth, and His will, then we may be quite certain that whatever goes, our truest riches will abide.

(2) The past is the mirror of the future for the Christian: we look back on all the great deeds of old by which God has redeemed and helped souls that cried to Him, and we find in them the eternal laws of His working. They are all true for to-day as they were at first; they remain true for ever.

(3) Not only does the record of what He has been to

others come in to bring material for our forecast of the future, but also the remembrance of what He has been to ourselves. Has he been with us in six troubles? We may be sure He will not abandon us at the seventh. He is not in the way of beginning to build and leaving His work unfinished. Feed your certain hopes for to-morrow on thankful remembrances of many a yesterday.

III. These words may be taken as the vow of a firm and lowly resolve. There is a future which we can but very slightly influence, and the less we look at that the better every way. But there is also a future which we can mould as we wish—the future of our own characters, the only future which is really ours at all—and the more clearly we set it before ourselves and make up our minds as to whither we wish to be tending, the better.

In that region it is eminently true, that "to-morrow shall be as this day and much more abundant." The law of continuity shapes our moral and spiritual characters. What I am to-day I shall increasingly be to-morrow. The awful power of habit solidifies actions into customs and prolongs the reverberation of every note once sounded along the vaulted roof of the chamber where we live. To-day is the child of yesterday and the parent of to-morrow. That solemn certainty of the continuance and increase of moral and spiritual characteristics works in both good and bad, but with a difference. To secure its full blessing in the gradual development of the germs of good, there must be constant effort and tenacious resolution. If we trust to the natural laws of growth and neglect our careful tending, we may sow much but we shall gather little. But to inherit the full consequences of that same law working in the growth and development of the evil in us, nothing is needed but carelessness. But if humbly we resolve and earnestly toil, looking for His help, we may venture to hope that our characters will grow in goodness and in likeness to our dear Lord; that we shall not cast away our confidence nor make shipwreck of our faith; that each new day shall find in us a deeper love, a perfecter consecration, a more joyful service, and that so, in all the beauties of the Christian soul, and in all the blessings of the Christian life, "to-morrow shall be as this day, and much more abundant."

As we grow in fears we shall grow in grace, until the day comes when we shall exchange earth for heaven. That will be the sublimest application of the text when, dying, we can calmly be sure that heaven's to-morrow shall be as earth's to-day, and much more abundant.

A. M.

CXVI. The Dwelling-place of God. Isa. lvii. 15.

"*For thus saith the high and lofty One that inhabiteth eternity, whose name is holy: I dwell in the high and holy place, with him also that is of a contrite and humble spirit, to revive the spirit of the humble, and to revive the heart of the contrite ones.*"

THERE are two very different aspects under which God may be thought of or spoken of by us. Sometimes we think of Him as the mighty Maker of all the things we see, a supreme Being of immeasurable strength and intelligence. Sometimes, on the other hand, our hearts turn to Him as a most kind and pitiful Father, who will hear when He is spoken to, and who makes Himself the friend and helper of feeble and sinful men. The one is the intellectual result of man's speculations about God, the other is the God specially as self-revealed in the Gospel and apprehended by the human heart.

Now both of these views are true, and though it is difficult for the mind at present to harmonize them in one act of thought, yet each of them must exert its due influence upon us if we are to attain a just or adequate attitude of soul towards the Almighty Father in heaven. To separate these two views so as to give unequal prominence to either of them, is to fall into a serious practical mistake, and the history of religion is full of the blunders which have arisen simply from pressing either aspect of the Divine to the prejudice of the other.

At present we are suffering from our exclusive devotion, in many quarters, to the divinity of the schools. With such an idea of God as philosophy can frame, the world as it is will not come into intellectual harmony. The more difficult facts of human history, especially the fact of sin, cannot be got to square with the philosophical conception of God. There is an intellectual irreconcilableness betwixt an absolute God and absolute evil. If sin be absolutely evil, such that no conceivable balance of resultant good can be the least equivalent for it, then the philosophical thesis that whatever is, is best, becomes simply unthinkable. Hence the constant temptation under which philosophy lies to under-estimate sin—to do so for the sake of harmonising the world with its ideal divinity.

Christianity need be under no such temptation to minimise the evil of sin, because its conception of God is not exclusively the philosophical one. Neither is it bound to construct a theory of optimism. It is because something is which is not right, that the whole Christian scheme exists. Perverted human wills do love and elect to do that which is wrong, wholly and immeasurably wrong; and no results you can show to follow from sin, be they what they may, can make the sin one jot less evil.

It is characteristic of all revelation that in this text the self-manifestation of God within human hearts, His manifestation to us under His human aspects, is represented to be an act of self-humbling or of condescension. God has, so to speak, two temple palaces, two sacred abodes, which He deigns to fill with a special manifestation of Himself, making known in each a divine side of His marvellous being. The one is His celestial residence, the palace home beyond the firmament, "the high and holy place," the seat of Him who is the King of kings and Lord of Lords. The other is the sacred house of the hearts of the contrite. It is the veiled, familiar, human-like Father of our Lord Jesus, who alone can revive, by inhabiting them, the hearts of the contrite ones, else should the spirit fail before Him and the soul which He hath made. The conditions under which God alone makes Himself known to man are moral conditions, conditions of heart and spirit. In the choice language of this verse, what may be called the natural distance of God from us is measured both on its physical and on its moral side. He is "high"—as the Maker, Master, Owner, Orderer of men, Jehovah inhabits the "lofty place!"

But there is also the distance of holiness from evil. He is "holy," and betwixt the Holy One in His holy place and us in our sin, the gulf is not a gulf of being, but a gulf of character. There is not a word here to hint that the first creates the least difficulty in His stooping to deal with us. The real difficulty is the moral one. There is nothing save sin which can hinder God from dwelling with any man. Moral fellowship is practicable only on the ground of moral affinity; and the beginning of moral affinity of man with God lies in the moral state described, a contrite and humble spirit.

It is a very reviving advent when to such a soul God comes to dwell. God is attracted by the crushed humility of the sinner who cannot do without Him. This is the attraction that drew Him once from heaven. It is strong enough to draw Him, with the same fatherly compassion, into every broken heart; and when He comes to take up His resting-place within the spirit of the penitent, to turn that into His earthly temple. It is in His own wondrous lowliness that He comes. He comes as He came at Bethlehem, showing all the tenderness and the sweetness and the graciousness of His nature. Like comes to like. See how the lowly comes unto the lowly. Even so make us contrite, Lord; even so to us come near, Lord Jesus!

J. O. D.

CXVII. The Year of Jubilee. ISA. lxi. 1. "*The Spirit of the Lord God is upon me: because the Lord hath anointed me to preach good tidings unto the meek: He hath sent me to bind up the broken-hearted, to proclaim liberty to the captives, and the opening of the prison to them that are bound.*"

THE allusion in these words is to the Jewish year of Jubilee. The evangelical sense of the term is confirmed by the fact that when the Saviour preached in the synagogue this was His text, and He announced the fulfilment of the prophecy from the advent of the Gospel dispensation. There are many analogies between the year of Jubilee which rejoiced the hearts of Israel, and that more comprehensive era which was to bring gladness to all people.

I. The Jewish jubilee commenced at the close of the day of atonement. This is a true type of the way in which spiritual blessings are exclusively introduced to mankind. There could be no jubilee for us, a race of lost and guilty sinners, unless an all-prevalent atonement had previously purchased our pardon. Peace and hope and joy for renovated man can come in happy jubilee only from the atonement of Christ. Because of His death there is proclaimed in all the world the acceptable year of the Lord.

II. The jubilee brought rest from exhausting labour. In a spiritual sense, is not rest for the weary just what we want? The Saviour's most gracious invitation, addressed to a world of the heavy laden, contains within it a promise of rest.

III. The Jewish jubilee brought the restoration of alienated property. We alienated our inheritance by sin. God's favour was turned away, God's fellowship was interrupted, God's image was defaced. Christ has rescued this forfeited inheritance, and will not refuse to enrich any man who comes to Him.

IV. The Jewish jubilee brought freedom to the slave. Christ has come to bring liberty to the captives. From the strongest chains Christ can deliver. "If the Son make you free, ye shall be free indeed."

Are you going to listen to the voice of the Gospel trumpet? or are you shutting your ears?

W. M. P.

CXVIII. Our Father. ISA. lxiii. 16. "*Doubtless Thou art our Father, though Abraham be ignorant of us, and Israel acknowledge us not: Thou, O Lord, art our Father, our Redeemer: Thy name is from everlasting.*"

THESE words were spoken by the prophet of God, in the name of the people whose sins he confessed, whose sorrows he deplored, and whose salvation he longed for. The voice of the nation went forth in this one voice, and in him there was a nation; in a man, in one man, all Israel; for he was inspired to pray this prayer offered here, and it was used by those who had faith, when the captivity came. If these words could be used by Jews—if they could use them, how much more Christians can. They belong not to Jews as such. They are the language of faith, and faith is of no country, no particular language, climate, no time, no dispensation more than another.

I. The preface of this declaration—"Doubtless." We lose much of our strength by giving way to the scepticism which we find about us. I say before I utter anything about my Father in heaven, *doubtless*. I am not to be sure about the weather, or the wind, or my life, or my health, or even about things which men take as types and proverbs of certainty; but I am sure of one thing, that God is my father. This is not the language of mere hope, but of fervent conviction. Some things are open to question, but this is not. Some things are matters of logic, which we may doubt, but this is a matter of revelation.

II. "Our Father." This brings the conclusion that God is a living person. There are different kinds of atheism about us. There is the atheism of carelessness. There are thousands and thousands of so-called Christians who are in reality atheists. There is an atheism abroad tinctured with devotion. Some of our writers are trying to divorce religion from God, and in some cases they actually believe in prayer. We say, "Our Father"; and the first doctrine is this, that God is a person, for you never say "Father" to a mist, or a number, or a thing. Sure as the Son is a person, the Father is also a person.

These words, "Our Father," are words that may be applied to God as the Father of human kind. All human life began in God: we are His offspring. When God's sons and daughters go wrong, does He care less than you do when your children go astray?

Again, we have found that He is our Father through Jesus Christ. In the third chapter of John, Jesus gives His first discourse about salvation, and tells us that we must be born again. Through Jesus we have new life—born in the first moment of true faith in Him. So being filled with faith and love, we can say, "Our Father," and with unwavering tongue. If we refuse this gift of Christ, not all the love of God can change us.

The Father never changes. The sun does not always rise with equal clearness, the dews do not always glisten, the river does not always gleam in splendour, but He is the Lord, He changes not.

III. The suggestion used to enforce the declaration: "Though Abraham be ignorant of us, and Israel acknowledge us not, Thou, O Lord, art our Father." The essence of this is, "Thou art our Father," though our earthly parents be ignorant of us and acknowledge us not. For instance, in consequence of death. The speakers were proud of having Abraham for their father; but he had long been dead. The time may come when our earthly parents may be ignorant of us by death. Though such changes come, though hearts grow still and eyes dim of those who love us best, we can say, "Doubtless, Thou art our Father."

Sometimes, through infirmity or age, our parents may acknowledge us not. There was a time when David had keen eyes, that if a child had cried in the wilderness to him he could have saved that child; but forty years after, when the life had gone out of the eyes, and the lissomeness out of the limbs, he could not. But we can turn our eyes heavenwards, and say, "Doubtless, Thou art our Father; Thy years shall not fail."

Earthly parents may not be able to acknowledge us by circumstances of distance. For instance, Joseph might cry, "Father," in the pit in vain. Once in the American war there was a general galloping at the head of his soldiers, and he had to pass his only son dying by the roadside; he could not help him. But whatever the helplessness of our dearest friends, God can help us.

Sometimes our earthly fathers cannot help us because they are reduced in circumstances. I have heard of a son coming back to the place where he was brought up, and finding the dear old garden trampled down by careless feet, and rough men handling furniture which was being sold. But all things are ours because God is ours.

We must turn this to practical account by praying. I want you to say, "Doubtless," and to pray. This is the first use we must make of the fact that God is our Father.

A Mussulman when travelling was joined by a Hindoo, and the two marched on together till darkness overtook them. Passing the night together, they resumed the journey in the morning and travelled all day, and again sought shelter for the night. The Hindoo, as was his custom, said his prayers and rested, and in the morning rose again and prayed once more and prepared to start. But he had not seen the Mussulman pray, and he wondered greatly. He watched for the third night to see if his companion would pray, but he neither saw nor heard anything of the

Mussulman's prayers. And at last he said, "Mussulman, do you not pray?" His companion replied, "Yes; it is binding on us to pray five times in the day." "Well," said the Hindoo, "what sort of a Mussulman are you? I have not seen you pray for three days." "I am marching all day," said the Mussulman, "and when we stop I am so tired that I cannot pray." Then the Hindoo said, "Are you too tired to travel? are you too tired to take food? are you too tired to speak to me? are you too tired to live?"

You understand and feel the point of this, you have *such* a Father. If at times you are tired—and you will be if you are to be of any good in the world—cast yourself on God through Christ, and through the depths of your heart pray to your Father, who is the Way, the Truth, and the Life.

C. S.

CXIX. The Way to Zion. JER. i. 5. "*They shall ask the way to Zion with their faces thitherward.*"

THE Israelites are seen by the eyes of God's prophet returning from a seventy years' exile, casting off their chains, and seriously asking their way home to Zion with their faces set thitherward. They are described in the context as "going and weeping." God has poured upon them "the spirit of grace and supplication," and its first effect is that "they look upon Him whom they have pierced, and mourn." The text suggests another thought, "They have been as lost sheep." The next verse says, "They have gone from mountain to hill, they have forgotten their resting-place." Once they lived there: it was their home; now for their sin they are banished, they have to ask the way to Zion.

Those who would make their future different from the past must cultivate two things.

I. The spirit of inquiry. Like these Israelites, we have been going "from mountain to hill," till we have forgotten our resting-place. There is but one resting-place for the creature—the love of God revealed in Jesus, apprehended by the soul, fled to, trusted to. There is always something beautiful in the spirit of inquiry, but of all inquiries the way to Zion is first. We all believe in a hereafter, in a heaven; the way to it is our question. The desire of every earnest soul must be to endeavour to anticipate the heavenly life—to live now in the life of God, to see Him now by faith, to follow Him now whithersoever, by His prophets, by His Word, by His Spirit, by the example of Christ, He leads. This is the way to Zion.

II. A spirit of determination. They who "ask the way to Zion," must have their faces thitherward. There is an inquiry about the way which is all speculation. There may even be a questioning about the way to Zion, with the back turned upon it. This is the case of inquirers who will keep some idol in their heart. This is the case of those who are only talking and not doing. Let each inquiry be a determination. Oh to think of asking the way, and then not taking it. The way to Zion is not intricate to the honest seeker. It lies very straight, though seldom smooth, before him who will enter by the Door.

C. J. V.

CXX. Battlements. JER. V. 10. "*Go ye up upon her walls, and destroy; but make not a full end: take away her battlements; for they are not the Lord's.*"

WE are impressed with the enormous impieties of Sodom, because that if there had been ten righteous found within, it would have been saved from the sulphur and the flame. But how deeply then must Jerusalem have transgressed, when the pardon was suspended not upon ten, but upon one. "If I can find but one man, if there be any that executeth judgment, that seeketh the truth; and I will pardon it." No wonder that a circumstance like this—this terrible depravity of the Jewish nation—should be to the patriot heart of the prophet an occasion of deepest sorrow.

I. There is implied in the words of the text the consciousness of danger. Battlements are erected for defence. In the spiritual condition of the world you will find indications of distrust and danger. Men agitated by the enigmas of existence, conscience apprehensive of horrors of whose existence it can hardly conceive, hearts failing them for fear, because of the destinies that are future and unknown. From this consciousness of danger you must find a refuge. Every one of us has got some tower, some battlements of real or fancied security in which we trust.

II. What are your battlements of defence? Are they your own or the Lord's? If they are your own battlements, then they are no sure defence in the hour of the battle and storm.

(1) Some make a battlement of denying the active government of God. He is no active governor now; He has retired into His pavilion, and if He knows the world at all He only knows it in some crisis of its history. There is no safety in this battlement. Come out of it.

(2) Some rest in mistaken notions of the Fatherhood of God. Some of man's worst disasters and errors have been born out of the sources of his richest hopes. To those who have a right to appropriate the Fatherhood of God there is nothing so delightful; but remember that God is only a Father to those who are in Christ.

(3) Some rest on mistaken notions of their own character and excellency.

III. The unassailable and perfect defence of those who trust in Jesus. As the mountains are round about Jerusalem, so the Lord is round about His people.

W. M. P.

CXXI. Balm in Gilead. JER. viii. 22. "*Is there no balm in Gilead; is there no physician there? Why then is not the health of the daughter of my people recovered.*"

THE prophecy of Jeremiah has been termed one long lamentation. His heart mourned over the results of the Chaldean invasion; but he had a deeper grief than even the national prostration and dishonour of his fatherland. The people had relapsed into idolatry. False prophets, who delivered lying messages and prophesied smooth things, abounded on every hand, and Jeremiah seemed to stand in single-handed witness to testify for the Lord of Hosts. "For the hurt of the daughter of my people I am hurt; I am black; astonishment hath taken hold on me. Is there no balm in Gilead?"

Let us apply these plaintive and solicitous words to ourselves.

I. The fact of disease. The spiritual malady under which all mankind are groaning, is represented in the Bible as making the whole head sick and the whole heart faint. The question of spiritual health, or sickness, becomes a question of immense importance, viewed in connection with the eternal duration of man's being. This malady was born with you, it has grown with your growth, and if you have not personally realized the transformation of the gospel, the leprosy hangs about you still. The cradled death is in your veins, and you are not shut up as other lepers are, just because everybody is a leper around you.

II. Seeing the disease, the question comes now to be asked, "Why is not the health of the daughter of my people recovered?" It is not because there is no cure. There is balm in Gilead; there is a dexterous and infallible physician there. If there be an infallible specific and a skilful physician, and if still the people die, the fault must be in themselves.

(1) There are many amongst us who will not admit themselves ill.

(2) There are men who will acknowledge themselves guilty and diseased but seek elsewhere for the remedy. In the cure of the soul's ailment there is but one balm and one Physician.

(3) There is another class who feel their danger, who come to the remedy, but who do not obey the prescriptions which the Physician has given. They are not far from the Kingdom of God, but nevertheless they are not in it.

The invitation is free to all—without money and without price. Come to the Physician that you may live.

W. M. P.

CXXII. The Swelling of Jordan. Jer. xii. 5.

"How wilt thou do in the swelling of Jordan?"

THE lesson to be enforced here is the fact that without Christianity, great spaces of our life are wholly unprovided for.

In laying down this proposition we are sustained by the observation and experience of common life. I promise you that if you build your house you will have for three hundred and sixty days in the year the gentlest wind, cloudless skies, soft rains. But the other five days of the year will present a very striking contrast to these halcyon days. They will be full of tempest, and the great thunderclouds will shut out the sun. Having thus forecast the year, for which portion of it will you build the house? For the five tempestuous days? You are right. But do not be a philosopher in logic and a fool in religion; be honest, self-consistent, face the consequences of your own premises.

The Gospel comes and says, "I only"—voice of God, word of Heaven—"I only can wrap myself round the whole compass of your life, touch every point of necessity, and take care of you in mortal crises, in final distresses. Surely a Gospel coming with such a message has the upper hand of the strongest reasoner, and only requires the moral consent of the most obdurate antagonist.

Look for a moment at the kind of life that is to be provided for. Life is but a vapour that appeareth for a little time and then vanisheth away. Put into it what sunshine you may, you do but add the possibility at least of proportionate shadow. Beautiful is the garden, and quiet the nest in which your life keeps itself warm, but the last wind kills the blossoms, and the tempest breaks the very branch on which your nest was built. Then you need a religion that stretches its blessed ministry around the whole compass of this existence, leaving no part without provision, descending upon youth like morning dew, accompanying middle life like a strong guardian, and comforting old age like a prophet.

There will come a day when learning will say, "Here we must part; I dare not go into the morrow that is coming upon your life. This poor little candlelight of mine would be blown out." There comes a time in life when pleasure says to you, "This is the last cup; drain it and let me go."

Let us now make one or two practical inquiries. What will you do in the day of uncontrollable trouble? What provision have you made for its coming? Into these regions nothing but the religion of Jesus can accompany you. What is true of great sorrows is equally true of great joys. If not balanced, and even chastened, joy will overdrive and overtax the soul, and turn itself into delirium. If your joy is to be continued and to be healthy, it must be connected with infinite lines. It is in Christ we find joy unspeakable; it is at God's right hand there are pleasures for evermore; it is in the sanctuary that light is added to light, until the glory becomes intense; it is in the holy place that the vision is strengthened to bear the ever-augmenting light. The joys will slay thee if they be not joys from Christ.

Christ meets the whole life; Christ goes everywhere; Christ walks upon the waters; Christ goes into the desert; Christ brings the last loaf and makes it a feast; Christ turns the water into wine. Now, " How will you do in the swelling of Jordan ! "

J. P.

CXXIII. A Divine Appeal. JER. xliv. 4. "*Oh, do not this abominable thing that I hate.*"

THE purport of the whole word of God may be compressed into this fervent appeal. Was there ever a more touching expostulation than this? Jehovah here appeals to men with all the infinite love of the Divine nature, and begs them not to do that which He detests.

With love, for though the term hate is used, observe that it does not describe hatred of the persons, but of the evil which they mean to commit. How wonderful this condescension and this love!

The text contains a statement and an appeal:

I. The statement that sin is that abominable thing which God hates. The language is very strong, and might, at first sight, appear inconsistent with the declaration that God is love. But a moment's reflection convinces us that the love of one thing is the hatred of its opposite; and when it is declared that God loves righteousness, that is only another way of asserting that he hates iniquity. He is love to all holiness, but just because He is so, He is all hatred to sin. Let us notice some of the grounds on which God's hatred of sin rests.

(1) Because it is a contempt of His authority and a defiance of His law.

If the sinner had his will there would be no God. That is the unuttered wish of his heart and that is the tendency of his conduct.

(2) Because it runs contrary to His whole nature. God is the impersonation of the law, and therefore disobedience to it is not a mere legal offence against an abstract statute, but it is personal animosity and antipathy to Himself.

(3) God hates sin, because of the consequences which follow in its train. It has come in to mar the happiness and derange the order of the moral universe; and to a Being whose name and whose nature is love, that which has been the cause of such misery to the human race must be the object of intensest loathing. It has blighted men's hearts, and blasted their lives, and seared their consciences, and contrasting them, sinful as they are, with what, sinless, they might have been, we cannot wonder that God should call iniquity "that abominable thing that I hate."

II. The appeal contained in the text, "Oh, do not this abominable thing."

It is not only by words that God seeks to dissuade us from following after sin. The expostulation of my text is made by all the mercies which we enjoy.

The same plea in another form is repeated by the voice of conscience within us. And that inward call is re-echoed and repeated by God's servants, as they come with His message to our souls.

God has made a yet more powerful, because a more direct appeal than any of these. Come to Calvary, that you may hear it plainly. Jesus did no sin, but all the griefs He felt were for our iniquities. Hear, again, how creation repeats at Calvary the same earnest cry, "Oh, do not this abominable thing." The sun is robed in darkness. The earth is heaving as with the swell of the ocean. The dead, as if awaked by some awful surprise, look out of their graves, all to cry out, "Why will men do that abominable thing which God hates?"

But God makes this appeal by the revelation of the future as well as through the cross of His Son. He takes us to the brink of the place of woe and gives us a glimpse only of its agony, that we may shudder and keep back. He says, "Be not deceived, God is not mocked; whatsoever a man soweth that shall he also reap." Why then will men recklessly rush on to this doom? God says, "Why will ye die?" You may escape it if you will, for you may be saved not only from the power, but also from the penalty of sin, through Jesus Christ.

Sinner, let this solemn appeal be heard by you, " Oh, do not this abominable thing that I hate."

W. M. T.

CXXIV.— A Vision of Ezekiel. EZEK. i. 4. *"And I looked, and, behold, a whirlwind came out of the north, a great cloud, and a fire."*

THE history of the Jews was a succession of startling paradoxes. Their most signal defeats were very often their most splendid triumphs, and in three several crises in their career—in youth, in middle life, and in old age—when they came into contact with Egypt, Babylon, and Rome, each time when they were almost annihilated, they started into new and more vigorous life. Their unmaking was their making anew. As a paradox the Babylonian captivity was the most striking of all. In their helpless, hopeless misery, and in the very abyss of their despair, above the howling of the storm the pæan of victory rises till the whole air is filled with the sound. No prophet is more confident of the future than the exile on the banks of Chebar. It is not that he sees only the bright prospects. No words can be more severe than those in which he denounces the sins of his countrymen. And yet as the prophet's eye ranges beyond the present, what does he see? He looks out on the desert: it is a scene of catastrophe, the ground is covered with bones, tossed hither and thither by the fury of the elements, or the hand of man. Is it possible that these bones shall live and move again? God only can say. But a moment more and the answer comes—there is a clattering of bones and they come together, bone to his bone, and the flesh and sinews cover them, and they start to their feet an exceeding great army. Then after the revival of Israel comes the opportunity to this army; the battle is still unfought, the victory has still to be won.

So the prophet is carried again by the Spirit, and he sees everything on a grander scale. His eye is arrested by a simple spring of water—fit symbol this of the Church of God. As he watches it, it rises and swells silently, it streams onward until it washes Moab and sweetens even the waters of the Dead Sea. A stream so puny and obscure in its source, so bright and beautiful in its issues, this mighty river of God.

So it has always been. God's chief revelations have ever flashed out in seasons of trial and perplexity. As in Ezekiel's days, there has been first the whirlwind, then the flame, and the light glowing amidst the blackness of the cloud. There is first the wild impetuous force rooting up all old institutions, scattering all old ideas, sweeping all things human and Divine into its abyss. Then the dark cloud of despair settles down upon them until the chariot of God emerges, blinding their eyes with its dazzling splendour, and after this the vision of a larger and purer worship. It was so at the epoch of the Babylonian captivity, at the downfall of the Roman empire, at the Reformation, and shall it not be so once again?

We are warned by the experience of the past not to overrate either the perplexities or the hopes of the present. Nearness of view unduly magnifies the proportions of events.

Yet it is surely true that the Church of our day is passing through one of those momentous crises which only occur at intervals of two or three centuries. It is the simultaneous occurrence of so many and various disturbing elements which form the characteristic feature of our age. Here is the vast accumulation of scientific facts, the rapid progress of scientific ideas; there is the enlarged knowledge of ancient and wide-spread religions, arising from the increased facilities of travel. Here is the sharpening of the critical faculty to a keenness of edge unattained in any previous age. There is the accumulation of new materials for its exercise from divers sources. These are some of the intellectual factors with which the Church in this age has to reckon.

And the social and political forces are not less disturbing. What must be our attitude as members of Christ's Church at such a season? The experience of the past will inspire hope for the future. "In quietness and confidence shall be your strength." As disciples of the Word Incarnate, the same eternal Word who is and has been from the beginning, in science as in history, in nature as in revelation, we shall rest assured that He has yet much to teach us; that a larger display of His manifold operations, however confusing now, must in the end carry with it a clearer knowledge of Himself. There is the whirlwind, there is the gathering cloud, but even now the keen eye of the faithful watcher detects a glimpse of blue in the sky.

The very essence of the revelation of the vision of the living creatures was that the Jews were taught to look for a new covenant, for a spiritual restoration. Three ideas are clearly connected with each other—mobility, spirituality and universality. The idea of mobility is the first, and it is significant in its contrast. The vision of Ezekiel is not a dead and dying story, it lives still as the very charter of the Church of the future. Any work for Christ's Church which shall be real, solid, abiding, must follow on the lines here marked out for us—mobility, spirituality, universality; these three ideas must inspire our efforts, not to cling obstinately to the decayed anachronisms of the past, not to narrow our intellectual horizon, not to stunt our moral sympathies, but to absorb new truths, to gather new ideas, to adapt, to enlarge, to follow always the teaching of the Spirit—the Spirit which, like the breath of the wind, will not be bound and imprisoned—the Spirit which in its very name speaks of elasticity and expansion, passing through every crevice, filling every interstice, conforming itself to every size and shape. This is our duty as Christians; remembering meanwhile that there is the fixed centre from which our thoughts must spread and to which all our hopes must converge—Jesus Christ, the same yesterday, to-day, and for ever.

J. B. L.

CXXV. God's Message and Man's Unbelief.

EZEK. xx. 49. *"Then said I, Ah Lord God! they say of me, Doth he not speak parables?"*

THERE is a tone of remonstrance and expostulation in these words of the prophet. He is conscious that because of something in the nature of his message that message will be unpopular with his hearers. Something mystic and dimly intelligible he had to tell the Jews, and they were irritated at the mysterious warnings. Why do you thus speak in parables? Let us have none of these mysteries, but plain speech. The request was a natural one, and the prophet was tempted to yield to it if possible. In this entreaty is implied a petition that he might be allowed to explain his parable. The desire was distinctly simple on both parts, though natural, for these words were God's verbal revelation, and were not the prophet's own to alter as he pleased.

I. Unbelief lay at the root of this request of the Jews, and also at the root of the prophet's willingness to yield to it. To say there is a God, and then to doubt whether that God is perfectly true and wise, is unbelief in its subtlest form. In reality the prophet was doubting whether the form in which God had cast His own message was the most perfect one, and forgetting that he was but the mouth-piece of His word, and that he might leave the results of His message to Him who gave it.

II. The sin of Israel and the temptation of Ezekiel exist now as truly as they did then. They are to be found wherever the Church of Christ, in discharging her great prophetic office for her Master, confronts an unbelieving world. She has words to speak that are full of mystery, words that sound like parables in the ears of those who listen to them. The mystery of the Incarnation, and the Resurrection, and Atonement, and Ascension, and the Holy Spirit's descent. In vain does the teacher seek to conjure the spirit of unbelief by attenuating the message which he has come to speak. The Church must be sternly faithful to her mission, and speak whatever parable or dogma God has given her.

III. Let the Christian Church beware of speaking her parables in addition to God's parables. W. C. M.

CXXVI. Why will ye die? EZEK. xxxiii. 11. *"As I live, saith the Lord God, I have no pleasure in the death of the wicked; but that the wicked turn from his way and live: turn ye, turn ye from your evil ways; for why will ye die?"*

THE love of sin is a species of infatuation. To make a wrong choice once is certainly possible for any soul, for did not Adam fall; but to persist in the wrong way after it has been proved wrong shows some obliquity in the moral nature. It is against reason. It is against self-interest even, when properly understood. It is as much a folly as a fault: for to go on in the way of sin is to go on in the way of death. It means this: that you choose a trifling and momentary gratification at the cost of endless pain. No man could make such a choice with his eyes perfectly open. Persistent sin can come only through shutting the eyes: it is like a spell or a charm, under the power of which a man does things which he knows to be foolish, as though he cannot help it. We may drink poison, but we must forget that it is poison before we can taste it.

It follows that every one who goes on wilfully in sin has to deceive himself, and a similar fraud has to be repeated as often as a man sins. Every man who sins, is led to believe a lie. It is in the face of their better self; and therefore to say the end of it is not hell, cannot excuse the guilt of their choice.

Now against this self-delusion or infatuation of the ungodly, God in His kindness is for ever fighting in a variety of ways. He fights by threats of penalty; He fights by the fate of other sinners whom punishment overtakes; He fights by men's own experiences; He fights, as in this text, by reason and expostulation; and this last, as a means for creating such a state of mind in men who rush blindfold on their fate, is often very effectual for making it clear to such men that they are in a desperate strait. The sinner is like a man rushing down hill. What can you do for him but shout to him to stop? It is all you can do—to reason and warn and appeal to his cooler sense. So precisely does the Almighty Friend of us men plead from His heavenly throne, and cry "Turn ye, turn ye from your evil ways; for why will ye die?"

I. On opening up the thoughts which underlie the reasoning and appeal of this phrase, I find to be implied that *death* is the inevitable end of a sinful life by a law as fixed as fate, a law which cannot be set aside. The evil of the commonwealth of the house of Israel entailed on it death, such a death as a commonwealth can die—bondage and oppression and dispersion. For an individual to persevere in ungodly ways means for him also death—such death as an immortal being can die. The one follows on the other in either case; death on persistent sinning. This is the first fact to which the attention of every unconverted man needs to be directed, I mean the inviolability of moral law In the one case just as in the other, if the *effect* is to be avoided the *cause* must be removed. Now this is not the way in which some people look on the matter. Some people imagine and say, that because God is merciful, He can save them at the last from the consequences of their ungodly ways. This is to say they do not turn from the way that leads to death ; they will not do that ; they deliberately go on in the way of sin as long as they have strength or time, yet they expect God to break on their behalf the law which dooms the sinner to suffer, and to make them happy after death, who did only evil in life. So they cast on God the responsibility of their saving or damnation. Is not this believing a lie ? In the first place, is it not your clear business so to live now as to ensure eternal life hereafter ? You must not neglect this, and then throw the consequences of your neglect on your Maker. Again, suppose God could cancel His own law to save you from the result of persistent sinning, is it at all clear that it would be *right* for Him to do so ? Would it be fair to make no difference in the end between those who listen and repent and obey and lead holy lives, and those who neither repent nor obey nor lead holy lives ?

But the simple fact is that not even the Almighty can do this; for, observe, it is no case of arbitrary penalty, of a mere punishment inflicted through the resentment of the eternal Law-giver, which, if He chooses to be merciful, He can remit. No ; the punishments of God are natural sequels, effects which follow of themselves when the cause is there. Given therefore the impenitent, sinful man, moral death follows. It follows the cause. There is no way to remove the effect, which is eternal death. Remove the cause. In physics if you move along any given line no power can stop you from reaching the point it leads to. So in sin ; if you continue in sin, you must reach the end, death.

II. Now, in the next place, what is involved here is that the responsibility for your final doom lies upon yourself, and not on God. To go forward as you are doing, means as we have seen, for you to perish. If you are not to perish, it must be by some change. Either you must turn your course, or the Almighty must turn His course. That He will not do, perhaps cannot do, certainly *will not* do. The change must be in you; " Turn *ye*, turn *ye* from your evil ways ; for why will ye die ? "

There is something awful in the solemnity with which God protests that the blame must lie with you. He does more than protest, He swears. Do you imagine it can give the Eternal Father, the ever-blessed and most merciful, any satisfaction to behold you rushing after death? Is He likely to put any stone, if it were but a pebble, in the way of your return to goodness, He who spared not His own Son to save you ? Dare you allege this is a hard law, because He does not violate for you the sequence of the moral constitution of the universe. With what eyes but are full of pity can the great Father of us all witness the insanity of His sons, who for a little pleasure fling away for ever their everlasting inheritance ? No; it is impossible God can take any pleasure in your dying. It lies with yourself to turn, O foolish, godless brother! Turn from your godless path, and the death to which it is taking you ; and if you turn, you will make God glad, and if you turn not, you will make God sad. You have before your soul to-day life or death. Which will you have ? But know this fully—I am now speaking to the unconverted—that to go forward as you are in irreligion and impenitence means nothing less than a moral suicide. Dare you undo your soul for ever ? Think of what you are casting away. Come to God ; say to yourself plainly, what it is you are dying for. Can you answer this question ? Why is it you are resolved to die ?

It is a question you dare not answer. But to tell the truth, the reasons for which sinners refuse to turn will not bear looking at. When a person's mind is set on an evil road, I cannot think he admits to himself what he is doing. Great are men's powers of self-deception. If the man will not admit to himself what he is doing, still less would he admit it to others.

There must be many of you who give far less attention to religion than you ought to; who seldom or never pray, who are covetous or vain, and live only for the passing day; and you know you are in a bad way. But if you were to be interrogated to-night, you would be at a loss to answer. You might say as hundreds do, "We have no time to attend to religion, for we are hard-working people, and it takes all our time to provide for our families, and to make ends meet." That is no answer at all. As if religion hindered work! As if the godly person could not attend to his business! The thing is too preposterous; your reasoning is not reasoning at all, it is the thinnest pretence. What religion does hinder is a dishonest trick for making money; what religion does discourage is anxiety about ends meeting which eats up the whole soul. But careful husbanding and honest labour and providing for one's family; it does not discourage this, it rather helps it on.

In what class of society do you find genuine Christians? among the squalid and beggarly, or among the hard-working and careful and well off? Is not the reasoning I have mentioned above a manifest falsehood?

Again, some people say there is no good in being religious because so many religious people are hypocrites, or because there are so many different beliefs, and they do not know which to believe. Is there any difference of opinion about the advantage of a good life over a bad one? Does any one really believe that he will be excused from the love of God because Christians go to different churches? Because many people say their prayers in a different way is it allowable for me to say no prayers at all? The truth is, all such talk is the flimsiest attempt on the part of ungodly persons to veil from themselves and from others the honest fact that they dislike religion and like their evil ways too well to abandon them. You may make what excuses you please, but depend upon it, this is at bottom the real reason. It is a sorry profession to make, that the irreligious life is more to our taste, that you prefer to run the risk of eternal death than to have pardon. And yet I can find no other reason for impenitent hearers of the gospel.

Why do not you turn? Try to be honest for once. It is not really for your making any gain that you sin; a few shillings would make up what you gain by sinning. Is it worth throwing your soul away? Is it the pleasure of drinking, swearing, or lewdness—a little of this tires us.

S

The game is not worth the candle. Why, then, is it? The real reason why we go on is this I suspect—we have such a distaste to religion, find it so dull, we cannot make up our minds to take up with it. Rather than that, we put it off from year to year, and in the meantime go on sinning. Is it not a fact that some of you think of religion and piety as a noisome drug, which might save our life at some time, but which you leave alone as long as you can? To keep God's day, to walk as the saints did—these things would be such a restraint upon you, and are so disagreeable, that you put religion on one side, and are growing grey very fast in the path of the destroyer.

Ask yourselves whether such conduct be wise. First of all, there is no denying that you are going on at a frightful risk, because to feel in that way about God and His service is to be religiously dead; and to go on in that condition without changing, is to be for ever unfit for His Heavenly presence, or the place where His disciples dwell. Anybody who does not like to praise Him, and to serve Him, and to fear Him, and do His bidding, cannot, it is plain, have the slightest chance of ever getting into heaven. As you are, eternal death stares you in the face.

In the next place, you are not getting a great deal for the terrific risk you are running. You are not even gaining present happiness, because you cannot have an easy life. You come to the church, you know the truth, you read the Bible, you feel the change must come one day, and you are in alarm lest you put it off too long. By shirking the disagreeable duty of repentance and a religious life, what are you gaining? Not happiness; at best a little respite from what you call restraint. But *is* religion so disagreeable that to put it off is worth all this? What if after risking your life you turn, repent, obey, be truly devout and follow God, and find it is not the irksome, dull, unpleasant weariness which you were silly enough to take it for? It is so to you now, I grant, before you turn. Of course it is, because your taste does not lie that way. You have long preferred ungodliness to God; but to turn, which God bids you do, means to acquire a new taste. Conversion, what does that mean? It means falling in love with piety, with Jesus Christ, and with God. Now to fall in love with anything transmutes its character in our eyes.

Once you are turned, therefore, all will be changed; the scales will drop from your eyes; you will be in a new world; and it will not be formidable, but gracious. It will not be irksome to us. Religion will not be your aversion, but will be your joy. "A new heart I will give you," says God. What a surprising change will come over us! The religion which appears to us now so dull, will be to your new-opened eyes and new-ravished heart the only true way.

What if this be so, and surely God would not call you unless it were so! Then what a fool you must be, and what a prodigious mistake you must be making! To what a blunder are you sacrificing your life! Oh, sirs, to turn to God with desire and love is to be for ever happy. But you will not do it, fearing it will make you wretched. Fatal blunder—oh, moral suicide for a blunder. Is it surprising, I ask you, that heaven looks on amazed, and Jesus weeps for pity, and God Himself, loving us like a father, pursues us with pitiable cries for us to stop, while we go on the fatal road? If men only would be wise and consider their latter end! If only they would pause and recollect whither the road is leading them, and what they are gaining by it. To *think* to them might be the first step of turning, and turning is the first step to light and blessedness. "Turn ye, turn ye from your evil ways; for why will ye die?"

J. O. D.

CXXVII. The Formalist and the Christian. EZEK. xxxiii. 30-33. *"Also, thou son of man, the children of thy people still are talking against thee by the walls and in the doors of the houses, and speak one to another, every one to his brother, saying, Come, I pray you, and hear what is the word that cometh forth from the Lord.*

"GOD hath made of one blood all nations of men for to dwell upon the face of the whole earth" so saith the Scripture. Though cavillers have tried their uttermost they have failed to shake the testimony. Such cavillers have a favourite theory that there were many distinct aboriginal races of men. We may argue successfully against this theory from the sad uniformity of evil, and from the reproduction in every age of the same types of character. Because of the strong family likeness which one age transmits to another, Scripture portraits sketched in the almost forgotten past may hang in our galleries to-day and may pass for very pictures of the living. Who can mistake the delineation of the character presented to us in the text? It is the description of the formalist.

Let us look at the points of resemblance and the points of difference between the Formalist and the Christian.

I. There is a resemblance to the spirit of hearing and in the respect which is felt for the temper and the minister of it? "Come, I pray you, and hear what is the word that cometh forth from the Lord."

II. There is a resemblance in their attachment to the ordinances of religion. "And they come unto thee as the people cometh."

III. There is a resemblance in their feelings being touched under the minister's discourse. "And, lo, thou art unto them as a very lovely song of one that hath a pleasant voice."

Thus far the resemblance between those who are only externally the Lord's and those who have felt Him in the heart and in the life. The difference is that in the formalist the heart is not right in the sight of God. The main hindrance is the over-weening preference for the present, the bondage of the soul to dense and external things. "They hear thy words but they will not do them." Why? "Their heart goeth after their covetousness."

Religion is a thing of the heart, it is not a mere timorous morality; it is not a faultless observance of devotion, it is a warm life welling up from a renewed heart: it is a new affection expelling or controlling the old. The formalist, if he remains such, shall remember too late the faithful minister's warning, "Then shall they know that a prophet hath been among them."

W. M. P.

CXXVIII. The Valley of Dry Bones. EZEK. xxxvii.

3. *"And he said unto me, Son of man, can these bones live? And I answered, O Lord God, Thou knowest."*

LIKE many other visions before and since, this vision of the valley of dry bones was partly shaped by the circumstances of the time. The horrors of the Chaldean invasion were still fresh in the memory, and in many a valley the army's track would have been marked by the bones of the slaughtered peasantry. What are we to understand by the dry bones of the vision of Ezekiel?

This is plainly the picture of a resurrection—not indeed of the general resurrection, because what Ezekiel saw was limited and local, but at the same time it is a sample of what will occur at the general resurrection.

I. These dry bones of Ezekiel's vision may well represent the lifeless condition of societies of men at particular times in their history, of nations, of churches, of less important institutions. The Jewish nation believes itself to be pictured in the vision as the dry bones. In the captivity little was left to Israel beyond a skeleton of its former self. At the restoration of the Jews from Babylon the promises in the vision were fulfilled. The Divine breath came upon the bones, and they lived. The remains of the past of Israel,—its sacred books, its priests, its prophets, its laws. These once more moved in the soul of the nation. We read of the completion of this restoration in the Books of Ezra and Nehemiah.

II. The dry bones of Ezekiel's vision may be discovered, and that not seldom, within the human soul. When a soul has lost its hold on truth or grace, all the traces of what it once has been do not forthwith disappear. There are survivals of the old believing life, fragments of the skeleton of the old convictions, phrases which expressed the feeling which once winged a prayer. These may remain on in the arid desolation, a very valley full of dry bones. Let these dry bones be respected. On them the breath of God may light. Habit which is only habit is not life, but it is better than nothing at all. A man may have ceased to mean his prayers, but let him not break with the little that remains of what once was life. The quickening power of Christ's resurrection may assert itself victoriously in that desert soul, so that like as Christ was raised from the dead in the glory of the Father, even so this soul should walk in newness of life.

H. P. L.

CXXIX. Authority. DANIEL xii. 9. "*And he said, Go thy way, Daniel: for the words are closed up and sealed till the time of the end. Many shall be purified, and made white, and tried; but the wicked shall do wickedly: and none of the wicked shall understand, but the wise shall understand.*"

IT is the manner of the Holy Spirit in sacred prophecy to pass rapidly from one future event to another foreshadowed by it. The prophet in this Scripture having revealed the sufferings which the Hebrew Church and nation would endure in the time of Antiochus Epiphanes, passes on by a quick transition to unfold the trials which await the Christian Church in the latter days. It is a subject for serious inquiry whether, in the history of the Church or world of late years, there has not been a gradual tendency towards a fulfilment of this prophecy.

I. In reviewing the past we may recognise a remarkable change in popular opinion concerning the origin and claims of authority, both civil and ecclesiastical. The belief taught by St. Paul and St. Peter that authority is derived from God, and that obedience is due to lawful authority in things not unlawful for the Lord's sake, has now been greatly weakened; and authority is commonly supposed to be derived from earth and not from heaven, and to have no other claim upon allegiance than that which depends on the voice of the people, and not on the will of God. Together with the change in popular opinion as to the claims of authority two other powers have grown up. Men crave protection, and admire strength. On one side some have almost deified the Roman Papacy, and on the other side some have been driven to defy all authority whether temporal or spiritual, and to cast away all belief in a Personal Ruler of the world, and in future rewards and punishments, and to place the people on the throne of God.

II. Our own duty in face of these events. We must endeavour to revive in the public mind a recognition of the Divine origin of authority. This feeling needs to be answered in rulers as well as in subjects. If parents, masters, and governors were resolved to act in the consciousness that their authority is received from God, and that He will call them to account at the Great Day, then they would use it as a sacred trust from heaven, and never abuse it to gratify their own selfish desires.   C. W

CXXX. The Way and the End. DAN. xii. 13.

"*But go thou thy way till the end be: for thou shalt rest, and stand in thy lot at the end of the days.*"

THERE are two things which mark out man from the lower creatures—he has a past and a future. They cannot live in memory, but man has the past in history and thoughts that wander back into God's eternity. They have no future—it is blank, black darkness. Man has a future—the future of this life and of God's great eternity—thoughts of which often give him great unrest. The past often brings up misery—he sees spectres in the future that threaten himself and God's world. So here with the prophet Daniel, "What shall be the end of these things?" What is the solution? This text is the answer to his questioning, and surely well suited to us in the present troubled state of things.

Let us then consider: First, some things contained in it; second, some people to whom this text is addressed.

I. (1) There is to be an end—"till the end be;" things are not always to remain perplexed and troubled. The face of the world, thoughtfully considered, teaches us this: the earth is limited and bounded, and yet with ever-increasing inhabitants the limit must be reached. Did not the maker take this into account? A house too small for the dwellers must be extended or pulled down. An artist with his picture must come to the end of his canvas. Surely the greatest architect and artist thought of this. If there is wisdom at all the world must end. Men of science tell us the same, that the earth is gradually nearing and narrowing its circuit round the central sun, till it must some day be burned up in it. There will be an end and dissolution. This world gives way to a new and higher world for those who love and trust God.

(2) There is to be a solution of difficult things at that end. Many things at present greatly trouble us. Let them rest, they will be solved at that great end. All these perplexities and doubts shall end. At the day of the revelation of Jesus Christ many doubts will flee away at one look at His face. His people will be sure then of their interest in Him, and of the righteousness of His working. Many Christians are troubled because the battle seems evenly

balanced, or even inclining to the side of evil. But then truth shall be set on the throne; judgment shall return to righteousness.

(3) There is a way for us to walk in till that end shall come. There is a secure way—happy to have a view of the end from an exceeding high mountain—often we have not that. When the sailor sees the heavens clear he is glad. But it is not always so. He is tossed up and down like the apostle, seeing neither sun nor moon nor stars. Still he has his chart and compass to guide him, though the higher lights are dimmed, and he finds his way by them. And we have always our chart to show us our way—the word of God; our compass, an enlightened conscience; our log-line of experiences, and using them we shall find our way to God. Our way, through Jesus Christ, to God's likeness, growing from glory to glory, and our way to true happiness seeking the fellowship of God. Nothing can pluck us from that way.

Each one has his separate way. Go then thy way. A way for thee—for thee—in this great highway. Yes, for each man and woman something he or she can do; no other can. Some influence which no other has. This is the reason why you are here in the world. Let this be a comfort to us that each has a way.

Christian people often trouble about which way. "If we only knew which road to take;" if we could only hear God saying, "This is the way, walk ye in it." But this way of doubt and perplexity may be the very way for thee, teaching thee to seek His Spirit and word. Thy way may be across an arid sand, or beset with thorns and thickets, where there seems no pathway. Thou hast to stand still, it may be, to see the salvation of God.

(4) To all such as are willing to take God's way, there will be rest and blessedness in the end: thou shalt rest and stand in thy lot. Thou shalt rest, rest meantime in thy heart, in thy peace of mind, finding true rest of spirit. Great peace have they, who love Thy law. A surface of trouble it may be, but a deep peace below where we rest in God. Peace I leave with you, a legacy, but peace I give unto you, a present gift, and also before the time of the end thou shalt have rest. Thy grave is a place of rest. The hand of the Lord Jesus lies on each grave to keep the dust

of His people distinct. And all the storm of tempest cannot touch it till He comes. When the winter is over, with a voice soft and strong—soft as breeze of spring, strong as the archangel's trump—He will call, saying, "Arise my love, my fair one, and come away."

The intermediate state is the darkest part of our existence. A deep shadow lies between the two worlds, but it will be a time of perfect rest. "To-day shalt thou be with Me." If these blessed souls had any disquiet, and should say, "O Lord, how long, holy and true?" He would bid them rest till the time be accomplished.

(5) Stand in their lot, figurative of the lot of tribes of Israel. They got their part in Canaan by lot, so this means here an appointed place in the great promised land of rest, in which great place there will be a wise and merciful appointment of the mansion to the person. Each way shall lead to its fitting place. Heaven is not a wide, monotonous, indiscriminate field, but an ordered place. Those who have lived together here, and cheered each other here, shall find themselves together there. Heaven is human and home-like, the present delivered from trial and sorrow.

A great thought to think of other company also. Moses, when his face shall not need to be veiled for its brightness; David, tuning his harp now to nothing but songs of gladness; Paul, and the rest; but better to meet the longed for and the lost, when God shall heal the breach of His people and bind the stroke of their wound.

II. Classes to whom this may be addressed:

(1) To those perplexed about prophecy, and the future of God's world; right to deal with these things, but not to be pre-occupied with them; leave them and attend to duties at thy feet. Some always perplexed about the Church. Every new form of infidelity which springs up they think the end of it is come. "Go thou thy way; thy way is clear. As for me and my children, we will serve the Lord."

(2) And so about other doubts and questionings, about predestination, freewill, etc. God did not give the Bible for speculation, but as a light to thy feet and lamp to thy path.

(3) To those troubled about future in this world, especially at this time when the future looks so clouded. What is to become of me? How is the wolf to be kept from the door? And if my friend die, am I to fall out like a weary

straggler from the ranks of men and be forsaken? Go on, thy bread shall be given. Take no thought for the morrow. Thought of its duties, yes, but not of the results.

(4) People troubled about future in another world. It is right to make calling and election sure, but they go beyond that. How if I am on the right, and my friend on the left. Shall I carry a sting of my sins? Heaven is human, but not carnal nor earthly. God will make all these things well to thee. Go and sin no more. I go to my Father and yours.

III. We should be very glad of two things: First, that there is an end; and secondly, a way.

(1) What if there were no end but this troubled life to go on; but this shall have an end; sin put down under His righteous feet.

(2) A way. What if there had been no way. I am the Way. The word is nigh thee, even in thy mouth and heart. In mouth, when you cry, Lord, save me; in thy heart when He says, Behold, I stand at the door and knock. All roads lead to Rome, says the old proverb. Take any path in the way of God, the humblest and lowliest, it leads to heaven. Not a drop in the moorland but what finds its way down into the streamlet and goes to the ocean. Not a thought that seeks to go God-ward but He will lead it thither. Beware of the end without the way.

J. K.

CXXXI. The Valley of Achor. HOSEA ii. 15.
" The valley of Achor for a door of hope."

HOSEA lived on the eve of a signal crisis in the history of Israel. Already when he wrote the Assyrian eagles were hovering over their prey, and soon the fatal swoop came. On the eve of this second captivity the prophet's thoughts reverted again and again to the lessons of the first. "When Israel was a child, then I loved him, and called my son out of Egypt." This is the suggestive analogy which runs through his prophecies, interwoven like a thread into their very texture. The prophet's voice, however mournful, is not the funeral knell of a dying people. Once more a mighty resurrection is ordained, and the sepulchre shall be made to yield up its prey. Before this new exodus is crowned with the triumph of the old, it must submit to the discipline and chastisement of the old. God will give them once more the valley of Achor, not that they may perish in their sins, but that the sin detected and put away may be the portal of a better hope. "The valley of Achor, or trouble, took its name from the trespass of Achan, the trouble which he brought upon Israel." In the incident there are three points to be noted,—

I. The nature of the sin. It was a hidden sin. This probably was its gratification in the eyes of the offender. No one else was wronged by it. This Babylonish garment would have been destroyed by fire if Achan had not concealed it for his own use. Does any one plead this excuse to himself for indulgence in any hidden sin? You yourself are the worse for it, that is surely sufficient answer, and doubly the worse because it is a hidden sin. Public opinion is a mirror in which we see our own faults. When this mirror is withdrawn, sin forgets its own hideousness. Your sin is working as a poison in your nature, and has infected the moral atmosphere you diffuse around.

II. The effects of such a sin on the man himself. It must pervade the whole character of the man. Untruthfulness is eating away his conscience, and his whole life is one continual lie. He is not one man, but two, and the one is arrayed against the other. In the conflict of good and evil he has a traitor in his own camp, the secret sin within makes overtures to the open evil without.

III. The detection and putting away of the sin. God's voice is heard, "Thou hast taken of the accursed thing, and thou hast dissembled." This conviction of self may be realized in many ways. It may be the random shaft of the preacher shot at a venture, or it may be a signal defeat sustained, which recalls you to yourself. The plague spot is detected. Then is the crisis. Will you put it away? Christ's atonement is not for you until you put away this evil thing.

J. B. L.

CXXXII. Patriotism and Christianity. Hos. xiii. 1.

"When Ephraim spake trembling, he exalted himself in Israel; but when he offended in Baal, he died."

THE principle asserted in the text is plain enough. Solomon embodies it in the words "Righteousness exalteth a nation." We have formulated it for ourselves, in our own saying, that "what is morally wrong can never be politically right." "Trembling." Some give this word as "tremblingly." Humility, according to this rendering of the text, is the root out of which this virtue grows,—so long as Ephraim was humble he exalted himself, when he became idolatrous his power turned to weakness. I am inclined to the view that we ought to read the passage with a stop after "trembling"—all that heard him *trembled*. It seems to say there was a time when Ephraim was very honourable, when his very speaking produced an impression upon all that heard him. Ephraim was the younger son of Joseph. When Joseph brought him and his elder brother to Jacob's death-bed to receive his blessing, Jacob crossed his hands over each other, so that his right hand rested upon the head of Ephraim, and Joseph sought to correct this mistake. But his father refused to change, assigning as his defence that Manasseh was to be a great people, but Ephraim was to be greater. And so it was. The blessing of Jacob was fulfilled. He was a fruitful bough, and it seemed for a time as if Ephraim was destined to exercise sovereignty over the whole people. Joshua was chosen from the tribe. Gideon turned away their wrath by a soft answer, and their influence was great for good or for evil. But they became turbulent and rebellious, and all through their history we trace the same spirit. It manifested itself to the detriment of the unity of the nation. When Jeroboam raised the standard of rebellion against the house of David, and tore the ten tribes from the kingdom of Judah, from that time Ephraim began to die. It was as a matter of policy, that the people might be kept from going to Jerusalem, that they instituted the worship of the golden calf. There were periods of prosperity and power, but its idolatry was to it the sentence of national death. Jeroboam perished by violence. Ahab's house was cut off. The people died themselves. Every nation without its borders had liberty to insult it. There seems to have been in the mind of the prophet some such notion as this when he spoke his burning words. A living lion, so long as he can roar is feared, but the most timorous creature may trample upon a *dead* lion. So this people, when they deserted the communion of their God, crouched to every one. The force of meanness could no further go. Ephraim was dead when their king could bring himself to speak after such a fashion. The carcase existed only for a time, because the surrounding vultures could not agree amongst themselves. And now I say that the law that determined the fate of Ephraim, will determine the fate of England. We love our country, for our fathers, our kindred are there, our children are there. Proudly she stands among the nations. Never was land so rich in privilege, or a people so laden with responsibility, a country so endowed with wealth. She speaks and there is trembling. She is exalted in Israel. Is this pre-eminence, and privilege, and responsibility, and power, destined to continue, or is it to share the fate of other nations who have been exalted to such a position? Tyre, Babylon, Nineveh, Carthage,—all empires that have risen and fallen, "art thou become like unto them?" Is this she that made the earth tremble, she that did shake the kingdoms? Here we are met by the objection: "You need not ask the question at all. Nations have had their birth, their maturity, their decay; a time to spread their branches; a time to yield their fruitbearing; a time for them to die." We are pointed to Tyre, to Carthage, to Rome, in support of such an argument; but the fact is ignored that the analogy is imperfect, from one single thing—they had not what we have, the gospel of Jesus Christ. Christianity has introduced a new factor into the problem. It is in itself a leaven of purity, which, operating freely, will leaven the whole lump. The past is not to be stated as if it were an infallible proof. The throne needs no alliance to defend it that is guarded by a generation of righteous men. There can be but one answer then. It rests with the Churches of our day to be faithful and England will not fail. If they are faithless, then, like Ephraim, England must die. But now, met by one objection, which we have disposed of, we are confronted by another.

Christianity does not sanction such an appeal as that we are making, does not sanction patriotism at all. Notice how extremes meet. The so-called spiritualistic class of Christians say : " Let things take their course ; our business is not to trouble ourselves about our country, but to save our souls." The infidel says "Yes, you need not go to Christian examples for patriotism, but to infidels ; Themistocles, Aristides, etc., are better examples of love of country than David or Paul or Jesus ! " Both parties are wrong. Christianity assumes patriotism. It does not re-thrash straw that has been thrashed already. But still further, carrying the war into the enemy's camp, I ask, is it in the poetry of Homer that we read " pray for the peace of Jerusalem, they shall prosper that love thee " ? Or the sentiment, " If I forget thee, oh Jerusalem, may my right hand forget her cunning " ? Was it from the pen of Seneca or Epictetus that the sentiment came, " For Zion's sake, I will not hold my peace " ? Was it Aristotle that said, " I would wish myself accursed for my brethren"? Has Regulus anything to equal the mourning cry of Jesus —" Oh Jerusalem, Jerusalem, thou that killest the prophets; how often would I have guarded thee as a hen guardeth her chickens under her wings," etc. It cannot but be that it is a right thing for Christian men to be patriotic and to care for the good of their country. I now proceed to specify the modes in which we may manifest this patriotism, this love of our country.

I. Personal influence on the side of goodness. Every sin that you and I commit threatens a permanent removal of the candlestick, every act of injustice is an unholy leaven in our country's peace ; every sin of which we are conscious is a playing with fire in the mines of gunpowder. Mercy, frugality, temperance, bring with them unity, peace, population. The opposite vices bring with them the national adversity in which the prophet may say : " And with so much ye bring in little ; ye eat, and have not enough ; ye drink, and are still athirst ; ye clothe you ; and he that earneth riches earneth them to put them into a bag with holes."

The first contribution a man can make to his country's prosperity is personal goodness.

II. Next to that is personal activity. *Doing* good is a

necessary adjunct to *being* good. Read the 4th chapter of the Epistle to the Ephesians. There you have the Apostolic idea of the Christian ministry, its origin and its results. The great mass of our congregations have a wrong idea of the minister's work. Ask them, and they will tell you that a minister's duty is to save souls. And they will say, "He is to conduct prayer meetings and cottage meetings, to distribute tracts, to alarm the unconverted, and generally to compel men to come in." But unless you know more about a minister's duty than the apostle Paul, this is not the minister's peculiar duty at all. The apostle says that the special work is for "the perfecting of the saints, for the edifying of the body of Christ." This does not mean that the minister is to be careless of the evangelization of the world. It does mean that the pastors are to preside in the church, and to keep the fountains of strength lovely and pure there. But the people who drink of those fountains, *they* are to bring the wanderers home, they are the stream; and they are to compel those who are not at the feast to come in. So much you see is taken for granted. It is not the especial ministerial function to evangelize the world, it is your function; it is the minister's duty to care for the development of the spiritual life. Were the functions of the Church properly fulfilled, it would not permit of an idle Christian, just as it will not admit of a drunken, a swearing, or a thieving Christian. Each member of the Church ought to be animated by the enthusiasm of humanity. You are standing all the day idle, waiting for some one to hire you, when the Lord has hired you already; you have a heavy account to face. Your ordinary excuses are refuges of lies which He will sweep away in the day of His fierce displeasure. You may creep into heaven, you will not find an abundant entrance. If it were possible to engrave such a conception of the Church on every Christian's heart as this, to write the thought in letters of fire that would burn up the dross of selfishness and of indolence, this were worthy a prophet or a prophet's song, and I would dare foretell a long future to England's power and England's glory. Next to personal godliness the best contribution is personal activity in the Church of Christ. But much more remains to be accomplished. We have not only to serve in the ranks, but to pay the war tax to support the soldiers who are working elsewhere. It was in accordance with this idea that our forefathers instituted missions across the sea. There were men dying for lack of knowledge, and the *Andrew Fullers* consulted with the *Careys*. They did not despair, they did not ask "what are these amongst so many," or say "it is useless to assault a citadel like that; its inhabitants are Anakim, while we are but grasshoppers." They besieged Jericho until the walls fell dow. Anxiety for the heathen abroad awoke anxiety for the heathen at home. And I would remind you that all the arguments which we recognise as arguments of force for Foreign Missions, are true of Home Missions. The master has equally commanded us to both. "Go out into all the world and preach the gospel unto every creature." I remind you that home—in a certain sense—home has a prior claim. "Blood is thicker than water," and the proverb has a force in the spiritual sense just as it has in the temporal sense. Suppose that to morrow we read in our newspapers that a new island had been discovered in the Pacific, that every one of the people on it were able to speak the English language. Englishmen of all characters—drunkards, criminals, honest men, decent and sober men amongst them—but that they had not got Christ's gospel. They might all be preached to of our Christ's gospel, no new language, no new book. What a talk there would be! Every church, every drawing room, every congregation would be full of it. Sirs, you do not need to go to the Pacific for the realization of the supposition, I tell you that round about you, under the very sound of your voices, when you come to worship God, there are men and women speaking the English tongue, living after English customs, who are going down to death, who care not for Christ, who will not live to God. If by any means we can reach them, speak to them, bring the cross and the gospel to them, let us be up and doing and succour the long lost for the glory and prosperity of our country. Evangelize England and you evangelize the world. Ask our missionaries who go abroad what their difficulty is, and they will tell you that the scums of civilization carry to their poor ignorant converts the deadly fire-water. That men who hold their heads high at home, are making their fortunes by the sale of opium. That merchants and sailors alike, when they leave England too often leave the restraints of civilization and of Christianity. If we could only evangelize our merchants, and our sailors, and our travellers, and our emigrants, before they leave England, how soon would the world be converted. As the most certain, and most effective way of bringing the world to Christ, then, I say, be true patriots, and bring the gospel to the door of every man and every woman in England.

J. A. M.

CXXXIII. The Restorer of Years. JOEL ii. 25.
"*And I will restore to you the years that the locust hath eaten, the cankerworm, and the caterpillar, and the palmerworm, My great army which I sent among you.*"

THERE is a difficulty which every teacher finds with the sublimities of the Bible. It is hard to take out the honey of a definite sense, and yet not mar the bloom of inspiration's loveliness. There is an attribute of God than which few can be more comforting, "The restorer of years." Blessed faculty of omnipotence! For who has not to lament over things that are gone? Who has not behind his back a dark train of lost opportunities following after him to the day of judgment?

Why are so many things—and those the best things—why are they no more? Hear God's answer, "The locust hath eaten them, the cankerworm, and the caterpillar, and the palmerworm, My great army which I sent among you." And the reason of God sending "that great army" was because your heart was not right with Him, and you did not profit by, nor give God glory in, His gifts. What does "that great army" mean?

I. Little things make God's great army when He sets them to do His works. Who has not learnt it, that it is the little things of life which have been his ruin?

II. What mean these vast puny desolaters, "the locust, cankerworm, caterpillar, and palmerworm."

(1) There came in fourth the "palmerworm" of the world, with its pleasures that ate into your spirituality and nipped the buds of early promise.

T

(2) Then came the "locusts," a thick swarming band of the evil passions of manhood.

(3) So came the "cankerworm" of the cares and ambition of life.

(4) A little way farther and there followed the creeping "caterpillar" of insidious unbelief, and life lay behind you a ruin of broken promises, and a waste of consumed desire.

III. It can all be restored, the ruined can be built up. God will do His own great work as the "restorer of years" if only you are willing. If the evil spirit returns sevenfold to the empty house, will not the good Spirit come back seven-fold—ay, seventy-fold—to a man in whose heart Christ is? Never forget to see this in the atonement, and be careful to inscribe upon the cross of Jesus, as one of the highest of its titles, "A restorer of years."

J. V.

CXXXIV. Pleasing God. MICAH vi. 6–8. *"Wherewith shall I come before the Lord, and bow myself before the high God? shall I come before Him with burnt-offerings, with calves of a year old? Will the Lord be pleased with thousands of rams, or with ten thousands of rivers of oil? shall I give my firstborn for my transgression, the fruit of my body for the sin of my soul? He hath showed thee, O man, what is good; and what doth the Lord require of thee, but to do justly, and to love mercy, and to walk humbly with thy God?"*

THIS is indeed a momentous question, and many and various have been the answers to it. In spirit and principle they reduce themselves to the three which, in these verses, are tacitly rejected, that the fourth may be established for all time.

I. Shall I do some outward acts to please God? Men are ever tempted to believe in the virtue of doing something; to ask, as they often asked our Lord, "What shall I do to inherit eternal life?"

External observances and good works without inward holiness are displeasing to God.

II. Can we please God by giving? Will the Lord be pleased with thousands of rams? Shall we, like the pagans, try to bribe God? While none of us is so ignorant as not to know the duty of charity, none of us is so foolish as to imagine that he can by gifts win his way one step nearer to the great white throne.

III. Shall I try to please God by suffering? This, too, has been fearfully attempted, and more persistently than any other, because in all ages men have invested God with the attributes of terror and of wrath. Can we judge of God when He looms dark and terrible through the crimson mist of haunted consciences and guilty hearts? No; when men have been able only to regard Him thus, then all the day long His terrors have they suffered.

IV. What is the prophet's answer to the question? If not by doing, not by giving, not by suffering, then how? By being. But by being what? By being just and merciful and humble before our God. This is what God requires, and thus alone can we live acceptably to Him, for this is to live in Christ. In Him was justice fulfilled; in Him was mercy consummated. God needs not our services, He needs not our gifts, least of all does He need our anguish; but He needs us, our hearts, our lives, our love. He needs it, and even this He gives us, shedding abroad the spirit of adoption in our hearts.

F. W. K.

CXXXV. The Vision made Plain. HAB. ii. 2.

"*And the Lord answered me, and said, Write the vision and make it plain upon tables, that he may run that readeth it.*"

THE attitude of the prophet is one of very earnest expectation and waiting for the Divine will, and he had a very earnest and practical desire to carry out that will so far as he might be enabled to do it. That is the spirit that always has been and always will be honoured of God. We all feel that it is what we should be distinguished by in all matters pertaining to our every-day life; for in all our ways we are to acknowledge God, that He might direct our paths; and in regard to more immediate Christian work and religious endeavour among those who know not the Lord, it is especially important that it should be so.

I. Let us notice the way in which it is the will of God

that the revelation of His truth shall be made known. He has declared that it shall be written: "Write the vision." It is in accordance with this that we have the Divine book of the revelation of God's word guaranteed to us with the evidence of Divine inspiration in every page of it, and proving in itself the Divine proof of its authority, and the Divine pledge of its ultimate triumph. We thank God for all the gifts of His creation, the bounties of His providence, and the blessings of His grace; but when we come to turn to the book of Divine truth we say, "Thanks be to God for His unspeakable gift."

II. We notice that God would have His will plainly revealed. "Make it plain." How full of condescension and grace is this! We find it so in all God's material works. They are open to the observation even of the illiterate and unlearned; and for those who cannot penetrate into their mysteries or fully appreciate their glories, they are plain enough to fill the most uncultivated mind with an appreciation that shall be full of pleasure, profit, and joy. There is nothing mean, nothing common, nothing that is not adapted to lift the soul up in meditation upon God. "The heavens declare the glory of God, and the firmament showeth forth His handiwork." Nature with open volume stands to spread her Maker's name abroad, and every labour of her hand shows something worthy of a God. You will find this same thing running through all the arrangements symbolized in the dispensation of the Old Testament, and realized in the New. Take the cities of refuge as an instance. They were all to be plain, not to be mistaken. Just in the same way about the King's highway abounding in wonders and mysteries that all the angelic intellect of all eternity cannot comprehend, and bearing the pilgrims who walk in it every day into grace which is already glory. We find our Lord giving thanks to the Father that He had "hidden these things from the wise and prudent, and revealed them unto babes." There was what the Saviour looked upon with complacency, and what we may think upon with gratitude.

The Gospel is unfathomable in its depth, but transparent in its clearness nevertheless. In the plainness with which it is revealed to us we see the Divine wisdom and grace of our God, and we can only say with adoring gratitude,

"Even so, Father, for so it seemed good in Thy sight." It becomes all who have to tell of the Gospel to others, to do it in the spirit that is enjoined in the prophet by the Lord, "Write the vision and make it plain."

III. Notice that the vision was to be written in a form so striking and impressive "that he may run who readeth it." Not as this passage is generally misquoted "that he who runs may read." The message is to be so plain and so striking that the man who sees it shall run in a moment to escape the evil of which it warns him, or to seek the blessing of which it tells him. There is an intimation of what is much needed now-a-days. We are too much afraid of anything like "sensation" in religion. The fear is that we may sink into its opposite extreme, and lose all life in the fear of being considered in any way victims of sensation. The tidings of the Gospel, instead of being reduced to the mere common-place platitudes that we sometimes hear, should be spoken and lived out in such a way that all might run that read it.

J. P. C.

CXXXVI. High Places. HAB. iii. 19. "*The Lord God is my strength, and He will make my feet like hinds' feet, and He will make me to walk upon mine high places.*"

"HIGH places" are just the best things in life and experience, those which lift a man up to God. Let us consider some of these "high places" up which God makes His people walk.

I. A mount of vision. On a mountain we generally see more clearly than at a lower elevation. Are there not seasons when we get clear views of Divine truth, when they appear in a new glory? True, the revelation is made—it is all in the book. But so is the landscape all laid down. Yet unless your feet ascend the high places, it is as though it were not there. So the revelation is in the book, but it is not in the soul. You must get up the mount of vision. For this you must labour, and it is worth it. There is as much difference between the man who gains a bright, clear view of truth, and the man who never rises to it, as between an ordinary man and a man of genius. Genius has been defined as "an infinite capacity for taking trouble." If we would have a clear, bright view of things we must take trouble to climb the heights whence it may be gained. We must keep the things in mind, and in their connections we must keep them in serene contemplation. Two men look at the same Scripture: the one sees little in it—to the other it is all bright and glorious; for that man has been on the mount of vision.

II. The mount of faith. On "high places" we see things at farthest distance, and so we may speak of the mount of faith. These things come into sight.

On "high places" not only is there nothing to come between you and the object gazed upon, but looking through a rarefied atmosphere there is the least possible obstruction to the vision. Moses on the heights of Pisgah saw the goodly land of promise spread out before him.

It is a beautiful type of faith. There is a Pisgah everywhere now, and we may ascend it when we will. Gazing upon the land which lies across the "narrow stream" a man may take out his title-deeds and contemplate his possessions. You have all in God. "All things are yours," because ye are God's. And to say you are God's is but another way of saying God is yours.

This claiming God is faith's highest exercise, faith's noblest act. And God is more than time and space—more than all contained within time and space.

In the picture the prophet's fancy draws in this psalm, he sees the fig trees without blossom, the vines without fruit, the fields yielding no crops, the fields without flocks, and the stalls without herds. Yet the Lord is more to him than all these, and so he can rejoice in Him. Having God a man has all.

III. In "high places" men breathe more freely. So pure and exhilarating is the rarefied air that it produces a kind of intoxication. So it is with the soul. "Be not drunk with wine wherein is excess, but be filled with the Spirit."

Drink in the quickening, inspiring influence of the Spirit. "Yield yourselves to God." "If you live in the Spirit, walk in the Spirit." Be spiritually-minded.

This pure spirit-life, so high and blessed, what is it? It is our own proper life. If we can only come to live it, it is the easiest and most natural of all life. God's natural man as He made him, lived that life. Redeemed man is to be brought back to it. In its best moments the redeemed life seems to enter Eden once more, the "feet are swift as hind's feet," and God makes the man to walk on his "high places."

IV. This, finally, is up the pathway of a free, steadfast, joyous obedience.

On the heights of a mountain a man can do more than on the low places of ordinary life. He becomes a wonder to himself. He can walk so far and resist fatigue so, that he seems to renew his youth.

This is an image and expression of a similar fact in the spiritual life. God makes a man's feet like "hinds' feet," and lifts him up to the "high places of an easy obedience. It comes to this at length. At first, when he began, there was little of the "hinds' feet," there was more of the elephantine tread. By-and-by there was the horse-like movement, which though lighter is often arrested by the little hills. It may be a good while before we see the "hinds' feet," but we may all get them if we will. They are not got supernaturally, but by the ordinary "means of grace." You may get them in common life.

Men have been likened to different animals and creatures, and in a great city you may meet with persons who have the likeness of almost every animal and creature there is. Man's nature may resemble that of the lion, the tiger, the wolf, the sloth, the mole, the serpent; but thanks be to God for the nobler resemblances in men to the doves in their windows, to the eagles in the rocks, to the hart on the mountain, and to the "hinds' feet." How many instances of ready, cheerful obedience are to be met with in city life. The "hinds' feet" are found in the warehouse, in the lanes of the city, in sickrooms, in all the various walks of life.

A. R.

CXXXVII. The Spirit of God the Strength of the Church. Zech. iv. 6. "*Not by might, nor by power, but by My Spirit, saith the Lord of hosts.*"

The Prophet Zechariah lived at a very important crisis of Jewish history. God in His mercy had visited His people, and they had been allowed to return from exile. A great national enthusiasm has been enkindled, and every hand is occupied in repairing the old waste places, and rearing afresh the ruined walls of the Temple. Prince Zerubbabel is foremost in this work, and the words of the text are sent by God to encourage him in his work. This whole book points forward to the spiritual temple which was to be reared in after days by the true Zerubbabel, the Lord Jesus, the Holy Building of which every Christian is intended to be a living stone.

I. We find in the text the statement of a fact. It is now a matter of history that the Church's rise and progress cannot be ascribed to human agencies. The strength of the infant Church was derived from the unseen presence of the Holy Spirit. So Christianity spread. So century after century in its own despite has the world been used as the scaffolding with which to rear this spiritual temple. So although the oracles of Greece are dumb, and Rome's most costly shrines are crumbling into dust, the religion which was founded by peasants of Galilee has for ages retained the allegiance of the most civilized nations of the world. "Not by might, nor by power, but by My Spirit, saith the Lord."

II. From this fact we derive much comfort for the future.

(1) As concerns the Church at large. Let the Holy Ghost be duly honoured in the Church, and be allowed to rule in it, and it will prosper. He who laid the foundation stone on the blood-stained heights of Calvary shall complete the fabric amid the overpowering glory of the Second Advent.

(2) As concerns the individual behaviour. Whatever be the difficulties and disappointments of the spiritual life by which you are cast down and disheartened, if only you will act upon the principle of the text you shall forge out of these very trials a Divine arrow, by which Satan shall be

pierced through and through. Be strong, not in yourself, not in your clergyman, but in the Lord, and in the power of His might. The fruit of the Spirit is joy. Uplifted by the Spirit you shall look away from self to Jesus. That is the secret of joy.

G. H. W.

CXXXVIII. The Day of Small Things. ZECH. iv. 10.
" For who hath despised the day of small things ?"

LOOK at these words in different applications, different connections.

I. First for application to common, secular or natural facts. " For who hath despised the day of small things?" Not you tradesmen, you say that pence makes pounds; and not lawyers, for they know the power of the littles at any rate; and not medical men, for they know that the question of a grain or a drop is often a question of life or death; and not the scholar, for the scholar knows that all scholarship must begin with A B C; and not the politician, for every one who knows the working of politics knows that, generally speaking, great doors turn on small hinges. Intelligence watches the work of God,—"Who hath measured the waters in the hollow of His hand, and meted out heaven with the span, and comprehended the dust of the earth in a measure, and weighed the mountains in scales, and the hills in a balance," and of whom it is said —" Behold, the nations are as the drop of a bucket, and are counted as the small dust of the balance: behold, He taketh up the isles as a very little thing,"— and sees that Being, so great that all the universe is but a type of His power, is always showing His character in little things. And intelligence watches the process and sees how that great Being who counts the isles as a very little thing, has crowded every leaf with millions of lives if they could but be discerned. The more we look into the life that teems in a little leaf the more do we grasp the idea that there is still more life there.

He it is who touches with all the colours of the rainbow and the fire of the sun the wings of the little insects who are born in the morning and die in the day. He does not despise little things, and how can we do so who delight in His work? Not a little blade of grass, not a little leaf wavering in the still air, not a bird on the bough but show forth the glory of the Lord; and not only the towering tree in Lebanon, but also the hyssop cometh from the Lord who is wonderful in counsel and excellent in working.

Who can despise the day of small things? Any Christian? Oh! no, if he understands himself. "Nature is Christian," says Bishop Horne. "Yes, Bishop," we say, "nature *is* Christian to Christian men." If any man be in Christ he has a new character, and creation is a new creation. Old things have passed away; all things have become new. Nature has nothing to say about the things of Calvary until we have looked at Calvary, and then it is full of them, and we learn that our Father cares for us. Do not think this an unpractical, unsentimental thought. There are times when we should be overpowered and ask, "Can God take any notice of *me*?" times when, having looked at the silent magnificence of night, each of us would be ready to say, "God can have no time to think about me." But Jesus says, "look at the small things;" and you notice that when He calls attention to nature He calls attention to small things, to little birds and little flowers and the very hairs of your head. God forbid that we should despise the day of small things. If any one here looks at God's work in nature, and in reference to things that occur in the sphere of nature says, "Who hath despised the day of small things?" then let him come up and speak for himself, or rather hear what God has to say for him.

II. Now next apply these words to the historical connection that called them forth—Zerubbabel laying the foundation of the Second Temple. It was a new day when he did it. In Scripture poetry the time of joy is spoken of as the day, and the time of sorrow as the night. The Jews had had a night of seventy-one years, when Jerusalem sat in gloom; a night when she looked in vain for her children, for they had been carried into captivity, and all her glory had lain in the grave. But there came a turning time, there was just a twinkle of dawn, and devout Jews were able to say, "see that," to the secular Jews; and the latter would answer, "Call that a day? If a day at all it is a day of small things." When the emperors, unconscious instruments of God, gave the Jews permission to return, it was a day of small things, and some despised it, while others were ready to say, "Our souls are filled with a dawn of light." When the first detachment went out, those who were worldly wise said it was a day of small things. About 50,000 went out under Zerubbabel, while as many as 600,000 went out from Egypt. There were many persons among them who had no stake in the country, and as men look up to men of money, men of weight looked at these men with simple contempt. However, they went out and travelled on as far as the city of their fathers' sepulchres; but even there they met those who despised them and their doings. They went to the city of stones with the hatchet and the pick to overcome the difficulties of building the city. It was hard to suffer from the sarcastic silence of their pretended friends, and the sarcastic speech of their foes. It would have been strange if amongst the followers of Zerubbabel some had not wavered. But the word of the Lord came saying, "The hands of Zerubbabel have laid the foundation of this house; his hands shall also finish it; and thou shalt know that the Lord of Hosts hath sent me unto you. For who hath despised the day of small things?"

It seemed to be a very unpromising enterprise just then; but another prophet had said, "The glory of the latter house shall be greater than the former." That temple which seemed to be glory in the air, filling the lookers-on with a pang of wonder—to be greater than that? Not greater in glory on this account, but because the Lord of the temple should stand there, the Lord to whom in past ages all sacrifice pointed, He Himself should stand there—glory itself should stand there, and when the building shall be completed it shall be no longer wanted, for the glory shall have come.

III. Let us proceed in the third place to apply this question or proverb to Christ, and the foundation of His Church. That Church has small beginnings. When the foundation of the temple was completed Zerubbabel set forth Christ, and the whole building of the temple set forth the building of the Church. If it had not been typical we could not understand why so much notice is taken of it in the Bible. The builder himself was a great man lineally, the descendant of the son of David; but he was greater typically, for he set forth Christ and Christ's work: "Behold the man whose name is the Branch; and he shall grow up out of his place, and he shall build the temple of the Lord. Even he shall build the temple of the Lord; and he shall bear the glory and shall sit and rule upon his throne; and he shall be a priest upon his throne; and the counsel of peace shall be between them both." This double idea was shadowed forth by the man and the building. There is no incongruity. Jesus speaks of Himself as at once the builder and the foundation of what He built; but there was a time when it was a day of small things in the history of the builder. See Jesus Christ, the Infant of Days, the little one. Small hands—but they were to grow until they grasped the sceptre. Small feet—but which would grow and would walk upon the waters and would be nailed by cruel men to the cross. The small voice which was heard from that rough stable was to still the tempest and raise the dead. This infant became the man, and the man became the Crucified One, and when it was done He said "It is finished," and in that act He laid the foundation of the Church. Foundation! it was only laying the beginning; but when that is finished, when the top-stone is brought forth with joy, then who will despise the day of small things, who will despise that Church, that mystical, spiritual, ineffably glorious structure which, when finished for eternity, shall call forth joys and deeper joy, and strokes of grander music, than were ever heard when the morning stars sang together and the sons of God shouted for joy over the temple of Creation?

The Church has had its day of small things, and has not quite got out of the small things yet, but let none here be found among those who despise the day of small things. Who can stop the day, and who can in the weakness of the Church keep it from advancing to perfection? Apply this also to the history of each individual Christian life. Oh, it is a day of small things for us individually, for me and for you! Small things what we call faith, hope, and charity: small prayers, small spirituality. Talk about matter under a microscope!—we must go under the microscope sometimes for the Divine growths to be seen; but it will go on, and shall any man despise it? It is not necessary for us to go from the first step to the second in one sudden stroke of miraculous enlargement. The flower never comes out of the unseen—scarcely unseen—seed all in a moment, and grace does not come up in a moment; you have to grow in grace, and is not this a comfort? But this should not be a comfort to make us indolent or to relax our efforts, but to make us grow. Let us not only in ourselves but in others apply this principle, and if we have grace in us we are apt to think of others. When we find Christians—Ready-to-halts and Much-afraids—let us keep this in mind: "For who hath despised the day of small things?"

It is an application of the principle of Christ: "Take heed that ye despise not one of these little ones." He speaks of poor Christians as little children who need so much care, and such a wealth of love and patience from those who have to deal with them. We are not to despise in them or in ourselves the day of small things. God is one in nature and in grace. He never stops and leaves a thing half finished; that which He has begun He will carry on. Then who shall despise the day of small things? Apply these things to Christian privileges. I am afraid we Christians are not where we ought to be, because we depise these things we have. Some walk with sorrowful feelings from the gloom to the glory: they are just able to bear with the present. If that is so are not we despising, as small things, those which are not small things except in comparison with the coming infinities? We get this idea perhaps from men of the world. They know Christians who say "we are passing through tribulation to the kingdom of Heaven;" they hear some warrior of the Christian faith say "O wretched man that I am! who shall deliver me from the body of this death?" and then they hear other Christians speaking as if they can just go on—as if they were bound to be content and give up what they would like to have of the pleasures of the world. Christians get the same notions, get it from the air they breathe, from the world, and consequently they get to underrate their privileges. I do so, and perhaps you also do. Is it a small thing to have the stone with a new name written upon it; is it a small thing to have the privileges we have; is it a small thing to have access always to the mercy-seat; is it a small thing to have an earnest of the inheritance; is it a small thing when our cares press upon us, and we are ashamed to speak about them to mortal ear, that we are welcome to speak about them to the Ancient of Days? Strangers may come unto the King on days of ceremony, but the children can always go to the Father.

Let us not despise small things. They are small in comparison with the things we shall have, but in themselves they are great. We have the privilege of telling God the tiny things; these are not things to be slighted, and when we also remember that these small privileges, as you call them, are but the leaves of a great forest, the dawnings of an everlasting day, who can, recollecting these things, despise the day of small things?

Can I apply this to acts of Christian obedience? Sometimes I find persons making an artificial distinction between great things and small things in God's commandments. I find that they make no difficulty in being themselves those who are to decide the question of great and small with reference to those things in God's law of grace. I find that they speak about things "essential," and things "non-essential." I find that Christian men and women after hearing what Christ has said choose those things which they call essential, and slight those things which are not to their taste!

Apply this also to service. We are called to service—the service of our King—and every Christian is as much a servant of Christ as was Paul who wrote with pride that title after his name, "Paul, a servant of Jesus Christ." Oh, does it not amaze you to find how much unemployed faculty there is in the Church of Jesus Christ, because many who are ordained servants of Jesus Christ keep back from doing anything until they can do something great? Some because they have not great things to give, give nothing. Some who have no difficulty in works of self-denial shrink from doing anything because it is conspicuous. Life is made up of small things, little things of truth, little things of spiritual life, little things of tenderness and persuasiveness. Let each one begin with the little thing which comes nearest if we are to do great things in the great strength of the great Saviour, having served our apprenticeship in doing the small things.

C. S.

CXXXIX. The Christian Life. ZECH. xiv. 6, 7. *"And it shall come to pass in that day, that the night shall not be clear, nor dark: but it shall be one day which shall be known to the Lord, not day, nor night: but it shall come to pass, that at evening time it shall be light."*

THESE verses present us with a most suggestive description of human history as a whole, and of each true godly life in that history. Let us consider the subject in its individual aspect. We have here:—

I. The mixed character of our earthly life. "The light shall not be clear, nor dark;" and again, "It shall be one day, not day, nor night." That is to say, the lot even of a good man is checkered. Every height has its hollow. And each earthly blessing has its accompanying and rectifying affliction. But no Christian is ever in absolute darkness. If the rough wind be blowing on him, God will take care that it be not also from the east.

We can all see more or less that through the trials of the past God has disciplined us into fitness for present duties. Present trials are the prophecies of future efficiency. Again we often see that our trials are frequently connected with our sins. Evil deeds are evil seeds which produce a harvest of bitterness which is a continual affliction to us. Again, our trials lead us to long for heaven, and wean us from the world.

II. The Christian's solace and support under this mixed experience. "It shall be one day which shall be known unto the Lord."

(1) Our condition is known unto the Lord.

(2) Our lot is ordered for us by Jehovah.

III. The happy termination of this mixed state of things to the Christian. "And it shall come to pass, that at evening time it shall be light." Relief shall come when it is least expected. Light is the synonym for joy, for purity, for knowledge. In heaven all the elements of darkness shall be absent. It shall be light.

W. M. T.

INDEX OF SUBJECTS.

Abraham's Seed, Blessing Through, 10.
Achor, The Valley of, 266.
Acquaintance with God, 97.
Aged, The Cry of the, 121.
Appeal, A Divine, 248.
Appeal, A Threefold, 214.
Authority, 262.

Battlements, 244.
Benediction, The, 35.
Benedictions of Life, The, 60.
Book, The Sealed, 191.
Broken Purposes, 94.

Calf, The Golden, 28.
Children, The Training of, 24.
Christ, Prophecy of, 95.
Christ, The Silence of, 221.
Christian Life, The, 287.
Christianity, The Origin of, 213.
Christianity, The Spread of, 140.
Clouds, Regarding the, 163.
Comfort, A Message of, 197.
Commandments, The Finality of the Ten, 49.
Courage, 55.
Covenant of Joshua, The, 59.
Creation, The, 1.
Creator of Man, The, 4.

Day of Small Things, The, 281.
Day which the Lord hath Made, The, 145.
Deliverance from Bondage, 142.
Depths, Out of the, 149.
Despondency, Spiritual, 210.
Development, Christian, 100.

Elijah's Farewell to Elisha, 73.
Elisha, The Call of, 71.

Esther's Prayer, 89.
Even from Thence, 43.
Ezekiel, A Vision of, 250.

Faith, Hindrances to, 11.
Fall of Solomon, The, 70.
Fears, 196.
Feast of Tabernacles, The, 51.
Formalist and the Christian, The, 259.
Friend, The Best, 160.
Fulfilment of the Promise, The, 152.
Future, The, 234.

Gilead, Balm in, 245.
Glory of the Lord, The, 69.
God, The Care of, 215.
God, The Dwelling-place of, 237.
God's Benefits, 137.
God's Doings in the Time of Old, 113.
God's Loving Kindness, 225.
God's Message and Man's Unbelief, 252.
God's Salvation, 119.
God's Still Voice, 61.
God's Thoughts and Man's Thoughts, 231.
God's Word, 232.

Harvest, 7.
Hermon, The Dew of, 151.
High Places, 277.
Hope in God, 111.
Hope, Unfailing 110.
Humility, 156.

Ideal, The Lost 208.
In the Way, 11.
Isaiah's Call, 169.

Is Life Worth Living? 124.

Jacob at Bethel, 18.
Jacob's Dream, 13.
Jordan, The Swelling of, 246.
Jubilee, The Year of, 239.

Kingdom, The Extension of the, 132.

Leader, Our True, 36.
Letter, The Spread, 81.
Life, A Worldly, 179.
Life, The Fountain of, 109.
Life, The Transitoriness of, 88.
Light, 3.
Light in the Clouds, The, 99.
Light of the Lord, The, 167.
Lord, The Coming out of His Place, 186.
Lot, Lessons from, 8.
Love, The Strength of, 166.

Missions in the Light of the Redeemer's Works, 219.
Mockers at Sin, 157.
Moses, God's Revelation to, 25.
Mysterious Providences, 19.

Naaman, 74.

Our Father, 240.
Our Weakness our Strength, 66.

Path, The Untrodden, 56.
Patriotism and Christianity, 268.
Peace, Perfect, 187.
Peace, The Price of, 174.
Penitence, 117.
Playing the Man, 62.
Pleasing God, 274.
Power of the Past, The, 79.
Prayer for a Complete Life, 135.
Prevailing Prayer, 9.
Promises, Precious, 120.

Rab-shakeh's Question to Hezekiah, 80.

Reality of the Invisible, The, 77.
Religion and Science, 131.
Restorer of Years, The, 273.
Returns, The Two, 165.
Revelation, Gradual, 189.

Sabbath, The, 45.
Salvation, The Wells of, 176.
Sanctuary, Help from the, 102.
Satan, The Insinuation of, 92.
Seeking the Face of God, 105.
Servant, God's, 206.
Sin and Mercy, 205,
Sojourners with God, 32.
Solitude of Christ in Redemption, The, 104.
Soul, The Dwelling-place of the, 52.
Sound, The Joyful, 126.
Spirit of God, The, 2.
Spirit of God the Strength of the Church, The, 280.
Stability, 19.
Success in God's Work, 57.

Thoughts of God, 122.
Times and Men, 85.
Time for Thee to Work, 146.
Trouble, Calling upon God in, 114.
True Aims and False Aims, 67.
Trust, The Secret of, 22.
Two Prayers, 39.

Valley of Dry Bones, The, 260.
Vanity of Vanities, 162.
Vision made Plain, The, 275.

Waiting for God, 185.
Walking with God, 5.
Way and the End, The, 263.
Way of the Lord, Preparing the, 200.
What is Man? 101.
Why will ye die? 253.

Zion, The Way to, 243.

INDEX OF TEXTS.

GENESIS.	PAGE
i. 1	1
,, 2	2
,, 3	3
,, 27	4
v. 24	5
viii. 22	7
xiii. 10–12	8
xviii. 32	9
xxii. 18	10
xxiv. 27	11
xxviii. 12	12
xxviii. 15	13
,, 16	16
xlii. 36	18
xlix. 4	19
l. 20	22

EXODUS.	
ii. 9, 10	24
iii. 6	25
xxxii. 1	28

LEVITICUS.	
xxv. 23	32

NUMBERS.	
vi. 24–26	35
x. 29–31	36
,, 35–36	39

DEUTERONOMY.	
iv. 29	43
v. 12	45
,, 22	49
xvi. 13–17	51
xxxiii. 27	52

JOSHUA.	
i. 5, 6	55

	PAGE
iii. 4	56
,, 5	57
xxiv. 25	59

RUTH.	
i. 8	60

1 SAMUEL.	
iii. 10	61

2 SAMUEL.	
x. 12	62

1 KINGS.	
iii. 3–7	66
,, 9	67
viii. 11	69
xi. 11	70
xix. 19, 20, 21	71

2 KINGS.	
ii. 9	73
v. 1	74
vi. 17	77
xiii. 20, 21	79
xviii. 19	80
xix. 14	81

1 CHRONICLES.	
xii. 32	85
xxix. 15	88

ESTHER.	
vii. 3	89

JOB.	
ii. 4	92
xvii. 11	94
xix. 25, 26	95

	PAGE
xxii. 21	97
xxxvii. 21	99

PSALMS.	
i. 3	100
viii. 4	101
xxii. 2	102
,, 11	104
xxvii. 8, 9	105
xxxvi. 9	109
xlii. 11	110
xliii. 5	111
xliv. 1	113
l. 15	114
li. 16, 17	117
lxvi. 16	119
lxxi. 9	121
lxxix. 3	122
,, 13	124
lxxxix. 15	126
xc. 2	131
cii. 15	132
,, 24	135
ciii. 2	137
cv. 24	140
cvii. 14	142
cxviii. 24	145
cxix. 126–128	146
cxxx. 1–8	149
cxxxiii. 3	151
cxxxviii. 8	152

PROVERBS.	
ii. 10, 11	156
xiv. 19	157
xxiii. 22	160

ECCLESIASTES.	
i. 2, 3	162

xi. 4	163	l. 10	210	xxxiii. 30–33	259
xii. 7	165	li. 1	213	xxxvii. 3	260
		„ 9–10	214		

SONG OF SOLOMON.

DANIEL.

		lii. 12	215		
xiii. 6	166	liii. 2	219	xii. 9	262
		„ 7	221	„ 13	263
		liv. 10	225		

ISAIAH.

		lv. 8	231		

HOSEA.

ii. 5	167	„ 10, 11	232	ii. 15	266
vi. 8	169	lvi. 12	234	xiii. 1	268
ix. 6	174	lvii. 15	237		

JOEL.

xii. 3	176	lix. 1	239		
xvii. 10, 11	179	lxiii. 16	240	ii. 25	273
xxv. 9	185				
xxvi. 20, 21	186				

JEREMIAH.

MICAH.

„ 3	187			vi. 6–8	274
xxviii. 10–13	189	i. 5	243		
xxix. 11	191	v. 10	244		

HABAKKUK.

xxxv. 4	196	viii. 22	245		
xl. 1	197	xii. 5	246	ii. 2	275
„ 3–5	200	xliv. 4	248	iii. 19	277
xli. 10	201				

EZEKIEL.

ZECHARIAH.

„ 22	205	i. 4	250	iv. 6	280
xlii. 1–4	206	xx. 49	252	„ 10	281
xlviii 18	208	xxxiii. 11	253	xiv. 6, 7	287

CHOICE STANDARD WORKS.

A NEW AND HANDSOME LIBRARY EDITION
OF
MILMAN'S COMPLETE WORKS,
With Table of Contents and Full Indexes.

IN 8 VOLS., CROWN 8VO, CLOTH.

PRICE, $12.00 PER SET. (Reduced from $24.50.

(Bound in Half Calf extra, $25.00 per set.)

THIS EDITION OF MILMAN'S WORKS, THOROUGHLY REVISED AND CORRECTED, COMPRISES

The History of the Jews, 2 Vols.
The History of Christianity, 2 Vols.
History of Latin Christianity, 4 Vols.

DR. MILMAN has won lasting popularity as a historian by his three great works, HISTORY OF THE JEWS, HISTORY OF CHRISTIANITY, and HISTORY OF LATIN CHRISTIANITY. These works link on to each other, and bring the narrative down from the beginning of all history to the middle period of the modern era. They are the work of the scholar, a conscientious student, and a Christian philosopher. DR. MILMAN prepared this new edition so as to give it the benefit of the results of more recent research. In the notes, and in detached appendices to the chapters, a variety of very important questions are critically discussed.

The author is noted for his calm and rigid impartiality, his fearless exposure of the bad and appreciation of the good, both in institutions and men, and his aim throughout, to utter the truth always in charity. The best authorities on all events narrated have been studiously sifted and their results given in a style remarkable for its clearness, force and animation.

MILMAN'S WORKS HAVE TAKEN THEIR PLACE AMONG THE APPROVED CLASSICS OF THE ENGLISH LANGUAGE. The general accuracy of his statements, the candor of his criticisms and the breadth of his charity are everywhere apparent in his writings. His search at all times seems to have been for truth, and that which he finds he states with simple clearness and with fearless honesty. HIS WORKS ARE IN THEIR DEPARTMENT OF HISTORY AS VALUABLE AS THE VOLUMES OF GIBBON ARE IN SECULAR HISTORY. THEY DESERVE A PLACE IN EVERY LIBRARY IN THE LAND. THIS NEW EDITION, in 8 vols., contains AN AVERAGE OF OVER 900 PAGES per volume. PRICE, $12.00 PER SET. (Formerly published in 14 vols. at $24.50.)

Sent on receipt of price, charges prepaid, by

A. C. ARMSTRONG & SON, 714 Broadway, New York.

CHOICE STANDARD WORKS.

A NEW EDITION OF
THE HISTORY OF THE CRUSADES.
A.D. 300–1270.
IN EIGHT PARTS, WITH AN INDEX OF 47 PAGES.

By JOSEPH FRANCOIS MICHAUD.

And a Preface and Supplementary Chapter by Hamilton W. Mabie.
3 vols., crown 8vo, Cloth. $3.75.

(Bound in Half Calf extra, $3 per vol.)

"The ability, diligence and faithfulness with which MICHAUD has executed his great task are undisputed, and it is to his well-filled volumes that all must resort for copious and authentic facts and luminous views respecting this most romantic and wonderful period in the annals of the world."

This work has long been out of print, and its republication is opportune. It narrates very fully and in a picturesque and interesting manner, the most striking episode in European history, and will add an invaluable work to the historical literature which has recently been put into the hands of the reading public in editions combining sound scholarship and reasonable prices. Of the first excellence as an authority, full of romantic incident, graphic in style, this new edition of that which is by universal consent

THE STANDARD HISTORY OF THE CRUSADES,
will have equal value for the student and general reader.

RIVERSIDE EDITION OF
MACAULAY'S ESSAYS,

Critical, Historical and Miscellaneous. With a Biographical and Critical Introduction from the well-known pen of Mr. E. P. Whipple. 3 vols., crown 8vo, Cloth, 3,000 pages. With a fine Portrait on Steel. Price, $3.75.

(Bound in Half Calf extra, $3 per vol.)

In this edition the essays have been arranged in chronological order, so that their perusal affords, so to speak, a complete biographical portraiture of the brilliant author's mind. It contains the pure text of the author and the exact punctuation, orthography, etc., of the English editions.

A very full index (55 pages) has been specially prepared for this edition. In this respect it is superior to the English editions, and wholly unlike any other American edition.

Sent on receipt of price, charges prepaid, by
A. C. ARMSTRONG & SON, 714 Broadway, New York.

CHOICE STANDARD WORKS.

NEW AND REVISED EDITION
OF
HALLAM'S COMPLETE WORKS,
With New Table of Contents and Indexes.

IN SIX VOLS., CROWN, 8VO, CLOTH.

PRICE, $7.50 PER SET. (Reduced from $17.50.)

(Bound in Half Calf extra, $3 per vol.)

THIS UNABRIDGED EDITION OF HALLAM'S WORKS COMPRISES

The Constitutional History of England, 2 Vols.
The Middle Ages, The State of Europe During the Middle Ages, 2 Vols.
Introduction to the Literature of Europe, 2 Vols.

REPRINTED FROM THE LAST LONDON EDITION, REVISED
AND CORRECTED BY THE AUTHOR.

MACAULAY, in his famous estimate of Hallam, says: "Mr. Hallam is, on the whole, far better qualified than any other writer of our time for the office which he has undertaken. He has great industry and great acuteness. His knowledge is extensive, various, and profound. His mind is equally distinguished by the amplitude of its grasp, and by the delicacy of its tact. His speculations have none of that vagueness which is the common fault of political philosophy. On the contrary, they are strikingly practical, and teach us not only the general rule, but the mode of applying it to solve particular cases. . . . Mr. Hallam's work is eminently judicial. Its whole spirit is that of the Bench, not that of the Bar. He sums up with a calm, steady impartiality, turning neither to the right nor to the left, glossing over nothing, exaggerating nothing, while the advocates on both sides are alternately biting their lips to hear their conflicting misstatements and sophism exposed."

This "STANDARD EDITION" of HALLAM'S WORKS, in 6 Vols., AVERAGES NEARLY 800 PAGES IN EACH VOL., and is sold at $7.50 PER SET (formerly published in 10 Vols. at $17.50.)

Sent on receipt of price, charges prepaid, by
A. C. ARMSTRONG & SON, 714 Broadway, New York.

CHOICE STANDARD WORKS.

THE MOST ELEGANT EDITION PUBLISHED
OF

CHARLES LAMB'S COMPLETE WORKS,

Including ELIA and ELIANA (the last containing the hitherto uncollected writings of Charles Lamb), corrected and revised, with a sketch of his life by Sir Thomas Noon Talfourd, and a fine Portrait on Steel.

3 VOLS., CR. 8VO, CLO. PRICE, $3.75 PER SET. (REDUCED FROM $7.50.)
(Bound in Half Calf extra, $3 per vol.)

With a volume of Letters and Essays collected for this edition by the industry of, and arranged with much taste and skill by, *J. E. BABSON*, Esq., of Boston, "*who literally knows Lamb by heart.*"

In Mr. Babson's preface to this additional volume, he says:

"Other writers may have more readers, but none have so many true, hearty, enthusiastic admirers as he. * * * With all lovers and appreciators of true wit, genuine humor, fine fancy, beautiful imagination and exquisite pathos, he is a prodigious favorite. Indeed, there is something—a nameless, indescribable charm—about this author's productions which captivates and enravishes his readers, and though Lamb found many admiring readers in his lifetime, since his death his fame and popularity have increased greatly. Then he was generally looked upon as a mere eccentric—a person of more quaintness than humor, of more oddity than genius. Now he is acknowledged to be a most beautiful and original genius—one of the 'fixed stars of the literary system'—whose light will never pale or grow dim, and whose peculiar brightness and beauty will long be the wonder and delight of many. * * * For years I have been hopefully and patiently waiting for somebody to collect these scattered and all but forgotten articles of Lamb's. * * * Without doubt, all genuine admirers, all true lovers of the gentle, genial, delightful 'Elia,' to whom almost every word of their favorite author's inditing is '*farsed with pleasaunce*,' will be mightily pleased with these productions of his inimitable pen, NOW FIRST COLLECTED TOGETHER."

As this "SUPERB EDITION" of LAMB'S WORKS, in 3 Vols., AVERAGING NEARLY 800 PAGES IN EACH VOLUME, is sold at the EXCEEDINGLY LOW PRICE OF $3.75 PER SET (formerly published in 5 Vols. at $7.50), the Publishers confidently believe IT WILL COMMEND ITSELF TO ALL FOR PERSONAL USE AND FOR LIBRARIES.

Sent on receipt of price, charges prepaid, by
A. C. ARMSTRONG & SON, 714 Broadway, New York.

CHOICE STANDARD WORKS.

A NEW EDITION
OF
D'ISRAELI'S COMPLETE WORKS.

Edited by his Son, LORD BEACONSFIELD,

With a fine Portrait on Steel. 6 Vols., Crown 8vo, Cloth.

PRICE, $7.50 PER SET. (Reduced from $15.00.)

(Bound in Half Calf extra, $3 per vol.)

THIS NEW EDITION OF D'ISRAELI'S WORKS COMPRISES

THE CURIOSITIES OF LITERATURE,	3 Vols.
CALAMITIES AND QUARRELS OF AUTHORS AND MEMOIRS,	1 Vol.
AMENITIES OF LITERATURE, SKETCHES AND CHARACTERS,	1 Vol.
LITERARY CHARACTER, HISTORY OF MEN OF GENIUS,	1 Vol.

A collection of literature which no judiciously selected library will fail to have, and no person of literary taste and culture willingly do without.

They are, in truth, a history of literature and of literary men, gathered from the writings of centuries and from living authors, philosophic and learned, yet easy and fascinating.

The Curiosities of Literature treat of everything curious in the literary kingdom. The formation of libraries, past and present, bibliomania, the oddities of authors, their labors, anecdotes, successes, failures, etc., containing a valuable mass of rare information.

The Amenities of Literature "is in a different strain, and treats of Language, the origin and growth of our own, the discovery and progress of the art of printing, the growth of literature, its patrons, followers and builders, and of other matters which have a broad and general bearing upon the subject in hand."

The Calamities and Quarrels of Authors "contains an account of authors' struggles, difficulties and poverty as a class * * * teaching them their failings and holding up the mirror for those who may be benefited by a view of the difficulties which beset authors."

Literary Character "is probably the most searching and distinctive treatise of its kind extant, made up, as it is, from the feelings and confessions of men of genius."

This NEW IMPRESSION of the famous works of the elder D'ISRAELI, IN 6 VOLS., PRICE $7.50 PER SET (formerly published in 9 Vols. at $15.00), has been aptly said to comprise the cream of English Literature of Europe from the times of Dr. Johnson to our own, and to constitute a whole library in themselves.

Sent on receipt of price, charges prepaid, by

A. C. ARMSTRONG & SON, 714 Broadway, New York.

CHOICE STANDARD WORKS.

A NEW AND SUPERIOR LIBRARY EDITION
OF

NAPIER'S PENINSULAR WAR.

FROM THE AUTHOR'S LAST REVISED EDITION.

With 55 Maps and Plans of Battles, 5 Steel Portraits and a Complete Index. Elegantly printed on toned paper, strongly bound in extra cloth.

PRICE, $7.50 PER SET. (Reduced from $12.50.)

(Bound in Half Calf extra, $3.50 per vol.)

THIS NEW AND COMPLETE EDITION COMPRISES THE

History of the War in the Peninsula

AND IN THE SOUTH OF FRANCE, FROM
THE YEAR 1807 TO 1814.

By GEN. W. F. P. NAPIER.

IN 5 VOLS., CROWN 8VO (IN A NEAT BOX).

"Sir Wm. Napier's History of the Peninsular War is the greatest military work in the English language, or indeed in any language, not even excepting the immortal commentaries of Cæsar. General Foy's 'Guerre dans la Peninsule' is written with vast ability, but is so marked by national jealousy and animosity, that it loses much of the authority to which it would otherwise be entitled from the author's consummate knowledge of the art of war, and his familiarity with the memorable scenes and events he undertakes to describe. In these two invaluable requisites Sir Wm. Napier was fully his equal; while he possessed an earnest love of truth, and a spirit of lofty magnanimity, to which we find no parallel in the French historian.

"It is creditable alike to Sir Wm. Napier and to the American people that in this country, this work has passed THROUGH SEVERAL EDITIONS, THE ONE BEFORE US BEING UNQUESTIONABLY THE HANDSOMEST AND THE MOST COMPLETE. To the student of History—especially to him who loves to dwell on the romantic character of Portugal and Spain—the marches, sieges, and battles of Wellington's armies during six long years, must always possess an interest which neither the Crimean war, nor the late great struggle in this country, can altogether efface. The soldier who is devoted to his profession, and who seeks great military principles and examples for his guidance, will pronounce Sir Wm. Napier THE MOST FAITHFUL AND THE MOST COMPETENT AUTHORITY TO BE FOUND IN ANY AGE OR IN ANY COUNTRY."—SCOTTISH AMER. JOURNAL.

Sent on receipt of price, charges prepaid, by

A. C. ARMSTRONG & SON, 714 Broadway, New York.

HENRY BOYNTON SMITH:

His Life and Work.

EDITED BY HIS WIFE.

With a fine Portrait on Steel, by Ritchie. One Vol., 8vo, 500 pages. Cloth, $2.50. (*Copies sent by mail, post-paid, on receipt of price.*)

This Memoir of the lamented Prof. Smith, gives a faithful picture of his character and public career. The story is deeply interesting, and while it fully justifies his reputation as one of the most accomplished scholars and theologians, it also shows him to have been a man of very rare personal attractions. The volume is enriched with recollections of him by Prof. Park, President Seelye, of Amherst ; Prof. A. S. Packard, of Bowdoin ; Rev. Dr. Withington, Dr. Cyrus Hamlin, Prof. Park, of Andover ; Prof. F. A. March, of Lafayette, and the Rev. Drs. T. H. Hastings and M. R. Vincent, of New York. Rev. Dr. Goodwin, of Philadelphia, and Rev. Dr. Prentiss have assisted in the preparation of the work.

EXTRACTS FROM NOTICES OF THE MEMOIR.

Philadelphia Presbyterian says : "Dr. Smith's life is here narrated largely in his own language. His letters are frank, bright, full, and frequent. These give to the book much of the interest of an autobiography—all the more interesting because he did not consciously compose it."

N. Y. Tribune : "This book is a picture of a character, and not of an intellect merely—others besides scholars may profitably read it—the beauty of Prof. Smith's character fully answered to the strength of his intellect and the richness of his culture—as the record of a scholarly career he had few equals on this side of the Atlantic."

N. Y. Evangelist : "The book is indeed one of the most attractive pieces of religious biography that we have ever read. The character of the departed scholar is outlined with great delicacy by the loving hand of her who knew him best."

N. Y. Christian Union : "This account of the man himself has a permanent value. The life was worthy of noble monuments and lasting fame, and no one can read this book without an impulse to higher effort and purer living ; and this will be more pleasing to the ransomed spirit—more in harmony with the wishes of his life here than sculptured marbles."

N. Y. Observer : "Dr. Smith's life was full of incident and adventure. His education was splendid. Foreign travel in youth broadened his view, enlarged his acquaintance with universities, with men, books, and life. The brightest intellects discerned his greatness. As a pastor, preacher, teacher, lecturer and professor, as a reviewer and editor, he always made the mark of a first rate workman, doing everything well. The loving hand of the wife has fitly held out to the eyes of the world, and bound up in this bundle such evidence of his greatness and worth, that the present generation and posterity will know something of what the Church lost when this light went out before eventide."

A. C. ARMSTRONG & SON, 714 Broadway, New York.

APOLOGETICS.

A COURSE OF LECTURES

By Henry B. Smith, D.D., LL.D.

Edited by William S. Karr, D.D.

In one volume, 12mo. Price, $1.00. *Sent by mail, post-paid, on receipt of price.*

"No treatise on Apologetics contains within the same narrow limits so much material for the defence of Christianity. Students and teachers of Apologetics will join on upon the systematizing here done for them by this able apologete, and follow out the lines of defence which he indicates. *In this way it must prove to be a stimulating and reproductive work."—Presbyterian Quarterly Review.*

"We cannot commend this book too highly. It is the matured thought of one of our maturest thinkers, on some of the most vital issues of our day. Believers and unbelievers who can appreciate clear definition, ponderous thought and cogent logic, ought alike to read this work. It is tonic to both intellect and faith."—*N. Y. Examiner.*

"No teacher in this country, and few anywhere, had a more thorough acquaintance with this large and abstruse subject, and with its enormous literature. His severe and carefully trained logical faculty, his cool and dispassionate judgment, his extensive learning, and his nervous and transparent style, lend to this, as to all his other productions, a profound interest and a peculiar charm. *It will be an invaluable manual, not only to the professional student, but to every thoughtful reader who seeks to justify the ways of God to man."—New York Tribune.*

"Compact and vigorous, characteristic of the mind and method of the lamented scholar and theologian. The Lectures relate to the following fundamental points: the supernatural in general, the knowableness of the supernatural, the supernatural in miracles. It seems to us that many intelligent persons, who have never been able to interest themselves in theological or metaphysical discussions, would nevertheless find much pleasure and profit in reading these chapters—so concise, distinct, natural and informing."—*N. Y. Observer.*

"They show a thorough mastery of the subject and of the literature bearing upon it, especially that of more recent date. Prof. Smith was one of this country's strongest theological thinkers."—*N. Y. Churchman.*

"Taken as a whole, this is the best book of its kind which has yet come from any American divine. It demands and is worth study."—*Standard of the Cross.*

A. C. ARMSTRONG & SON, 714 BROADWAY, NEW YORK.

www.ingramcontent.com/pod-product-compliance
Lightning Source LLC
Chambersburg PA
CBHW021955220426
43663CB00007B/826